POSITIVE
and
NEGATIVE
SYNDROMES
in
SCHIZOPHRENIA

Assessment and Research

Clinical and Experimental Psychiatry

Monograph Series of the Department of Psychiatry
Albert Einstein College of Medicine of Yeshiva University
Montefiore Medical Center
Bronx, N.Y.

Editor-in-Chief Herman M. van Praag, M.D., Ph.D.

1. CONTEMPORARY APPROACHES TO PSYCHOLOGICAL ASSESSMENT
Edited by Scott Wetzler, Ph.D., & Martin M. Katz, Ph.D.

2. COMPUTER APPLICATIONS IN PSYCHIATRY AND PSYCHOLOGY
Edited by David Baskin, Ph.D.

3. VIOLENCE AND SUICIDALITY: PERSPECTIVES IN CLINICAL AND
PSYCHOBIOLOGICAL RESEARCH
*Edited by Herman M. van Praag, M.D., Ph.D.,
Robert Plutchik, Ph.D., & Alan Apter, M.D.*

4. THE ROLE OF SEROTONIN IN PSYCHIATRIC DISORDERS
*Edited by Serena-Lynn Brown, M.D., Ph.D.,
Herman M. van Praag, M.D., Ph.D.*

5. POSITIVE AND NEGATIVE SYNDROMES IN SCHIZOPHRENIA:
ASSESSMENT AND RESEARCH
By Stanley R. Kay, Ph.D.

Clinical and Experimental Psychiatry Monograph No. 5

POSITIVE
and
NEGATIVE
SYNDROMES
in
SCHIZOPHRENIA

Assessment and Research

STANLEY R. KAY, Ph.D.

*Chief of Schizophrenia Research Program
and Associate Clinical Professor
Department of Psychiatry (Psychology)
Albert Einstein College of Medicine of Yeshiva University
Montefiore Medical Center
Bronx, NY*

BRUNNER/MAZEL, *Publishers* • NEW YORK

Library of Congress Cataloging-in-Publication Data
Kay, Stanley R.
    Positive and negative syndromes in schizophrenia : assessment and
research / Stanley R. Kay.
        p.   cm. — (Clinical and experimental psychiatry ; 5)
    Includes bibliographical references and index.
    ISBN 0-87630-608-3
    1. Schizophrenia. I. Title. II. Series.
    [DNLM: 1. Schizophrenia.   W1 CL664EH v. 5 / WM 203 K23p]
RC514.K33   1991
616.89'82—dc20
DNLM/DLC
for Library of Congress   90-15113
                                                                    CIP

Published by
BRUNNER/MAZEL, INC.
19 Union Square
New York, New York 10003

Manufactured in the United States of America

10 9 8 7 6 5 4 3 2

A Note on the Series

Psychiatry is in a state of flux. The excitement springs in part from internal changes, such as the development and official acceptance (at least in the U.S.A.) of an operationalized, multiaxial classification system of behavioral disorders (the DSM-III), the increasing sophistication of methods to measure abnormal human behavior and the impressive expansion of biological and psychological treatment modalities. Exciting developments are also taking place in fields relating to psychiatry; in molecular (brain) biology, genetics, brain imaging, drug development, epidemiology, experimental psychology, to mention only a few striking examples.

More generally speaking, psychiatry is moving, still relatively slowly, but irresistibly, from a more philosophical, contemplative orientation, to that of an empirical science. From the fifties on, biological psychiatry has been a major catalyst of that process. It provided the mother discipline with a third cornerstone, i.e., neurobiology, the other two being psychology and medical sociology. In addition, it forced the profession into the direction of standardization of diagnoses and of assessment of abnormal behavior. Biological psychiatry provided psychiatry not only with a new basic science and with new treatment modalities, but also with the tools, the methodology and the mentality to operate within the confines of an empirical science, the only framework in which a medical discipline can survive.

In other fields of psychiatry, too, one discerns a gradual trend towards scientification. Psychological treatment techniques are standardized and manuals developed to make these skills more easily transferrable. Methods registering treatment outcome—traditionally used in the behavioral/cognitive field—are now more and more requested and, hence, developed for dynamic forms of psychotherapy as well. Social and community psychiatry, until the sixties more firmly rooted in humanitarian ideals and social awareness than in empirical studies, profited greatly from its liaison with the social sciences and the expansion of psychiatric epidemiology.

Let there be no misunderstanding. Empiricism does *not imply* that it is only the measurable that counts. Psychiatry would be mutilated if it would neglect that what is not yet capturable in numbers and probably never will be. It *does imply* that what is measurable should be measured. Progress in psychiatry is dependent on ideas and on experiment. Their linkage is inseparable.

This monograph series, published under the auspices of the Department of Psychiatry of the Albert Einstein College of Medicine/Montefiore Medical Center, is meant to keep track of important developments in our profession, to summarize what has been achieved in particular fields, and to bring together the viewpoints obtained from disparate vantage points—in short, to capture some of the excitement ongoing in modern psychiatry, both in its clinical and experimental dimensions. Our Department hosts the Series, but naturally welcomes contributions from others.

Bernie Mazel is not only the publisher of this series, but it was he who generated the idea—an ambitious plan which, however, we all feel is worthy of pursuit. The edifice of psychiatry is impressive, but still somewhat flawed in its foundations. May this Series contribute to consolidation of its infrastructure.

—HERMAN M. VAN PRAAG, M.D., PH.D.
Silverman Professor and Chairman
Department of Psychiatry
Albert Einstein College of Medicine
Montefiore Medical Center
Bronx, New York

Contents

APPENDICES

Foreword

Stanley Kay died suddenly and unexpectedly at the 17th Congress of the Collegium Internationale Neuro-Psychopharmacologicum held in Kyoto, Japan, from September 10-14, 1990, shortly after he had given a presentation. His death was dramatic and untimely. I was terribly shocked when I received the message. This is not an empty phrase for the occasion, but a true *cri de coeur*.

Stanley was much too young to die, much too productive, much too valuable. Valuable above all for his family. Valuable also for psychiatric research. As in all types of human endeavor, research is conducted on different echelons. There are those flying high and those flying lower. Stanley belonged to the top in schizophrenia research. I consider the scales he developed to assess the psychopathology of schizophrenia as the best available and his research on the clinical significance of the positive-negative symptom dimension as pioneering.

Stanley was a *pur sang* researcher—industrious, always raising questions, fond of data, delighting in their analyses. For him, there were no distractions such as private practice and no indulgences such as membership on multiple committees; he did not even have time for much socializing. Research was the purpose of his life.

Finally, for our Department, Stanley was of incalculable value. Not only because he was a top-notch researcher, but, more important, because he was an outstanding human being. Loyal to the Department, he was always willing to help if a job had to be done. He was a patient and lucid teacher, always in good humor and, above all, reliable. If asked to do something, one could be certain it would be done, thoroughly and expeditiously. He was a kind man, somewhat reserved, the opposite of pompous; he was, indeed, an honest man.

The book you have in your hands summarizes Kay's work over the past 10 years. He finished it before he passed away. There were no gaps to be filled by someone else. It is entirely his book.

I am a religious believer in that I see God as a metaphor for the most noble, creative, and sublime aspirations and intentions that mankind—in its best representatives in their best moments—generates. "The human soul is God's lamp," a Proverb reads (20:27). It is only in that light that the beauty and dignity of His countenance manifests itself.

The Sabbath after I learned about Stanley's death I went to the synagogue to pray, to say Kaddish for him. I don't know whether it did him any good, but it did me good. May he rest in peace.

HERMAN M. VAN PRAAG, M.D., PH.D.
Silverman Professor and Chairman
Department of Psychiatry
Albert Einstein College of Medicine
Montefiore Medical Center
Bronx, New York

Preface

Schizophrenia is perhaps the most common, devastating, and perplexing of the psychotic disorders. If afflicts about one in every 100 Americans and singly accounts for the greatest number of beds occupied in public psychiatric hospitals. The cardinal symptoms include delusions, hallucinations, disordered cognition, and various deficits in thinking and relating to one's environment. If not resolved within the first two years, schizophrenia tends to run a deteriorative course and to endure, at least in some facets, for one's lifetime. In the later stages, the patient may appear as a mere shell of his or her former existence, lacking a wide range of basic intellectual, emotional, social, and communicational skills.

New hope for schizophrenia was raised in the 1950s with the introduction of neuroleptic drugs, such as chlorpromazine and haloperidol. These medications have revolutionized the treatment of schizophrenia, bringing remission or stabilization to many patients. The neurochemical action of these medications, which involves blocking transmission of dopamine in the brain, led to the hypothesis that schizophrenia may be explained by a dopamine excess. The "dopamine hypothesis" remains the prevalent model even today.

Although neuroleptic medications are now routinely prescribed for schizophrenia, not all patients and not all symptoms respond adequately. There has been increasing recognition that this illness is far more complex than previously thought and that the dopamine hypothesis is too simplistic. The resistance of schizophrenia to treatment and even to scientific scrutiny may be due to its heterogeneity, which has been described by Bleuler (1908) and Kraepelin (1919) as early as 80 years ago. It is generally recognized that schizophrenic patients differ in their premorbid history, symptom profile, drug response, course of illness, and prognosis. The traditional ways of subtyping this condition, such as paranoid-nonparanoid and acute-chronic, have not adequately explained its diversity or led to better tailored treatments.

In the past several years, however, there has emerged a new approach which recognizes the systematic differences in the symptomatic presentation. It was proposed that symptoms can be classified as "positive" (productive) and "negative" (deficit), and that this distinction may reflect separate syndromes or processes that underlie schizophrenia. Accordingly, the positive-negative mode held out hope for guiding us to better tailored treatment strategies. Considerable research over the past decade has accumulated on this distinction, which is rapidly becoming a standard way to characterize schizophrenia. In recognition of its importance, the positive-negative model is now described in the latest textbooks on abnormal psychology.

Our exploration of this area began in the early 1980s as an extension of our research on the treatment of schizophrenia. The available instruments to assess positive and negative syndromes were, in our view, not sufficiently objective or sensitive for scientific research. Our starting point, therefore, was the development and standardization of a new, better operationalized method to provide reliable and valid assessment of the symptom profile. With the resulting instrument, known as the Positive and Negative Syndrome Scale (PANSS), we embarked on a series of investigations that probed the significance of positive and negative dimensions from several research perspectives.

Our strategy included cross-sectional, longitudinal, typological, psychopharmacological, drug-free, phasic, and prospective follow-up studies that examined patients in both the acute and chronic phases of illness. From the aggregate of our work, involving over 240 schizophrenic patients, we found that these syndromes are associated with significant differences in one's early development, family history of psychiatric illness, intellectual and neurological profiles, response to psychotropic medications, and long-term outcome. The positive-negative distinction, therefore, appears to tease apart fundamental variations within schizophrenia and to carry distinct implications for understanding the origins, optimal treatment, and prognosis of the illness.

Our findings, however, indicate important modifications to the original positive-negative model. Our data suggest, for example, that a negative syndrome may predict a better rather than worse long-term outcome; that early neurodevelopmental disorders involving the prefrontal region play a major role in the pathogenesis of certain forms of schizophrenia; that the positive-negative distinction embodies independent psychopathological processes but not "subtypes" of schizophrenia; and that a more thorough understanding of schizophrenia requires a broader conception than the positive-negative model, one that accounts for a fuller range of symptoms. In regard to the latter point, we have described a "pyramidical model" of schizophrenia, which places the positive and negative dimensions within

the context of other syndromes and the traditional typology of schizophrenia.

The present monograph serves as a comprehensive and up-to-date review
of our work in the field. As indicated by the title, this volume focuses on
two general themes surrounding positive and negative syndromes: the
method of assessment and the consequent research findings. The introduc-
tory section summarizes key issues and controversies in schizophrenia to
provide a background for the positive-negative model and our studies
thereof. The second section is concerned with the development, training,
use, and standardization of our new instrument for assessing the spectrum
of psychopathology in schizophrenia. Further initiatives and extensions of
this psychometric method, including a two-tier diagnostic interview and assessment for schizophrenia, are presented in the third section. The fourth
section describes research with this instrument that elucidates the nature
and significance of positive and negative syndromes in different phases of
the schizophrenic disorder. The fifth and final section culminates in our recent expansion of the positive-negative model and in the conclusions and
synthesis of our findings with other research.

It is intended that this volume will inform the reader of the importance
of positive and negative syndromes for understanding, treating, and study-
ing the different processes that underlie schizophrenia. We further consider
that our presentation may correct some misconceptions and add new
knowledge about the meaning of these syndromes, while offering a useful
tool for their assessment. Our hope is that, with more light cast onto the
various components of this disorder, it will become less of a mystery, and
that the path to novel and more efficacious forms of treatment will be
thereby illuminated.

Acknowledgments and Dedication

This volume is the product of more than a decade of research in which many persons made valuable contributions.

Man Mohan Singh, M.D., a friend and esteemed colleague for 20 years, inspired the pursuit of different underlying processes in schizophrenia. He has long championed the need to devise more objective assessment methods, to clarify a developmental component in schizophrenia, and to consider the role of cholinergic mechanisms in its pathophysiology.

Lewis A. Opler, M.D., Ph.D., with whom I have collaborated since 1981, channeled our research directions toward a scrutiny of the positive-negative distinction, this in recognition of its theoretical importance and its implications for newer treatment strategies.

Abraham Fiszbein, M.D., participated assiduously in most phases of data collection and was central to the standardization of our new rating instrument as well as to its Spanish translation.

Jean Pierre Lindenmayer, M.D., Arnold Merriam, M.D., Reuven Sandyk, M.D., M.Sc., S. Shalom Feinberg, M.D., and Lauren B. Marangell, M.D., separately took leads in investigating different facets of the positive-negative distinction, namely its relationship to affective processes, neuropathology, and psychopharmacology.

Lisa M. Murrill, M.A., participated materially in the coordination and compilation of data and patient follow-up, and Serge Sevy, M.D., assisted in computerized data analysis. Ms. Murrill, Betty Newkirk, and Sukhwinder Singh, M.D., graciously helped in the preparation of the manuscript.

Finally, Herman M. van Praag, M.D., Ph.D., Martin M. Katz, Ph.D., Marlene Lopez, and Victor Rosado, M.D., provided the administrative support and encouragement that made this work possible.

To all these individuals, and to the many research assistants, clinical support staff, and patients who took part in these investigations, I owe my sincere thanks. In gratitude for their vital role, this book is dedicated to them.

PART I

Toward an Understanding of Schizophrenia

1

The Schizophrenia Puzzle

Schizophrenia, so named to describe the splitting of the mind from reality, actually represents a tragic split on many levels. In fact, we see at a glance so many splits and disassembled pieces that the disorder may be likened to a jigsaw puzzle. The patient with this affliction is separated from his own thoughts and feelings, typically experiences alienation from his family and society, and suffers years—possibly a lifetime—of personal, social, and occupational incapacity. Often, the sufferer describes his experiences as we would a nightmare: a kaleidoscopic sequence of sudden, inexplicable events that isolate, torment, and terrorize one, and from which there is no escape. But unlike the dreamer, the schizophrenic may never fully waken.

The anguish is real both to the victim and the victim's loved ones, who long for the return to a full, rich life which may forever remain a memory. Even when the patient responds to treatment, showing signs of returning to a healthier mental state, some stubborn symptoms tend to remain, disabling the daily routine and serving as a constant reminder of the deterioration wrought by the illness. For example, there may be persistent delusions, a restriction in emotional responses, or loss of ability to think in abstract and symbolic terms. All too often, even the limited recovery proves to be a temporary resurrection rather than the reclaiming of a normal existence. Each time the patient relapses and the condition deteriorates, the family experiences the revived disappointment from yet another false hope. As the patient gradually changes into a hollowed shell, a pale replica of a once functional being, the likelihood of a full recovery becomes ever more remote.

THE SCHIZOPHRENIC EXPERIENCE

Schizophrenia afflicts approximately one of every 100 Americans in a lifetime. It is the single condition that accounts for the majority of beds occupied in public psychiatric hospitals, costing society an estimated $10–20

3

billion each year (Torrey, 1982). The problem is just as rampant in other industrialized nations as in the United States.

But the epidemiological data and economic consequences tell only society's story, and not the personal devastation of the victim. As a psychosis, schizophrenia represents a severe mental disorder that significantly impairs the individual's capacity to function; when it occurs, the patient's relationship to his environment is radically transformed. Alien thoughts and sounds may invade one's consciousness, strange ideas may take hold, and uncontrolled feelings of anger, fear, suspicion, and anxiety may dominate. Attention is usually diverted while arousal level is heightened, as though one's system is operating in a constant overdrive. The ability to think clearly and rationally and to exercise sound judgment is affected, and normal social relations are typically strained as the patient becomes increasingly preoccupied and seclusive. Under these circumstances, it becomes difficult to get on with one's social, educational, and occupational life. Even simple activities, such as greeting a friend and sitting quietly at a dinner table, are disrupted in the florid state of schizophrenia.

Subjectively, the patient may experience intense feelings of depression, and this is associated with a high prevalence of suicide in schizophrenia (McGlashan, 1984; Prasad & Kumar, 1988). Consider, for example, the following excerpt from a letter written to me by a schizophrenic woman in outpatient treatment. This autobiographical prose was entitled "A Phantasy or Dream-like Image":

> "In her agonizing despair and hopelessness at NEVER AGAIN retrieving her lost spiritual affinities, she gave up on life. The fierce Wind of Destiny enveloped M＿＿＿＿ within a cloud-shadow of obscure phantasmagorian, endless sorrow. M＿＿＿＿ finally ceased to struggle against the hostile, embittered Winter Wind, as she now floated lifelessly, relinquishing all hope of a tomorrow. There poured forth from the depth of her being a plaintive sound—TOO TRAGIC TO BE REAL."

If a picture is worth a thousand words, then perhaps we can learn much about the mental state of a schizophrenic from self-portraits. Clinical experience and empirical research suggest that human figure drawings can serve as a window to the inner processes of severely psychotic patients (Di Leo, 1973; Kay, 1978). Figures 1:1 to 1:4 are self-portraits of actively ill, unmedicated schizophrenic patients who, on clinical examination, displayed disorganization of thoughts, bizarre ideation, and hallucinatory activity. Like the drawings, their world is a combination of confused, dissociated elements, an everchanging display of conflicting emotions, and strange, even

Fig. 1:1. Female, age 19, schizophrenic, catatonic subtype, 4 years of illness

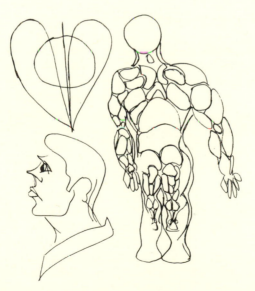

Fig. 1:2. Male, age 19, schizophrenic, paranoid subtype, 1 year of illness

Fig. 1:3. Female, age 25,
schizophrenic,
disorganized subtype,
4 years of illness

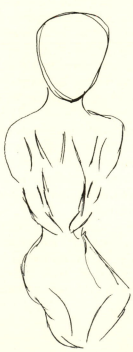

Fig. 1:4. Female,
age 27, schizophrenic,
chronic undifferentiated subtype,
5 years of illness

contradictory ideas that permeate consciousness and distort one's sense of reality. In addition, we see from these portraits a direct reflection of the emptiness, the vacuous state that comprises an amalgam of deficits, including the very loss of one's sense of identity.

THE SCHIZOPHRENIC TRANSFORMATION

What makes schizophrenia especially tragic, however, is its timing and course. It tends to develop during the years of adolescence to the early 20s, a time crucial for achieving the final intellectual, social, and occupational milestones as one makes the transition from child to productive adult. Even a temporary psychotic interlude would constitute a serious disruption to a person's development and directions in life. Yet the illness often is relentless; it tends to be persistent and recurrent, with a bleak prognosis after a two-year duration (Brown, 1960).

On initial presentation, approximately one-third of schizophrenic patients make a successful recovery, one-third improve partially or temporarily, and the remaining one-third are essentially unchanged (Torrey, 1983). Even for those patients who do respond to interventions, schizophrenia is regarded as a lifelong illness for which there is no cure; like diabetes, it requires ongoing drug therapy to guard against relapse. But unlike the diabetic, the treated schizophrenic usually shows significant impairments, some of which directly interfere with healthy judgment and insight into the illness, and therefore into the role of continued medical care. The result frequently is a failure to persist with outpatient treatment, leading almost invariably to relapse and rehospitalization (Nimatoudis et al., 1989). Indeed, the rate of rehospitalization for schizophrenia is estimated to be 30–40 percent within six months of discharge, 40–50 percent after one year, and as high as 75 percent by the third to fifth year (Anthony, Cohen, & Vitalo, 1978; Anthony & Farkas, 1982).

Unfortunately, with each readmission the chance for recovery tends to diminish, the reconstitution is less complete, and the likelihood of a long-term institutional career increases. As the years pass with continued illness, normal interests, ambitions, and emotional responses seem to be lost, and the personality may undergo a gradual and possibly irreversible transformation.

In many cases, too, the family is transformed by the emotional jolt. Some express a misguided sense of guilt for the condition of their son or daughter, and some express feelings of impotence as the patient's life is distorted by the psychosis. Most commonly, the loved ones share with the patient the roller coaster ride of emotional highs and lows, unable to distance themselves from the painful experiences of the patient, unable to react normally to an abnormal situation, and confused about what they may have done wrong or how they may help. Above all, the families feel angry and depressed at their own helplessness.

SCHIZOPHRENIA: A CLINICAL PUZZLE

The frustration and puzzlement of the family are to some extent paralleled by similar feelings on the part of the clinician who treats the patient. For despite the major advances in various fields of health research, our understanding of schizophrenia—its nature, its course, and its treatment—has advanced with painful slowness since its description by Eugene Bleuler (1908) and Emil Kraepelin (1919) in the early part of this century. These pioneering psychiatrists viewed schizophrenia from the standpoint of its symptomatic expression and downhill course. Thus, the illness was described as a "dementia praecox," characterized by precocious loss of mental capabilities that leads to a demented state while the patient is still in the prime of life.

During the subsequent decades, the field has experienced remarkable growth in biological approaches to treatment and assessment. Two developments in particular stand out. Neuroleptic drugs were introduced in the 1950s for treating schizophrenia and have since become the standard and primary mode of therapy. The success of dopamine blocking agents in countering psychotic symptoms has led to the dopamine hypothesis of schizophrenia, still prevalent today, which relates the disorder to excessive transmission of dopamine in the brain. Secondly, in the 1970s and 1980s, neuroradiological and other methods of brain imaging have further advanced our knowledge of brain structure and chemistry. Data from these techniques have helped to characterize the impairments in the brain anatomy and functioning of schizophrenic as compared to healthy persons and other psychiatric patients.

Both these scientific advances, therefore, have spawned important theories of the schizophrenic illness that seem to bear the promise of achieving a "major breakthrough." Thus far, however, the biological findings have been heuristic but by no means conclusive. Even as a treatment modality, the neuroleptics have helped some schizophrenics but not others, and many are helped only to a partial extent. One possible explanation for the stalemate in research, which will be elaborated on shortly, rests in the heterogeneity of the condition, which operates against consistent and replicable findings.

A second reason is that the technological sophistication of some biological measures has not been matched by accurate clinical assessment methods. Even the very diagnosis of schizophrenia, which is not generally recognized as an organically based disease, is determined not by biological methods but by a survey of the symptoms and course of illness. Currently, the Research Diagnostic Criteria (Spitzer, Endicott, & Robins, 1978) and the derivative DSM–III–R (American Psychiatric Association, 1987) are used standardly in the United States for defining the condition. The presence of several prototypic symptoms, such as hallucinations, bizarre behavior, and disorganized thinking, that are sustained over a six-month period is taken as evidence of schizophrenia, provided that features of other competing diagnoses, such as affective disorder and organic brain syndrome, are absent.

The publication of widely accepted diagnostic criteria for schizophrenia has immensely improved the reliability of diagnosis, but not necessarily its validity. In other words, clinicians using the same standards for diagnosis are now more likely to agree on whether a patient suffers from schizophrenia, but this does not guarantee that their assessment is correct. The validity of a diagnosis depends on showing correspondence between diagnostic judgments and independent sources of confirmation. The problem, of course, remains that no clear-cut yardstick of schizophrenia exists for comparative purposes. Consequently, the diagnostic criteria may conceivably represent a superficial, impressionistic view of what constitutes the disorder rather than its essence.

Schizophrenia, in fact, is known for its variability, which makes it especially difficult to pin down. The disorder takes on myriad forms, characterized by multiple symptoms that, in an untreated state, may fluctuate in intensity. Thus, two patients with a confirmed diagnosis of schizophrenia may bear little resemblance to one another and even to themselves over the course of time.

Their clinical presentation, furthermore, may be highly similar to what is seen typically in other mental disorders. For instance, schizophrenics often show cardinal symptoms of a depressive illness. In addition to sad mood and increased suicide risk, they frequently exhibit lack of interest in their environment, loss of energy, amotivation, and disturbed sleep. Cognitively, these patients are disabled to the point where a significant number could be characterized as having a mental deficiency (IQ of 70 and below). A large-scale review of IQ studies (Payne, 1973) reports the average intelligence scores of schizophrenics to fall in the "dull normal" range (IQ in the 80s), and the average for unremitted chronic schizophrenics is within the subnormal region (IQ in the 60s). Consequently, diagnostic confusion with mental retardation becomes a common problem (Kay, 1989a). The nature of the cognitive impairment, in fact, often resembles that of retardation in terms of apparent developmental deficits and a childlike mode of thinking (Blatt & Wild, 1976). Alternatively, the thinking of schizophrenics is known also to have an "organic" quality, including impoverished and perseverative ideation; indeed a large proportion of such patients—between 84 percent and 94 percent by our estimation (Kay, 1986; Vardy & Kay, 1983)—score in the "brain damaged" region on standard neuropsychological tests, such as the Memory For Designs and Bender-Gestalt tests.

The clinical puzzle of schizophrenia, therefore, involves piecing together the crucial elements of the disorder so that a recognizable entity emerges, one which has unique hallmarks that render it distinguishable from other clinical syndromes. Without a clear perspective on the condition and its components, our understanding of schizophrenia is likely to be inaccurate and, at best, superficial.

SCHIZOPHRENIA: A RESEARCH PUZZLE

As already suggested, despite the volume of publications on schizophrenia, little has been resolved about its fundamental nature. At present, we feel reasonably capable of describing it, treating it pharmacologically with partial success, and arriving at crude judgments about prognosis. In terms of understanding the pathogenesis, however, we are still in a stage of assumption and speculation, so that the requisites for prevention and cure are lacking.

Two likely reasons for the slow progress of research on schizophrenia have been alluded to: the variability of the condition and the lack of suitable clinical assessment methods. The net result is that the disorder is difficult to identify and its nature remains elusive. Patients diagnosed with schizophrenia can differ markedly from one another not only in their clinical presentation but also in their outcome with treatment. To address such problems, nosologists have attempted to subclassify schizophrenia according to symptomatic expression (e.g., paranoid, disorganized, catatonic), stage of illness (acute, chronic), nature of onset (early vs. late, gradual vs. sudden, reactive vs. process), and prognostic outlook (atypical-schizophreniform vs. typical-nuclear).

The actual treatment decisions, however, have benefited little from these nosological distinctions. The choice of neuroleptics and other facets of treatment planning, for example, is usually not determined by the schizophrenic subdiagnosis. And finally, from a scientific standpoint, there is no clear evidence that these diverse categories of schizophrenia represent separable disease entities. Thus, we are left with the dilemma of an apparently nonunitary disorder which, by virtue of its great variability, seems to defy subcategorization.

The consequence of this heterogeneity for research is that what is found in one study, with one particular group of schizophrenic patients, may not be confirmed with a different group that bears the same diagnosis. In such cases, the findings are said to lack "external validity" and may be rejected as a research error. More commonly, however, the variability will be present even *within* the patient sampling, and therefore within the study. The result is that true effects tend to "wash out" due to lack of internal consistency or to a self-cancellation of opposing patterns in the aggregate.

Studies on the psychophysiological basis of schizophrenia, for example, have yielded confusing and often conflicting data (Kay, 1981). Some studies report evidence of overarousal, some underarousal, while others find no clear evidence for either conclusion. Aside from differences in techniques of measurement, in the arousal systems under study, and in the drug status of the patients surveyed, schizophrenic subtypes differ systematically in their arousal levels (Kay & Singh, 1975b). Thus, the averaging of values obtained for autonomic arousal on catatonic patients (who show a mean resting pulse rate of 92.4) with those of paranoid patients (who show a mean resting pulse rate of 76.5) would militate against finding differences from a normal control group.

In this example, two reliable observations would be obscured by the failure to recognize significant differences among schizophrenics. It demonstrates that an accurate portrayal clearly requires full appreciation of the diverse phenomena that constitute what sometimes is referred to as "the schizophrenia spectrum disorders." A blindness to the systematic variations in schizophrenia is a blindness to the very nature of the illness. Fresh insights will come from discerning the consistencies within subsets of schizophrenic patients and determining the reasons for their differences from others.

In summary, progress in schizophrenia research depends very much on identifying distinct subgroups of dimensions rather than on classifying together all who meet DSM–III–R or other criteria for the diagnosis. Progress in treatment likewise demands a syndrome-specific approach rather than a general, "one size fits all" prescription. In seeking a solution to the schizophrenia puzzle, therefore, first we must *recognize* it to be a puzzle, that is, a composite of numerous pieces that will make sense only once the interrelationships are understood. Next we must arrive at a reliable and objective way to measure these components in order that one may subject them to scientific scrutiny. This has been our approach to the investigation of schizophrenia, as will be described in the forthcoming chapters.

2

The Positive-Negative Distinction

THE DOPAMINE HYPOTHESIS

In the previous chapter it was observed that schizophrenia, after decades of research, remains one of the most prevalent, devastating, and enigmatic of the psychiatric disorders. We presented the view that its resistance to scientific study seems to be rooted in its heterogeneous nature. Since the early writings of Bleuler (1908), it was recognized that schizophrenia comprises diverse conditions, and any attempt to understand it must take into account its various guises or components. The treatment of schizophrenia must likewise be geared to the particular disorder that is encountered.

The diversity in symptoms, history, and course of illness raises serious doubt about the efficacy and even the logic behind our principal treatment, the neuroleptic drug. The use of dopamine blocking agents, such as chlorpromazine and haloperidol, best fits a unitary or single-factor model of schizophrenia, one characterized by excessive dopaminergic activity. However, the limitation of these drugs, hence of the dopamine model as well, is revealed by their lack of efficacy for a large segment of schizophrenic patients and for many symptoms, even among those who are partially recovered and capable of hospital discharge.

The dopamine hypothesis itself has been challenged on several counts (Lader, 1983): (a) dopamine blockade cannot be directly equated with antipsychotic drugs; (b) dopamine agonists, such as amphetamine, exacerbate symptoms of actively psychotic schizophrenic patients, but not those in remission; (c) several predictions that should follow from excessive dopaminergic activity, such as low prolactin concentrations and incompatibility of parkinsonian with schizophrenic symptoms, are not supported; (d) the dopamine level in schizophrenia, as measured by dopamine turnover from cerebrospinal fluid homovanillic acid, is not consistently elevated except among those with motor hyperactivity; (e) postmortem studies of the brain of schizophrenic patients, after taking into account their experience with neuroleptics, do not reveal a clear-cut dopamine excess; (f) those postmortem studies that do indicate increased number of D_2 type dopamine receptors are contaminated by recent use of antipsychotic drugs, which also increases the D_2 receptor number; and (g) dopamine excess is not evident in patients who terminated drug treatment at least one month prior to death.

These observations, of course, do not contradict the beneficial role of dopamine blocking drugs in schizophrenia, which would suggest that dopaminergic activity is in some way involved in the symptomatic expression of the illness. We may conclude, however, that disorder of the dopamine system is not likely to represent a causal agent and does not account for the entire disorder.

A TWO-FACTOR MODEL OF SCHIZOPHRENIA

The need for a revised and expanded view of schizophrenia has, accordingly, become increasingly evident. One of the major advances in recent times has come from Strauss, Carpenter, and Bartko (1974), who proposed that at least two separate symptom profiles may be distinguished in schizophrenia. A positive, or productive, symptom is described as an abnormal feature, such as hallucinations, delusions, and disorganized thinking, that is present in the mental status. A negative, or deficit, symptom is defined as the absence of normal functions and, thus, includes features such as blunted affect, emotional withdrawal, and cognitive deficiency.

Based on this model, Timothy Crow (1980a, 1980b) in Great Britain hypothesized that the positive-negative distinction may embody separate disorders in schizophrenia. He proposed that these arise from unrelated neurological conditions and predict differences in drug response and in the ultimate course of illness (see Table 2:1). According to Crow, positive symptoms prevail in the acute stage and may signify an excessive transmission of dopamine in the brain. Patients of this type were thus characterized by a neurochemical abnormality that, logically, would be expected to respond well to neuroleptics and lead eventually to a good outcome. Negative symptoms, by contrast, were thought to prevail mainly in the chronic stage and to signify a structural brain abnormality, such as indicated by enlarged ventricles in the brain, hence cell loss and cortical atrophy. Patients of this description were expected to be neuroleptic resistant and to carry a poor prognosis.

Crow summarized his position by suggesting that "The two syndromes are related to distinct pathological processes—a disturbance of dopamine transmission being related to the drug-responsive [positive] syndrome and a quite separate and perhaps encephalitic-like process being associated with

TABLE 2:1
Crow's Two-Factor Model of Symptoms in Schizophrenia*

| | Symptoms | |
Area of Difference	Positive	Negative
Characteristic symptoms	Productive: hallucinations, thought disorder	Deficit: affective flattening, poverty of speech, loss of drive
Characteristic phase of schizophrenia	Acute	Chronic
Response to neuroleptics	Good	Poor
Intellectual impairment	Absent	Usually present
Pathological processes	Increased dopamine receptors	Cellular loss and structural changes in the brain

*Based on Crow (1980a).

the [negative] syndrome" (Crow, 1980b, p. 383). In this way, the dopamine hypothesis might be rescued by the position that it is applicable to only a subset of symptoms in schizophrenia.

Negative or deficit features of mental illness were identified by Pinel as long ago as 1801. The origins of the positive-negative terminology are usually attributed to Hughlings Jackson (1887), a British neurologist who drew this distinction not to describe unrelated symptoms of schizophrenia, but rather as a way to delineate primary from secondary neurological phenomena. Although not employing this terminology, Bleuler (1908) and Kraepelin (1919) provided a conceptual framework for its current application to schizophrenia by identifying symptom complexes that today would be recognized as positive or negative clusters.

Kraepelin's contention was that the core of schizophrenia is defect state which runs a deteriorative course; the more florid manifestations, such as hallucinations and delusions, were regarded as "accessory symptoms." In the years to follow, this position was gradually overtaken by emphasis on productive features as pathognomonic of schizophrenia and, in fact, a prerequisite for its diagnosis. This was evidenced, for example, in the diagnostic criteria for schizophrenia as put forth by Kurt Schneider (1959), Feigner et al. (1972), the Research Diagnostic Criteria (RDC) (Spitzer, Endicott, & Robins, 1978), and the DSM–III and DSM–III–R (American Psychiatric Association, 1980, 1987). Therefore, what were earlier construed as ancillary features of schizophrenia were later regarded as central or defining features, in all likelihood because of their ease in being reliably identified and assessed (Andreasen, 1982).

The comparative difficulty in measuring negative symptoms, of course, does not render these less important. The need to incorporate both negative and positive features into a model of schizophrenia was brought out by the factor analytic studies of the 1960s and, particularly, the research of Strauss, Carpenter, and Bartko (1974), who adapted Hughlings Jackson's terminology for classifying different profiles in schizophrenia.

Whereas Crow's seminal model viewed the positive and negative symptoms as unrelated facets of schizophrenia that may reflect separate pathological processes, Nancy Andreasen (Andreasen & Olsen, 1982; Andreasen et al., 1982) in Iowa proposed instead a typological model. She described positive and negative symptoms as *opposing* features which characterize different subtypes.

More recently, William Carpenter argued that negative symptoms do not form a stable and unitary construct and, therefore, should be replaced by the concept of a "deficit syndrome" (Carpenter, Heinrichs, & Alphs, 1985; Carpenter, Heinrichs, & Wagman, 1988). The latter term would additionally denote intractibility over a period of time and, in this respect, would by definition concur with some of the key attributes of the negative profile as described by Crow (see critique by Kay & Opler, 1989).

Although the viewpoint on positive and negative symptoms has thus branched out into rival models, the distinction retains an obvious appeal. It offers a simple dichotomization of schizophrenia, one that is rooted in different forms of neuropathology and proposes to embrace much of the diversity. If the positive-negative distinction is validated by empirical research, it would constitute a milestone in clarifying systematic differences in the etiology, pharmacotherapy, and prognosis of schizophrenia. After some 30 years of domination by the dopamine hypothesis, it would become the first major conceptualization that replaces (or, more accurately, incorporates) this post-neuroleptic model and expands our thinking from a one-factor to a two-factor perspective on schizophrenia.

EMPIRICAL STUDIES OF THE TWO-FACTOR MODEL

The empirical research, unfortunately, has not consistently supported the principal tenets of the positive-negative distinction (see reviews by Kay & Opler, 1987, and Pogue-Geile & Zubin, 1988). In particular, studies of its relationship to differences in drug response, brain structure, phase of illness, and prognosis have yielded mixed results. The Crow hypothesis was admittedly speculative and inferential. It was tied to a few experiments that revealed: (a) in acute schizophrenia, positive symptoms respond preferentially to neuroleptics (Johnstone et al., 1978a); (b) brain atrophy in chronic

TABLE 2:2
Effects of Amphetamine vs. Neuroleptics on Positive and
Negative Features of Schizophrenia*

Symptoms	Baseline mean	Change with Medication					
		Amphetamine			Neuroleptics		
		Mean	Direction	p	Mean	Direction	p
Positive	21.3	26.6	↑	<.001	15.4	↓	<.001
Negative	8.1	8.9	↑	<.05	7.7		n.s.
Emotional withdrawal	3.5	4.4	↑	<.001	2.9	↓	<.02
Motor retardation & blunted affect	4.7	4.5		n.s.	4.9		n.s.

*Based on Angrist, Rotrosen, & Gershon (1980). P refers to significance of increase (↑) or decrease (↓) from baseline (paired *t* test, two-tailed).

schizophrenia, as indicated by enlarged cerebral ventricles, is correlated with intellectual deficit and negative symptoms (Johnstone, Crow, et al., 1978b); and (c) dopamine receptors are increased in the postmortem brain of schizophrenics (Owens & Johnstone, 1980). These observations, though supportive, do not *demand* the interpretation given by Crow. As already discussed, methodological artifacts might well explain the postmortem findings. Moreover, the attempts to replicate and expand on these observations have not always been successful (Pogue-Geile & Zubin, 1988).

One pillar of support for the Crow hypothesis has been the seminal research by Angrist, Rotrosen, and Gershon (1980) at New York University. Their comparison of clinical response to amphetamine vs. neuroleptic treatment was taken as demonstration that neuroleptics target the positive symptoms alone. The investigators examined 21 schizophrenic patients on both drug regimens after six to 15 days off medication. They found significant worsening of all symptoms on amphetamine, while neuroleptics led to improvement of a positive but not negative symptom cluster rated on the Brief Psychiatric Rating Scale (BPRS) (Overall & Gorham, 1962). Yet, emotional withdrawal, which was one of the three items constituting the negative factor, actually *improved* significantly with neuroleptics in the same manner as the positive symptoms (see Table 2:2).

Another landmark study, reported by the Andreasen group, proposed in line with Crow that schizophrenics with a prominent negative syndrome are characterized by ventricular enlargement, reflecting cell loss in the brain (Andreasen et al., 1982). From a cohort of 52 schizophrenic patients, they compared the 16 with the largest ventricular brain ratios against the 16 with the smallest. Although the authors cited "trends" in the hypothesized direction, in fact, of the 10 symptoms depicted as positive or negative, only one—bizarre behavior—reached statistical significance. In all other respects the groups were clinically similar.

Next, the researchers divided their sample into those with predominantly positive or negative symptoms, as well as a "mixed" group which could not be classified decisively (Andreasen & Olsen, 1982). They found the negative type to show poorer premorbid functioning in terms of educational attainment, employment status, and Phillips (1953) ratings of premorbid social adjustment. No other sociodemographic characteristics distinguished the groups. They also reported what they considered evidence of greater neurological impairment in the negative subtype: larger ventricular brain ratios, fewer right-handers, and poorer scores on the Mini-Mental status (from Mini-Mental State Exam) which includes cognitive ratings.

One interpretational problem, however, comes from the questionable validity and specificity of the Mini-Mental status as a cognitive and, particularly, a neuropsychological test. A yet more serious issue concerns possible sampling artifact: the negative group had far greater experience with electroconvulsive therapy (56 percent of cases vs. 5 percent of the positive group, $p < 0.05$). This disparity could well explain the reported differences in neurological and cognitive functioning (Friedberg, 1961).

More recent neuropsychological studies have indeed failed to support the models of Crow and Andreasen. For example, Bilder et al. (1985) found aspects of *both* positive and negative syndromes to correlate with an extensive neuropsychological battery conducted on 32 chronic schizophrenics. Recent study by Peuskens et al. (1989), as well as Andreasen's own later work, has failed to replicate the association of negative syndrome with enlarged cerebral ventricles. On the other hand, information-processing research seems to concur in finding a negative syndrome associated with slower information-processing capacity (Green & Walker, 1984; Cornblatt et al., 1985; Weiner et al., in press). The most promising and consistent leads, therefore, have involved differences in premorbid adjustment and in cognitive, though not specifically neurological, functioning.

LIMITATIONS IN METHODOLOGY

The varied and, at times, discordant research findings, however, do not necessarily discount the validity of the positive-negative distinction. It has been noted that this still young area of research is beset by fundamental weaknesses in the methodology, which are likely to augment type II error, i.e., to militate against consistent findings (Sommers, 1985; Zubin, 1985; Kay & Opler, 1987). Let us consider here six common pitfalls.

First is the reliance on scales that are not fully operationalized and standardized, thus promoting measurement that is weak, inaccurate, or simply invalid. As will be more carefully described in the next chapter, the scales that are available for research (e.g., Overall & Gorham, 1962; Andreasen & Olsen, 1982; Lewine, Fogg, & Meltzer, 1983; Heinrichs, Hanlon, & Carpenter, 1984; Iager, Kirch, & Wyatt, 1985) provide neither a standardized interview nor specific rating criteria to decide between different levels of symptom severity, such as mild vs. moderate.

These methods also have been criticized for uncertain content and construct validity as well as lack of retest reliability (Zubin, 1985; Kay, Fiszbein, & Opler, 1986a; Liddle, 1987). Carpenter and colleagues (1985) have persuasively argued that several of the symptoms which have been classified as negative (e.g., "attentional impairment" and "disorientation") may actually be *secondary* to positive features, such as hallucinations or hyperarousal. Thus, a patient who is floridly psychotic may seem more distracted, isolated, confused, or dysfunctional without presenting a true deficit syndrome. The research at Columbia University (Bilder et al., 1985; Cornblatt et al., 1985) and at our own facility (Kay, Opler & Fiszbein, 1986; Kay, Fiszbein, Lindenmayer, & Opler, 1986) confirms that an attentional impairment, for instance, clusters equally with negative and positive phenomena.

Second, it is noteworthy that many studies analyze the negative syndrome in a vacuum, without due consideration for how it may differ from the positive syndrome, depression, or other facets of the illness. Unless the significance attributed to the negative syndrome is *particular* to that cluster of symptoms, the conclusions will be grossly misleading, having perhaps more to do with the severity than with the character of the disorder. Studies on negative psychopathology, therefore, require a psychometrically comparable measurement of other symptoms that serve, in effect, as "controls" to provide this relational perspective.

A third pitfall is the tendency to study syndromes cross-sectionally. The popularity of cross-sectional designs could have much to do with their congeniality for quick and large-scale data collection. It is important to recognize, however, that the cross-sectional perspective offers only a "snapshot" view that is static rather than dynamic. Thus, it tells us little about hypothesized processes and cause-effect relationships. By its very nature, this perspective does not allow one to examine the stability, course, and mutability of symptoms over time. This is a crucial shortcoming, since negative phenomena have been hypothesized to show specific longitudinal characteristics, such as prominence in the chronic stage, lack of response to neuroleptics, and poor outcome. Without a research design that can test these assumptions, a meaningful validation study is not possible.

Fourth, the relatively few investigations that examine positive and negative syndromes longitudinally seem to apply only a short-term design that covers several (usually three to six) weeks of neuroleptic treatment, or else a retrospective view of the course of illness. For example, the longitudinal studies of Pogue-Geile and Harrow (1984, 1985), though highly informative, were derived from retrospective assessment of symptoms rather than from concurrent baseline analysis and subsequent follow-up. Without a prospective design, we cannot establish the predictive significance of a positive or negative presentation, and without long-term follow-up we cannot presume to know its prognostic import.

Fifth, the sampling has generally been limited to small groups and to patients in the chronic phase of schizophrenia. Often, the duration of illness is not specified, or data from acute, subchronic, and chronic schizophrenics are indiscriminately combined. As we shall see later (Chapter 10), it is not correct to assume that the meaning of these syndromes is the same at different stages of illness. The failure to take this into consideration may lead to sampling variability that cancels out the findings within a given study and contributes to systematic differences between studies.

Sixth, the overwhelming majority of the research on these syndromes has not investigated patients in the more natural, drug-free state. As a result, the observations may be contaminated by prior clinical response to neuroleptics, which will obviously alter the psychiatric picture in specific ways. Alternatively, the very selection of patients whose positive or negative features are uncorrected by drug treatment may result in an unrepresentative refractory sample. Indeed, one cannot reasonably assume that the negative profile carries the same meaning in a drug-treated as in an unmedicated patient, whose negative symptoms have gone unchallenged and, therefore, may still subside with the intervention. Finally, as has been amply stressed (Rifkin, Quitkin, & Klein, 1975; Carpenter, Heinrichs, & Alphs, 1985), the assessment of negative symptoms in medicated patients may be confounded by extrapyramidal drug side effects that restrict verbal, motor, and social functions and perhaps mimic negative phenomena.

PROGRAMMATIC STUDY

Mindful of these methodological pitfalls, our research group has embarked on a series of investigations aiming for a sharper and fuller perspective on the validity and significance of the positive-negative distinction in schizophrenia. This direction was inspired by separate trends in our earlier longitudinal research that applied both psychopharmacological and developmental frameworks.

First, we noted that the prototypic neuroleptics, such as chlorpromazine

TABLE 2:3
Cognitive Abnormality in Schizophrenia: A Dual-Process Model*

Distinguishing Features	Two Processes in Chronic Schizophrenia	
	Arousal-Related	Developmentally-Rooted
Onset of symptoms	Overt psychotic phase	Premorbid
Cognitive & social profiles	Disorganized, excited	Deficient, primitive
Diagnostic subtype	Catatonic	Hebephrenic, simple
Prognostic subtype	Schizophreniform (good outcome)	Nuclear (poor outcome)
Neuroleptic response	Fuller remission	Residual cognitive and social deficits
Course	Labile	Stable
Prevalent syndrome	Positive	Negative

*Based on Kay & Singh (1979).

and haloperidol, seemed to act more quickly and effectively on arousal-related disorders in schizophrenia, such as confusion, disorganized state, and sleeplessness, as compared with such deficit symptoms as difficulty in abstract thinking and passive social withdrawal (Singh & Kay, 1975a, 1975b). Our own clinical observations (Kay & Opler, 1985), backed up by scattered reports in the Australian and Japanese literature (Buchanan et al., 1975; Inanaga et al., 1975; Ogura, Kishimoto, and Nakao, 1976), suggested that psychotropic drugs which promote rather than block dopamine transmission (e.g., L-dopa) produce quite the opposite pattern of symptomatic changes. This implied the existence of two kinds of symptoms with converse neuropharmacological bases.

Secondly, our research in the 1970s examined schizophrenia in terms of developmental (Kay & Singh, 1975a, 1979) and ethological principles (Singh, Kay, & Pitman, 1981a, 1981b) to seek fresh insights into the fundamental nature of cognitive and social dysfunctions. These studies evaluated cognitive developmental impairment according to Piagetian theory (Piaget, 1952) and abnormal territorial behavior according to Tinbergen's (1972) evolutionary concept. Using pharmacotherapy as a dissective experimental tool, we monitored changes in patients' functioning from placebo baseline across 16 to 20 weeks of neuroleptic treatment. From this work we found that certain cognitive and social processes are particularly resistant to drug therapy. Such disorders are characterized by a primitive, often childlike quality and seem to be present both before the onset of florid symptoms and even after their resolution with neuroleptics.

These observations led us to a "dual-process model" of schizophrenic abnormality (Kay & Singh, 1979), which posits two separate components (see Table 2:3): (a) a neuroleptic-resistant developmental component, observed mainly in hebephrenic and nuclear subtypes, which precedes the manifest psychosis and remains as the residue in otherwise reconstituted patients; and (b) a neuroleptic-responsive arousal-related component, seen mainly in catatonic and schizophreniform subtypes, which represents a temporary state of disorganization and remits more fully. These distinct stable and labile processes seem to correspond to what we today term the negative and positive syndromes.

Our strategy for investigating the positive-negative distinction began with the development and standardization of a well operationalized method for assessing syndromes (Chapter 3). With this instrument, we undertook large-scale, multidimensional studies of schizophrenic patients at various phases of the illness. The research designs included cross-sectional comparisons, longitudinal study with prospective baseline measures, and either drug-free evaluation or independent control ratings of drug side effects.

It will be seen that the cumulative findings support the reliability and validity of the negative syndrome in schizophrenia as a pathological process distinct from the positive syndrome. Our data suggest that the "dual-process model" indeed embodies the positive-negative distinction. A negative syndrome in chronic schizophrenia seems to signify a more ominous condition that arises developmentally, responds less favorably to traditional neuroleptic medications, is associated with familial schizophrenia, and culminates in sustained multimodal deficits. The delineation of independent positive and negative syndromes, hopefully, may lead to a more comprehensive understanding of the processes that underlie schizophrenia and to better conceived strategies for treatment. Our findings, however, do not support the models originally proposed by Crow and Andreasen. Contrary to their views, (a) positive and negative syndromes do not necessarily decrease or increase over time; (b) their import seems to differ systematically at different stages of the illness; (c) their distinction in response to neuroleptics varies according to the particular compound selected; and (d) alone, the two syndromes are insufficient to explain the full range of schizophrenic phenomena.

The forthcoming chapters will describe in detail our new method for assessing these and other facets of the schizophrenic disorder. Thereafter, the results from our series of investigations, as based on this technique, will be systematically reviewed. In the last section, we will describe a "pyramidical model" for conceptualizing the clinical dimensions of schizophrenia and their relatedness to the conventional diagnostic subtypes. Finally, we will propose a novel interpretation of the positive and negative features, one built on a unifying hypothesis about the pathophysiological mechanisms that underlie these manifestations.

PART II

Assessment of the Syndromes

3

Methods of Positive-Negative Assessment

THE IMPORTANCE OF STANDARDIZED MEASUREMENT

In the preceding section we presented the view that delineation of positive and negative syndromes may at least partly explain the heterogeneity of schizophrenia and, thereby, offer important new leads toward understanding and treating this condition. Yet as also noted, the studies of these syndromes have yielded diverse and often conflicting results. Investigators still disagree on the distinctiveness of these syndromes, their relatedness to neuropathology, their different response to neuroleptics, and their stability over the long-term course of illness.

Research findings, of course, are no more trustworthy than the measures on which they are based. Instruments that are of narrow scope will necessarily limit the range of one's findings, for obviously we cannot discover what we fail to examine. Instruments that are unreliable or of low validity can be expected to produce weak or inconsistent results (a "type II" research error, or false negative) or, worse yet, misleading data (a "type I" research error, or false positive). Therefore, the methods used for positive-negative assessment can be a fundamental source of variance between studies and even within studies.

Despite the importance of newer and better standardized assessment methods, it is striking that in our era of rapid technological growth, clinical evaluation is essentially at an impasse. Most investigators still use the rating techniques from the late 1950s and early 1960s, which had been introduced to assess symptomatic changes with neuroleptic drugs. In general, these methods could at best be considered *partially* operationalized and standardized, as they are founded on poorly described interviews, minimally defined criteria, and incomplete validation studies (see discussion by Kay, in press-b). This laxity is of serious consequence, since the "law of the lowest common denominator" dictates that the reliability and validity of one's findings are limited by the reliability and validity of the weakest instrument in one's battery. Thus, even the most sophisticated and accurate neurobiological measurement will be adulterated when paired with a crude clinical rating.

In view of the recent interest in negative symptomatology, newer assessment methods have been originated, but these have tended to follow the older pattern of only partial operationalization and standardization. In the sections to follow, we shall review the requisites for a sound positive-negative symptom scale and the formal psychometric characteristics of those most commonly used, in order to spotlight their strengths and limitations.

REQUISITES FOR ASSESSMENT

The profession of psychology has established rigorous technical guidelines for test development (American Psychological Association, 1985) to ensure that the psychometric qualities are optimized and that the test is, in effect, scientifically grounded. These guidelines, however, often are not adhered to when psychiatric assessment methods are devised, particularly symptom rating scales. The present discussion will revolve around three areas that need to be addressed in developing a positive-negative scale: operational criteria, scale construction, and standardization.

1. Operational Criteria

For a psychiatric rating instrument to be objective and reliable, it is essential that it be thoroughly operationalized in all facets. Most scales present symptom definitions, but typically fail to provide detailed criteria for measuring symptom severity. Thus, the single-word descriptors, such as "mild," "moderate," and "moderate-severe," are not tied to precise definitions and so, by default, are judged on the basis of one's subjective frame of reference. Most positive and negative symptom scales also offer no detailed guide to the clinical interview, which is the actual data source or "test" itself. Since the material that is elicited from the patient depends directly on the vagaries of the interview, the lack of a formal and/or structured procedure compromises the validity of the assessment and may lead to great variation among observers.

Even the training process must be made standard in order that different rating teams utilize the method in a comparable manner. Without such uniformity in training, each research center ultimately evolves its own interpretations and conventions on interviewing and rating. For similar reasons, international use of a scale requires the availability of official translations that are suitably adapted to the different cultures and, preferably, are standardized against the original scale.

2. Scale Construction

A useful, versatile instrument is constructed with a sufficient number of rating points as well as a balanced and broad range of items to permit maximal sensitivity and an ample scope of assessment. The content of a scale, i.e., the item selection, is of obvious importance. A first principle for establishing good content validity is suitable representation from different facets of the construct (Nunnally, 1978). Thus, if a scale purports to assess negative phenomena, it must sample these manifestations from different functional spheres that are presumed to be involved, such as the cognitive, social, emotional, and communicational. It would be misleading, for example, to describe as a negative symptom scale one that looks at only the social or emotional processes.

A second principle of content validity is the inclusion of a relatively large number of items, since this helps to cancel out random error variance and, thereby, improves reliability. Likewise, it is also desirable that the major subscales—i.e., the positive and negative clusters—be composed of an equal number of items, so that their potential reliabilities are equated. If one applies a method such as the Brief Psychiatric Rating Scale (BPRS) (Overall & Gorham, 1962), which presents 11 positive but only three negative items, the positive score will tend to be more reliable and sensitive to change; in these basic respects it will not be comparable to the negative score. Since reliability imposes an upper limit on validity, the two subscales will be imbalanced in terms of validity as well. Thus, it would be a serious mistake to conclude from longitudinal therapeutic study with such a scale that the positive cluster is more treatment-sensitive than the negative: this is a feature of the scale itself and not necessarily of the presumed construct. Yet, since the BPRS has been the most frequently used scale in psychopharmacological research of schizophrenia (Hedlund & Viewig, 1980), there is a prima facie reason to be skeptical of the conclusions on positive and negative syndromes.

Perhaps the most difficult task in test or scale construction is the establishment of construct validity, which requires demonstration that the instrument is truly isolating and measuring the phenomenon of interest—and nothing else (Nunnally, 1978). There is indeed considerable doubt that the prevalent scales for assessing negative symptoms achieve this (Sommers, 1985; Zubin, 1985). As has been duly stressed (Carpenter, Heinrichs, & Alphs, 1985), the negative items must depict the deficit condition and not manifestations that are secondary to positive symptoms. For example, poor attention, disorientation, and social avoidance are three symptoms commonly included in negative scales that could well be associated with positive symptoms, such as overarousal, confusion, and hallucinations. The distinction between negative and positive symptoms is most clearly drawn by a more conservative item selection for the negative scale, inclusion of a parallel positive scale for comparative purposes, and provision of a composite (positive minus negative) index. The latter "difference score" permits judgment of the predominance of one syndrome in relation to the other, thereby facilitating typological evaluation and screening selection.

The negative symptom assessment also, however, needs to be distinguished from depression, which is prevalent in schizophrenia (Knight & Roff, 1985) and may likewise manifest itself in diminished social, motor, and cognitive functions (Carpenter, Heinrichs, & Alphs, 1985; Lindenmayer & Kay, 1989). Less fully recognized, but equally important, is the need to separate negative phenomena from other facets of psychopathology, including global severity of illness, with which it tends to strongly covary (Kay, Opler, & Fiszbein, 1986). This requires, in effect, a *full range assessment* of psychopathology in order that the negative dimension be viewed relationally, as properly embedded within the overall profile of symptoms. To do otherwise—to look at the negative picture in a vacuum— is to hazard a false interpretation, one that attributes to the negative syndrome properties which, in reality, are not specific to that syndrome.

3. Standardization

Once a test or scale is constructed, an intensive series of large-scale studies must ensue to establish its psychometric properties. There are many separate aspects of reliability and validity that need to be demonstrated (Nunnally, 1978; American Psychological Association, 1985), of which the positive-negative scales have tackled only a few, most notably interrater agreement. It is a serious but common error to compare and select rating methods on the basis of this sole parameter. One must recognize that interrater reliability does not imply validity: the fact that people agree on their judgment does not necessarily mean that the judgment is correct, relevant, or interpretable.

In addition to interrater concordance, it is essential to demonstrate that the scale is internally consistent, stable over time, and reliable when used repeatedly on the same subject. In terms of validity, the standardization studies should include evidence of content and construct validity (see above) to ascertain that the scale is truly depicting the purported dimension. Also crucial are data on factorial validity to establish the nature and purity of components; criterion-related validity to specify the scale's association with external variables; and, from the longitudinal standpoint, predictive validity and sensitivity to change. The final step in standardization is the provision of norms and percentile ranks, which allows the scale user to interpret the scores statistically with respect to the reference group. The percentiles further can provide an empirical predefined criterion for screening and classifying patients.

COMPARISON OF POSITIVE-NEGATIVE SCALES

Several different scales for assessing negative and/or positive symptoms have been applied by researchers, contributing to the discrepancies in findings. Table 3:1 summarizes the characteristics of those used most commonly, as based on the original articles that describe their standardization.

KMS

We begin our comparison with the Krawiecka-Manchester Scale (KMS) (Krawiecka, Goldberg, & Vaughan, 1977), which has been relatively popular in Great Britain and continental Europe, due in large part to its use by Dr. Timothy Crow and his colleague, Dr. Eve Johnstone. The principal advantages of the KMS are the fairly precise operational criteria for interviewing and rating, which are enhanced by the availability of videotapes for training. The procedure was not developed, however, as a negative symptom scale but, rather, as "an ideal instrument to use where large chronic psychotic populations have to be screened with a certain amount of rapidity" (Krawiecka, Goldberg, & Vaughan, 1977, p. 302). Thus, the interview is brief; the scaling entails only five points; and the assessment is limited to eight symptoms in total. Of these items, only three (poverty of speech, flattened incongruous affect, and psychomotor retardation) may be considered negative, and yet all three are potentially secondary to depression or positive symptoms. Crow (1985) and Johnstone et al. (1978a) have accordingly used a modification of the KMS that separates out "incongruous affect" and deletes "psychomotor retardation" from the negative assessment, but this now leaves only two symptoms (poverty of speech and flat affect) to represent negative schizophrenia.

The standardization study of the KMS (Krawiecka, Goldberg, & Vaughan, 1977) samples a mere "10 known psychiatric patients" of unspecified diagnosis, and it presents no validation data and no reliability analysis other than interrater agreement. The interrater reliability, in fact, appears

TABLE 3:1
Comparison of Negative Symptom Scales*

	Negative Symptom Scale					
Dimension of Comparison	KMS	SANS/ SAPS	BPRS	NSRS	QLS	PANSS
Operational Criteria						
• Items defined?	No	Yes	Yes	Yes	Yes	Yes
• Detailed criteria for each level of symptom severity?	Yes	No	No	No	No	Yes
• Comprehensive patient interview?	No	No	Yes	No	No	Yes
• Detailed interview guide?	Yes	No	No	No	No	Yes
• Structured clinical interview available?	No	No	No	No	No	Yes
• Videotape training available?	Yes	Yes	No	No	No	Yes
• Translations?	?	Yes	Yes	?	?	Yes
Scale Construction						
• Number of scaling points?	5	6	7	7	7	7
• Number of negative symptoms?	3	5	3	10	4	7
• Number of positive symptoms?	3	4	11	0	0	7
• Number of total symptoms?	8	9	18	10	4	30
• Balanced no. of positive & negative items?	Yes	No	No	No	No	Yes
• Number of functional spheres represented in the negative scale?	3	4	2	3	3	4
• Secondary negative symptoms excluded?	No	No	No	No	No	Yes
• Composite (positive vs. negative) index?	No	No	No	No	No	Yes
• Depression scale included?	Yes	No	Yes	No	No	Yes
• Other symptom clusters assessed?	No	No	Yes	No	No	Yes
• Global psychopathology score obtained?	Yes	No	Yes	No	No	Yes
Standardization Data Reported						
• Size of standardization sample (N)?	10	52+26	112	33	111	101+82
• Interrater reliability (negative items)?	.50−.73	.70−.88	.62−.72	.65−.97	.58−.94	.70−.89
• Internal reliability?	No	Yes	No	No	No	Yes
• Longitudinal reliability?	No	No	No	No	No	Yes
• Stability?	No	No	No	No	No	Yes
• Factorial validity?	No	No	Yes	No	Yes	Yes
• Content validity?	No	No	No	No	Yes	Yes
• Construct validity?	No	No	No	No	No	Yes
• Criterion-related validity?	No	Yes	No	Yes	No	Yes
• Predictive validity?	No	No	No	No	No	Yes
• Sensitivity to change?	No	No	No	No	No	Yes
• Normative data and percentile ranks?	No	No	No	No	No	Yes (N=240)

*Based on Kay (in press, b). See text for abbreviations and explanations.

to be weak, with a reported Kendall correlation that averages .64 for the negative items.

SANS

The Scale for Assessing Negative Symptoms (SANS) (Andreasen, 1982; Andreasen & Olsen, 1982), as the first method devised specifically to measure negative phenomena in schizophrenia, has gained ascendance in the United States. Its main asset is a detailed and internally reliable inspection of five negative symptoms: affective flattening, alogia, avolition-apathy, anhedonia-asociality, and attentional impairment. When used with the four-item companion Scale for Assessing Positive Symptoms (SAPS), a comparison with positive symptoms is made possible, although this is to some extent mitigated by imbalance in the number of items in the SANS vs. SAPS.

A more serious criticism is that the global ratings, which determine the final scores, are poorly defined and impressionistic. In addition, the six levels of symptom severity for the global ratings also lack adequate anchoring definitions, and the interview itself is not well structured or formalized. Consequently, many investigators report feeling "uncomfortable" with the SANS and having difficulty in establishing good reliability (personal communication).

Of crucial importance, one of the five negative items in the SANS (attentional impairment) covaries equally with positive symptoms both conceptually and statistically (Bilder et al., 1985; Cornblatt et al., 1985; Kay, Opler, & Fiszbein, 1986). Meanwhile other aspects of psychopathology, such as depression and general severity of illness, are not evaluated for comparative purposes. In terms of standardization, most facets of reliability and validity remain to be demonstrated. Recent comparison by Thiemann, Csernansky, and Berger (1987) found that the SANS contributes nothing beyond the assessment provided by the much older BPRS (Overall & Gorham, 1962).

BPRS

The BPRS, as already noted, is the most popular and universally used psychiatric rating scale, particularly as applied to drug studies (Hedlund & Viewig, 1980). Besides being a "tried and true" instrument, its benefits include a fairly comprehensive three-phase interview (Overall, 1976) and an 18-item symptom evaluation that yields five factor scores, including depression (Guy, 1976). A significant drawback, however, is the lack of a detailed interview guide and also the absence of definitions for the seven anchoring points along the scale.

For the present purposes, the primary problem with the BPRS is that it was not devised to measure negative phenomena and, in point of fact, includes only three negative items—blunted affect, emotional withdrawal, and motor retardation. These symptoms have been variously found to correlate with depressive and catatonic states (e.g., Bucci, 1987; Prosser et al., 1987) and to be confounded with extrapyramidal symptoms (e.g., Kane et al., 1985; Prosser et al., 1987). As mentioned in the previous chapter, these three negative items respond differentially to neuroleptics (Angrist, Rotrosen, & Gershon, 1980), suggesting that they are conceptually distinct and may not be combined.

In terms of the scope of assessment, the BPRS negative or "withdrawal-retardation" subscale, as it is sometimes referred to, considers only two spheres of function, the emotional and the motoric. The anergia factor of the BPRS, which some investigators have utilized as a negative scale, subsumes these same three items plus disorientation, which is a multidetermined symptom that could be associated with confusion, withdrawal, or neuropathology.

NSRS

The Negative Symptom Rating Scale (NSRS) (Iager, Kirch, & Wyatt, 1985) has been critiqued by us elsewhere (Kay, Fiszbein, & Opler, 1986) and will not be reviewed in detail here. Although it comprises 10 negative items, several of these (speech content, attention, orientation) are inseparable from positive symptoms. The interview and ratings are not fully operationalized, and the scale does not permit comparative assessment of positive features, depression, or other components or psychopathology. The standardization study (Iager, Kirch, & Wyatt, 1985), which included only 33 patients of variable diagnosis, provides minimal data on reliability and validity.

QLS

The Quality of Life Scale (QLS) (Heinrichs, Hanlon, & Carpenter, 1984) consists of 21 items which condense to four factors that reflect on three functional spheres. By contrast to the other scales, the QLS is more firmly rooted in social, occupational, and behavioral data rather than on psychopathology judgments. Nevertheless, it shares some of the same limitations as the NSRS: weak operational criteria and lack of basis for comparison with other aspects of the illness. While the standardization sample is impressive in its size and in its factorial analysis, the study neglects many fundamental issues on reliability and validity.

POSITIVE AND NEGATIVE SYNDROME SCALE (PANSS)

The Positive and Negative Syndrome Scale (PANSS) (Kay, Fiszbein, & Opler, 1987; Kay, Opler, & Lindenmayer, 1988, 1989) was developed specifically to address the foregoing psychometric limitations, and therefore it is no coincidence that it stands apart from these other scales as one which is more strictly operationalized, more comprehensive in its range of assessment, and more thoroughly standardized. Table 3:1 summarizes the psychometric properties of the PANSS as compared to the five other negative symptom scales just described. The details about its standardization will be reviewed later (Chapter 5).

The PANSS measurement derives from behavioral information plus a four-phase 35–45 minute clinical interview. This is followed by seven-point ratings on 30 symptoms, for which each item and each level of symptom severity are defined. The ratings provide summary scores on a seven-item positive scale, seven-item negative scale, 16-item general psychopathology scale, and a composite (positive minus negative) index.

The seven positive items, which encompass five realms of functioning, include delusions, conceptual disorganization, hallucinatory behavior, excitement, grandiosity, suspiciousness-persecution, and hostility. The seven negative items, which sample from four spheres of functioning, were selected as characteristic of a primary deficit syndrome: blunted affect, emotional withdrawal, poor rapport, passive/apathetic social withdrawal, difficulty in abstract thinking, lack of spontaneity and flow of conversation, and stereotyped thinking. Since the PANSS incorporates all items in the BPRS, it also yields factor scores for five other psychopathology clusters, including depression.

The interview guide presents specific lines of questioning to elicit psychopathology (see Appendix A). More recently, we have developed a Structured Clinical Interview for the PANSS assessment (see Chapter 7) and one that provides for its use with the DSM–III–R (see Chapter 8), thus enabling combined diagnostic and functional-dimensional evaluations. A children's edition of the PANSS interview and ratings also has been newly developed for systematic assessment of psychopathology in patients ages 6–16 years (Fields et al., 1990).

For purposes of multicenter study, videotapes have been prepared to automate and standardize the interview and rater training (Kay, Opler & Fiszbein, 1989a, 1989b). The PANSS Rating Manual (Kay, Opler, & Fiszbein, 1990) has been translated into 13 languages for international use (see Appendix B) and, thus far, has been restandardized in French (Lepine, Piron, & Chapotot, 1989), Italian (Pozzi, 1989, personal communication), and Spanish (see Chapter 6). The psychometric studies have involved large samples of schizophrenic inpatients and have addressed the multiple facets of reliability and validity

(Chapter 5). Data have been reported, for example, on the validity of the PANSS in relation to premorbid, genealogical, course-related, psychopharmacological, and prognostic variables (Kay, Fiszbein, & Opler, 1987; Kay & Opler, 1987). The Rating Manual currently includes normative data and percentile ranks on 240 medicated schizophrenic patients (Appendix C).

The psychometric advantages of the PANSS may be summarized as follows: (a) operational criteria for eliciting and rating psychopathology; (b) broad spectrum of assessment that includes negative, positive, depressive, and general features of schizophrenia to enable profiling of syndromes; (c) content sampling that is balanced, encompasses several functional spheres, and excludes from the negative scale items known to correlate with positive or depressive features; (d) standard videotape training; (e) comprehensive standardization studies; (f) normative tables that provide an empirical basis for patient screening and interpretation of ratings; and (g) availability in several languages, which can foster multinational and crosscultural studies.

DEVELOPMENT OF THE PANSS

The PANSS was originated, therefore, as a more rigorously operationalized method for evaluating positive, negative, and other symptom dimensions in schizophrenia. Initially, it had been formulated as a special adaptation of two psychiatric rating scales, the BPRS (Overall & Gorham, 1962) and the Psychopathology Rating Schedule (Singh & Kay, 1975a), which culled items that optimally represent the positive and negative features of schizophrenia. As it evolved, however, we recognized the need for greater psychometric sophistication to successfully standardize the technique, including more detailed guidelines for eliciting and evaluating psychiatric symptoms. Accordingly, the interview procedure and all rated items were modified and expanded to provide precise instructions for conduct of the PANSS interview, clear-cut definitions for each parameter to be rated, distinct criteria for all seven levels of psychopathology, and what we judged as equivalent distance between rating points on each item.

The PANSS categorizes positive and negative symptoms according to the original conceptualization of Crow (1980a, 1980b). The selection of items was guided by five considerations, in the following order of importance: (a) items must be consistent with the theoretical concept of positive and negative psychopathology as representing productive features superadded to the mental status vs. deficit features characterized by loss of functions; (b) they should comprise symptoms that can be unambiguously classified as positive or negative and which, by most accounts, are regarded as primary rather than derivative; (c) they should include symptoms that are consensually regarded as *central* to the definition of positive syndrome (e.g., hallucinations, delusions, and disorganized thinking) and negative syndrome (e.g., blunted affect, emotional withdrawal, and impoverished communication); (d) to optimize content validity, they should sample from diverse realms of functioning, such as the cognitive, affective, social, and communicational; and (e) for practical and psychometric reasons, such as facilitating cross-comparisons and equalizing reliability potential, the number of items in the positive and negative scales should be the same.

In addition to the seven positive and seven negative items, 16 symptoms that cannot be linked decisively to either syndrome are included and comprise a general psychopathology scale (see Appendix D for listing). As described by Guy (1976), five factor scores are also obtained by summing statistically related items; these factors are anergia, thought disturbance, activation, paranoid-belligerence, and depression. The general psychopathology and factor scores serve as reference points, or control measures, for interpreting the positive and negative syndrome scores.

PANSS INTERVIEW PROCEDURE

The PANSS ratings are based on the totality of information pertaining to a specified period, normally identified as the previous week. The information derives from both clinical interview and reports by primary care hospital staff or, if the patient is not institutionalized, reports by family members. The information on daily functioning is an essential source for assessing social and behavioral deviations, particularly the items on emotional withdrawal, passive/apathetic social withdrawal, poor impulse control, active social avoidance, uncooperativeness, hostility, excitement, and motor retardation. Staff or family reports contribute also to assessing the severity of various other dimensions of psychopathology insofar as these are manifested in the realms of social interactions, general behavior, and adaptive functioning.

Most of the PANSS ratings, however, accrue primarily from a formal 35–45 minute formalized psychiatric interview that permits direct observation of affective, psychomotor, cognitive, perceptual, attentional, integrative, and interactive functions. The interview may be conceptualized as involving four phases, as outlined in Table 3:2.

Phase I

In the first 5–10 minutes (the "nondirective phase"), patients are encouraged to discuss their history, circumstances surrounding their hospitalization, their current life situation, and their symptoms. The object of the

TABLE 3:2
**Organization of the Positive and Negative Syndrome Scale (PANSS)
Clinical Interview***

Phase	Approx. Time	Objectives	Interview Strategy	Areas of Inquiry
Preinterview	5 min.	Obtain specified data on functioning outside the interview situation	Inquiry from primary care staff or family	Social behavior, emotional involvement, motor functions, life functions, hostility, impulse control, and management problems
I	5–10 min.	Establish rapport; Observe spontaneous organization of ideas, abnormal behavior, and pathological themes	Unstructured; Nondirective	History, onset of illness, events that led to hospitalization, and special concerns
II	15 min.	Systematically pursue areas of psychopathology to ascertain the presence and severity of symptoms	Semistructured; Use of leading questions that become progressively more focused	Impaired insight, delusions, hallucinations, suspiciousness, and guilt feelings
III	5–10 min.	Directly assess subjective feelings, orientation, and abstract reasoning	Structured; Use of specific sets of questions	Mood state, anxiety, orientation to three spheres, and abstract reasoning ability
IV	5–10 min.	Clarify information; Assess full range of psychopathology; Observe response to stress and vulnerability to disorganization	Directive; Testing of limits	Further probe of responses that were avoided, ambivalent, or illogical

*Based on Kay, Opler, & Fiszbein (1990).

interview at this point is to establish rapport and allow the patient to pro-nounce on areas of concern. Therefore, the interviewer at first assumes a nondirective, unchallenging posture in order to observe, as unobtrusively as possible, the nature of thought processes and content, judgment and in-sight, communication and rapport, and affective and motor responses.

Phase II

Deviant material from the first segment of the interview is elucidated sys-tematically during the second ("semi-structured") phase, lasting another

15–20 minutes, by use of leading questions that progress from unprovocative, nonspecific inquiry (e.g., "Are you special in some ways?") to more direct probe of pathological themes (e.g., "Do you have special or unusual powers?" "Do you consider yourself famous?"). The prototypic questions for eliciting different areas of psychopathology are presented in Appendix A or, alternatively, in the SCI-PANSS (Chapter 7). The object now is to measurably assess productive symptoms that are judged mainly from patients' report and elaborations thereof, such as hallucinations, delusional ideation, suspiciousness, and impaired insight. For this purpose, the interviewer attempts to establish first the presence of symptoms and next their severity in terms of prominence, frequency, and interference in activities of daily living.

Phase III

The third and most focused segment of the interview (the "structured" phase), which requires another 5–10 minutes, involves a series of specific questions to secure information on mood state, anxiety, orientation to three spheres, and abstract reasoning ability. Typical questions used for these probes are included also in Appendix A and in the SCI-PANSS. It may be noted that difficulty in thinking abstractly is evaluated by questions on similarities and proverb interpretation in order to test concept formation and abstract reasoning, respectively. These items are varied and rotated when using the PANSS for repeated or longitudinal assessment.

Phase IV

After all the essential rating information is obtained, the final 5–10 minutes of interview (the "directive" phase) are allocated for more direct and forceful probe of areas in which the patient appeared defensive, ambivalent, or uncooperative. For example, a patient who avoided acknowledging a psychiatric disorder in a forthright manner may be challenged for a decisive statement. Likewise, if the patient seemed to vacillate in describing mood state, this contradiction is pointed out in an attempt to resolve it. In this last phase, therefore, the patient is subjected to greatest stress and "testing of limits"; this may be necessary to proceed beyond the social demand characteristics that are inherent in the interview situation and to explore the patient's hostile or impulsive tendencies, as well as susceptibility to disorganization.

The interview thus lends itself to observation of physical manifestations (e.g., tension, mannerisms and posturing, excitement, blunting of affect), interpersonal behavior (e.g., poor rapport, uncooperativeness, hostility, poor attention), cognitive-verbal processes (e.g., conceptual disorganization, stereotyped thinking, lack of spontaneity and flow of conversation), thought content (e.g., grandiosity, somatic concern, guilt feelings, delusions), and response to structured questioning (e.g., disorientation, anxiety, depression, concreted thinking).

PANSS GENERAL RATING INSTRUCTIONS

Data gathered from this assessment procedure are applied to the PANSS ratings. Each of the 30 items is accompanied by a specific definition as well as detailed anchoring criteria for all seven rating points (see Glossary). These seven points represent increasing levels of psychopathology, as follows: 1—absent; 2—minimal; 3—mild; 4—moderate; 5—moderate severe; 6—severe; 7—extreme.

In assigning ratings, one first considers whether a symptom is at all present, as judging by the item definition. If the symptom is absent, it is scored 1, whereas if it is present the rater must determine its severity by reference to the particular criteria for the anchoring points. The highest applicable rating point is always assigned, even if the patient meets criteria for lower ratings as well. In judging the level of symptom severity, the rater must utilize a holistic perspective to decide which anchoring point best characterizes the patient's functioning and rate accordingly, whether or not all elements of the description are observed.

The rating points of 2 to 7 correspond to incremental levels of symptom severity. They are keyed to the prominence of symptoms, their frequency during the observation phase, and above all their disruptive impact on daily living. In general, a rating of 2 (minimal) denotes questionable, subtle, or suspected pathology, or it also may allude to the extreme end of the normal range. A rating of 3 (mild) is indicative of a symptom whose presence is clearly established but not pronounced and interferes little in day-to-day functioning; it often is disclosed as a result of the assessment but otherwise may not be apparent. A rating of 4 (moderate) characterizes a symptom which, though representing a serious problem, either occurs only occasionally or intrudes on daily life only to a modest extent. A rating of 5 (moderate severe) indicates marked manifestations that distinctly impact upon one's functioning but are not all-consuming and usually can be contained at will (e.g., suppressed during the course of interview). A rating of 6 (severe) represents gross pathology that is present very frequently, proves highly disruptive to one's life, and possibly calls for direct supervision. A rating of 7 (extreme) refers to the most serious level of psychopathology, whereby the manifestations drastically interfere in many or all major life functions (eating, sleeping, grooming, etc.) and typically necessitate close supervision or assistance in several areas.

Each item is rated in consultation with the definitions and criteria provided in the Glossary. The ratings are rendered on the PANSS Rating Form (Appendix D) by encircling the appropriate number following each dimension.

PANSS SCORING INSTRUCTIONS

Scores for the positive, negative, and general psychopathology scales are arrived at by summation of ratings across the component items. Therefore, the potential ranges are 7 to 49 for positive and negative scales and 16 to 112 for general psychopathology. Scoring for the five psychopathology factors also is achieved by summing the constituent items, as identified on the PANSS Rating Form (Appendix D). This yields separate scores for anergia (range, 4–28), thought disturbance (range, 4–28), activation (range, 3–21), paranoid/belligerence (range, 3–21), and depression (range, 4–28). In addition to these measures, a composite scale is scored by subtracting the negative from the positive scale score. This produces a bipolar index that ranges from −42 to +42, which is essentially a difference (delta) score that reflects the degree of predominance of one syndrome in relation to the other and may serve for purposes of classification. Finally, one may add together all 30 items to provide a total psychopathology score (range, 30–210) that reflects on the severity of illness across parameters.

To achieve optimal reliability with the PANSS, it is recommended that raters with clinical background be selected and trained until they demonstrate an interrater reliability of at least 0.80. It is also advised that, whenever possible, two or more trained raters simultaneously but independently perform the PANSS assessment on the basis of the same interview. In such cases, the PANSS ratings and scale scores should derive from the arithmetic mean of all raters, or else from the consensus among raters after post-rating discussion of each item.

Interpretation of this dimensional scoring procedure is aided by reference to the provisional table of norms from a sample of 240 schizophrenics with a confirmed DSM–III diagnosis (see Appendix C). The age range of this group was 18 to 68 years (mean = 33.1, SD = 10.21), and the duration of illness since onset was between one month and 42 years (mean = 10.7, SD = 8.90). Demographically, the sample consisted of 179 males and 61 females, and ethnically there were 106 blacks, 60 whites, 72 of Hispanic origin, and 2 Asians.

Appendix C provides for conversion of raw scores to percentile ranks on all four scales plus five clusters from the PANSS. In cases where the actual raw score value is not indicated on the table, its corresponding percentile rank may be computed by simple interpolation. The percentile rank compares the individual's score to that of the normative population in terms of the percent that it surpasses. For example, a PANSS negative score of 34 is at the 97th percentile and so is extremely high, exceeding that of 96 percent of schizophrenics on whom the scale was normed.

As is customary for psychometric measures, the percentile ranks on the PANSS may be broadly interpreted as follows:

Percentile	*Range*
95 and above	Very high
75–94	High
26–74	Average
6–25	Low
5 and below	Very low

In addition to interpretation of scale scores, percentile ranks provide an objective anchor for comparing groups, evaluating changes, and screening patients for study (i.e., deciding on cutoff scores for inclusionary and exclusionary criteria). The PANSS Rating Form (Appendix D) thus provides space for entry of the patient's raw scores, percentiles, and ranges.

Beyond the dimensional scoring method described above, the PANSS may be used for typological assessment when it is necessary to classify schizophrenics as having a predominantly positive or negative syndrome (i.e., positive or negative schizophrenia). We have described two methods, one more stringent but exclusionary, and one less stringent, which permits subtyping of virtually all patients.

The more stringent system involves counting how many ratings of 4 (moderate) or higher are obtained on the positive and negative scales (Lindenmayer, Kay, & Opler, 1984; Opler et al., 1984). Patients are classified as "positive subtype" if they score three or more moderate ratings on the positive scale but fewer than three moderate ratings on the negative scale. Patients are classified as "negative subtype" if they exhibit the opposite pattern, i.e., at least three moderate ratings on the negative scale but fewer than three on the positive scale. Patients who score at least three moderate ratings on *both* scales are regarded as "mixed type," while those who reach this criterion for neither scale are considered "neither type."

The more inclusionary system for typological assessment (cf. Singh, Kay, & Opler, 1987) utilizes the difference score from the composite scale. Patients with a positive composite scale score valence (i.e., > 0) are classified as "positive subtype," and those with a negative valence (i.e., < 0) are classified as "negative subtype."

Finally, one may choose a stringency level to suit particular research objectives, using the empirically established percentile ranks, shown in Appendix C, as the criteria. This procedure declares, in effect, that a person with a decidedly high positive or negative profile is one who scores at the extremes of the schizophrenic sample distribution curve on the PANSS composite scale. For example, it may be resolved to consider as "positive" all those who fall above the 75th percentile (composite score > 3) and as "negative" all those below the 25th percentile (< -7). A far more rigorous criterion would be the 95th and 5th percentiles (composite scores of 11 or higher and -15 or lower, respectively).

CLINICAL APPLICATION OF THE PANSS

From the clinical vantage point, the percentile ranks describe the special characteristics of the patient's symptomatic profile. In addition, the clinician can visually inspect the areas of notable psychopathology by turning the PANSS Rating Form (Appendix D) onto its side, i.e., horizontally. The result is a profile of 30 symptoms in which the most prominent manifestations are denoted by the higher elevations, and absence of symptoms by the lowest elevation. The scanning of scores thus quickly reveals the most disabling symptoms and, conversely, the areas in which the patient is symptom-free.

The clinical application of the PANSS at Bronx Psychiatric Center has found it useful in adjudicating upon difficult diagnostic cases and in preparing comprehensive psychological reports. For example, patients with a major depressive disorder were distinguished from negative symptom schizophrenics by their extreme scores on the depression factor (> 95th percentile) and comparatively low scores on the negative syndrome and thought disorganization factor.

Special clinical problems have also been disclosed by inspection of the PANSS profile. For instance, a schizophrenic inpatient who had been referred for evaluation seemed to be a promising candidate for hospital discharge, having apparently made a remarkable recovery from a florid psychotic state. The lack of positive symptoms was confirmed on the PANSS. The patient, however, was found to rate consistently high on the negative scale, including passive/apathetic social withdrawal, and extremely high on lack of judgment and insight. On this basis, it was predicted that the patient would lead an idle, isolated life upon discharge and might not see any reason to continue his outpatient follow-up or medications—two factors that would place him at high risk for relapse (Nimatoudis et al., 1989). Accordingly, it was recommended that he undergo further counseling and rehabilitation in preparation for discharge.

---------- 4 ----------

PANSS Training Practicum

STANDARDIZATION OF TRAINING

The importance of standardized assessment to achieve objective and valid measurement was discussed in Chapter 3. Although some test developers go to great length to standardize their instrument, the need to standardize the training as well is often overlooked. Such a process is usually not necessary for so-called "objective" tests, in which the administration and scoring are dictated entirely by the instructions and, therefore, can vary minimally across examiners. But for clinician-rated evaluations, in which some degree of judgment is inevitably required, the quality of measurement may be compromised by a poorly trained assessor. In such cases, a standard program of training is highly important for reliability and validity.

The standardization of training provides quality control for potential users of a rating scale, and it also ensures that the training is identical across persons and across research centers. Unless we are confident that different raters are using the instrument in the same way, we cannot know whether differences in findings are genuine (representing true variations between patients) or an artifact (constituting variations between raters). We need to be able to rule out training differences when, for example, we apply a clinical instrument to monitor changes in a patient, to contrast different patients or patient groups, and to compare results from different studies and, particularly, from diverse cultures.

Videotape training, which is available for the Positive and Negative Syndrome Scale (PANSS) (Kay, Opler, & Fiszbein, 1989a, 1989b), is an especially valuable method for standardizing the use of rated assessments and boosting reliability (Katz & Itil, 1974). It uniformly provides for all trainees exposure to the same interviews and an explanation of how the patients' responses and behaviors translate into specific quantified judgments. In so doing, it automates the tutorial process and also makes possible self-training and self-testing. Another strength of the video tutorial is the capability of freezing the action or later reviewing any particular segment that will

43

elucidate the psychopathology of the patient who was rated. This review process is especially helpful in sharpening rating skills and in resolving disagreements among raters.

The PANSS training videotapes display five interviews of schizophrenic patients, and in two of the cases, the rationale for the selected ratings is carefully explicated. This is aided by flashbacks to the point of the interview that best illustrates the symptoms being assessed.

ESTABLISHING INTERRATER RELIABILITY

The goal of rater training is to ascertain that the novice utilizes the scale in the same manner as other raters, particularly those experienced in its application. This is demonstrated by a high concordance among raters, which is expressed by the coefficient of interrater reliability. In this pursuit, the new rater may train with others, be apprenticed with a veteran user, or learn by the videotape technique. In all cases, the procedure for establishing high interrater reliability on the PANSS is similar.

First, the trainee must familiarize himself with the formal interview guidelines and rating criteria, as presented in the previous two chapters. Next, he must observe and/or participate in the PANSS patient interview. The trainee (and even the advanced rater) is expected to take notes of pertinent information from the interview and, immediately thereafter, to perform the ratings independently, in consultation with the Manual of Definitions (Kay, Opler, & Fiszbein, 1990). These ratings are then compared with those of others, and the reasons for any differences are explored through discussion in order to clarify misunderstandings and improve rating skills. Generally, the discrepancy may be traced to differences in what was noticed from the interview or to differences in one's comprehension of symptom definitions or rating criteria. In the case of videotape training, one has the opportunity to selectively replay segments to help achieve consensus. A disparity of ± 1 point on the seven-point items is considered within the range of agreement; a disparity of greater than one point is considered a true disagreement.

The interrater reliability may be computed *statistically* using intraclass correlation, Kendall coefficient of concordance, or (for two raters only) Pearson correlation. Alternatively, it may be calculated *descriptively* by determining, for each item, the proportion of obtained to potential rater agreements. For example, if four raters (A, B, C, and D) train together, there are six possible paired comparisons (A–B, A–C, A–D, B–C, and C–D), hence six potential rater agreements for each item. Our task is to determine how many paired agreements are actually obtained out of these six. If, in the present example, the team assigns ratings of 4, 2, 5, and 6 to item P1 (Delusions), there are only two agreements (4–5 and 5–6) out of the six that are possible, yielding an obviously poor interrater concordance of 0.33. If for the next item the ratings are 2, 2, 3, and 4, this is somewhat better, there are only two true disagreements (2–4 and 2–4), yielding an interrater concordance of 0.67.

The percent agreement can be calculated for each of the PANSS scales as well as for the total 30-item instrument by averaging across the constituent items. An interrater coefficient of 0.70, which is typical for less well defined psychopathology scales, is considered a minimally acceptable level for use of the PANSS. One that exceeds 0.80 is regarded as satisfactory, and one in the 0.90 range is highly reliable.

Next, we shall review the abbreviated transcript of an actual PANSS interview of a schizophrenic inpatient. This will be followed by an explanation of ratings, which will permit us to evaluate our own initial rating skills and to become aware of sources of disagreement. It needs to be cautioned, of course, that the written text cannot display essential information on a patient's affect, motor behavior, and vocal characteristics, which would be evident from the live or videotaped interview. Therefore, these audiovisual features, as well as the relevant information on ward behavior that was derived from interview of the hospital staff, will be summarized here in order that the full range of psychopathology can be appreciated. In reviewing this transcript, it should be noted that the period of assessment covers the week up to the point of interview.

Sample Interview*

James L. (fictitious name) is a large, 31-year-old black man who has been hospitalized on a locked psychiatric ward for approximately one year. The case records indicate that this is his first admission and that he has shown little change in his mental status since the onset of illness. For the past month, his drug treatment has consisted of fluphenazine, 25 mg per day.

The ward staff report that Mr. L.'s personal self-care is good and that socially he is fairly active. He participates consistently in therapeutic community meetings, engages spontaneously in conversation with other patients and staff, and is well liked by all. Ordinarily he is not a management problem, although he may become agitated by the level of noise and activity on the ward. During the past week, however, there has been no evidence of uncooperativeness, aggressive outburst, or motor excitement. He was not

---

*Edited from the *PNSS Training Videotape, Volume II* (Kay, Opler, & Fiszbein, 1989b) and reprinted with permission courtesy of Janssen Research Foundation, Richard C. Meibach, Ph.D., director of Clinical Research, CNS Department.

observed talking or muttering to himself, and his sleep and appetite have been normal.

On interview, Mr. L. was found to be friendly and open in his communication. He was neatly dressed and groomed, and his movements were smooth and seemingly relaxed. Facial expression showed a restricted range of affect and a dreamy, preoccupied expression, with eyes often staring off into space and rarely fixed on the interviewer. Nevertheless, he seemed suitably animated, and he gestured appropriately with his hands and arms. His speech was soft but halting, and frequently there were long lapses between sentences.

Dr. Kay: Good afternoon. We're going to spend a little time talking about you and the reasons for your being here. Perhaps you can start out by telling me a bit about your background and what brought you to the hospital.

Mr. L.: Well, I grew up in Europe; born, raised in Europe; came to the United States, worked as a Metropolitan; arranged the ranks of me to go from Metropolitan to Lieutenant to Captain. Well, I got my start, then I had to go back to Attorney General, and after I got into my office I married my wife, settled down, saved up a little money, and it's been pretty good ever since that. I like the United States, but I like Europe too: it's old fashioned.

Dr. Kay: In which part of Europe were you born and raised?

Mr. L.: All of Europe.

Dr. Kay: *All* of Europe? It's a wide continent, you know.

Mr. L.: Well . . . it's got castles. . .

Dr. Kay: So you must speak other languages than English.

Mr. L.: Well, I speak Spanish, a little Italian, a bit of Pig Latin, just a little bit.

Dr. Kay: Which is your native language?

Mr. L.: My native language? English.

Dr. Kay: In which part of Europe, then, were you raised?

Mr. L.: Well, I was raised up in Europe, but . . . the places you went was just like you went to town. See, I'm kind of old. There were no names then. We just know where we live at and everything.

Dr. Kay: What year were you born in that you're so old?

Mr. L.: I was born in the Roman numbers, but I ain't telling my age!

Dr. Kay: O.K., but it sounds like you're hinting that you're over 1,000 years old. I must say you don't look quite that old.

Mr. L.: Yeah, I don't look old as I am, but I got a little gray in the top of my head.

Dr. Kay: How could it be that you're over a 1,000 years old when most people live only 70, 80, or maybe 90 years?

Mr. L.: Well, I say if you get old you get some refraction . . . uh . . . infriction . . . uh . . . you can live a long life.

Dr. Kay: To me it sounds as if there's something special about your history. Is that correct?

Mr. L.: There *is* something kind of special.

Dr. Kay: Maybe you can explain that.

Mr. L.: Back in my history I fought in the Civil War, and the South won, and that's all there is to it.

Dr. Kay: So you've been around a long time. What is the secret of your long life?

Mr. L.: I think just taking care of yourself eating. Now since I've been in this place I used to weigh 169 lbs. and in a year gained over 45–50 lbs.

Dr. Kay: Is that a problem for you?

Mr. L.: Yeah, it is a problem. It makes me sluggish, you know.

Dr. Kay: Now you've described one way in which you're special, and that is in being much older than anyone else. Is there any other way in which you're special?

Mr. L.: Well . . . mmmm . . . I'd say I'm just like anyone else.

Dr. Kay: So you're no different from most people?

Mr. L.: Well, yeah, from most *regular* people.

Dr. Kay: What makes you different?

Mr. L.: Uh . . . mmm . . . I'm a spirit.

Dr. Kay: What do you mean by that?

Mr. L.: Well, years ago I was on Earth and I was the Chosen One. So I disappeared off Earth, went up, and everything's been beautiful. But I don't see really that I'm special. You see, some of my cousins are spirits too.

Dr. Kay: Tell me, what abilities does a spirit have that regular people don't?

Mr. L.: A spirit produce the laws of his Father's ways, go by the Holy Koran, read the Holy Koran, help people out, heal people. . .

Dr. Kay: You can heal people? You have that power?

Mr. L.: Sure.

Dr. Kay: You cure people from what illnesses?

Mr. L.: Cancers and . . . mostly breast cancers. See, I'm a scientist too, and I made some medication. Quite a few people that I know had cancer, and I injected needles in them.

Dr. Kay: If someone came to you with terminal cancer, could you cure him?

Mr. L.: Sure, if I made up the right medication.

Dr. Kay: But what about your spiritual powers?

Mr. L.: You know I can go on a spirit—that's if I got my gown with me.

Dr. Kay: What gown is that?

Mr. L.: That's my gown that I wear up on the planet.

Dr. Kay: What planet?

Mr. L.: Uh . . . Can't call it; it's got no name.

Dr. Kay: Well, what does this planet have to do with you?

Mr. L.: It's just like this: I'm the Commanding General, so me and three others have to provide for the government, provide for the people. I say a word or two and food come out of the air, cattle come out of the air for the butcher, and you know, stuff like that.

Dr. Kay: Are you in charge of this planet?

Mr. L.: Mm . . . I could say so.

Dr. Kay: Does that make you a king or ruler? How would you describe it?

Mr. L.: Not on the planet, but up there in the bubble, I say the right word, think the right thought, and feed the people.

Dr. Kay: You mentioned before about being "the Chosen One." Who chose you, and for what purpose?

Mr. L.: My father chose me for this purpose. See, on the planet people call me "Konk." I say the word and houses come out of the ground and food is provided, and just things that people can look forward to me for.

Dr. Kay: It sounds almost as if you have a position like that of God, at least for that planet.

Mr. L.: That's true, that's true, yeah.

Dr. Kay: You *are* God?

Mr. L.: Well, if you read the Holy Koran, you'll know more about me than that. My name is Toby Christie, but I go by the name of Zeus Christ. When I was working over here I went by the name of Clark Kent to hide my identity, because my kinfolk, they'll be going around talking about me.

Dr. Kay: How did you find out about all your powers?

Mr. L.: I just went up into space and my father told me to read the Holy Koran, so I learned Latalian and that's how it was.

Dr. Kay: Considering all the powers you have, are you able to hear the voices of people when the people are not actually there?

Mr. L.: No, not unless they're really there.

Dr. Kay: Have you ever had visions—seen things that aren't really there?

Mr. L.: Well, yeah, I've seen those, and they scared me. Last year two or three times a little girl just came into my visions and said, "Please help, please help." It scared me.

Dr. Kay: Have you had any visions or heard any voices in the last week?

Mr. L.: No, not in the last week.

Dr. Kay: How do you spend most of your time these days?

Mr. L.: Oh, I keep busy, I read some, I watch TV, I spend the time with the other folks.

Dr. Kay: Do you have a lot of friends?

Mr. L.: Oh, yeah.

Dr. Kay: Are there some people, though, that you don't really trust?

Mr. L.: Well, I don't trust men that much; I stay around with ladies. And it's not whites: I don't trust blacks.

Dr. Kay: So you feel suspicious about blacks or about men?

Mr. L.: Yeah, cause they always fool around.

Dr. Kay: Have they ever hurt you?

Mr. L.: They do all the sodomy and molesting upstairs. I've been sodomized, I've been molested everywhere you can think of.

Dr. Kay: Is it one person who sodomized and molested you, or is it a group of people?

Mr. L.:   It's a group of people.

Dr. Kay: Are they particularly targeting you?

Mr. L.:   Well, everybody I know's been molested, but they're particularly after me.

Dr. Kay: But why?

Mr. L.:   Because they don't like who I am or they don't like the way I dress, 'cause I always used to go around and say I'm the handsomest man in the world.

Dr. Kay: Would you say, though, that you're in danger because of these people?

Mr. L.:   Well, I would say I was in danger.

Dr. Kay: Do you think that there might actually be a plot to harm you?

Mr. L.:   Yes, I do.

Dr. Kay: Is there one person in particular who's behind the plot?

Mr. L.:   I've heard around that the Government was in it, the Commissioner was in it, and the District Attorney was in it.

Dr. Kay: What's their interest in you, though?

Mr. L.:   I think they want their jobs. See about 30 years ago I was the governor, I was the commissioner, I was the district attorney.

Dr. Kay: If I may ask you a more personal question, have you ever had any kind of mental problem?

Mr. L.:   Not that I know of. And I studied a little of . . . well, you could say I studied *all* of psychiatry. If something was wrong with me, they wouldn't have to kidnap me and put me here.

Dr. Kay: Do you know where you are now?

Mr. L.:   Sure . . . I'm in this room.

Dr. Kay: O.K. But this room is in what hospital?

Mr. L.:   What hospital? Well, you all may know the name of it, but it's not a psychiatric hospital anyway.

Dr. Kay: Oh, it's not?

Mr. L.:   No, it's a medical hospital.

Dr. Kay: What are you doing in a medical hospital?

Mr. L.: I think people want to play games, fix it up so they can get a check. I mean because I own the company, and I did four, five million operations in the hospital, and I use to cure them everyday. They then took it over and threatened the people.

Dr. Kay: But would you say that you have any medical problems that we should know about? Problems with your body or with your health?

Mr. L.: No. I once had an operation, long ago, but that don't bother me now.

Dr. Kay: And you've never had any psychiatric problems in your life—is that right?

Mr. L.: That's right.

Dr. Kay: Are you taking any kinds of medicine at this point?

Mr. L.: Yeah, but it really don't make me sleepy or make me relaxed or nothing.

Dr. Kay: But is there a reason why you're taking medicine?

Mr. L.: I guess they want to put me on it. But I don't need it.

Dr. Kay: They're wrong then?

Mr. L.: Yeah, they're wrong, because ain't neither one of them no doctor.

Dr. Kay: Well, who is your doctor?

Mr. L.: He goes by the name of Forbes, but he's not really a doctor.

Dr. Kay: Yes, Dr. Forbes. I know him. But is he really just masquerading as a doctor?

Mr. L.: They put him here. He's just a creation to me. He don't have no guts, no heart, no lung, no kidney.

Dr. Kay: Who is your social worker?

Mr. L.: My social worker? Miss . . . uh . . . Agor, Afrin, uh . . . Efrin?

Dr. Kay: Your nurse?

Mr. L.: My nurse? She's not a nurse either; that's the reason why I don't call her a nurse.

Dr. Kay: Well, what's her name?

Mr. L.: Miss Peterson.

Dr. Kay: Why do you say she's not a nurse?

Mr. L.: She's *not* a nurse. When they first put me on medication, see, and she was serving medication, I asked her for her license. She said, "Don't worry about my license." I said, "Well, produce your license, and then I'll take your medication." She can't produce it, so I wouldn't take no medicine, and then they sent out four or five men who gave me a needle.

Dr. Kay: Do you get into trouble on the ward or get into fights?

Mr. L.: No. I ain't been in no fights since I've been here.

Dr. Kay: Now, would you know exactly what is today's date?

Mr. L.: It's the 30th.

Dr. Kay: Of what month?

Mr. L.: November.

Dr. Kay: Yes, that's right. And in what year?

Mr. L.: I see you don't know how to read the date either.

Dr. Kay: What do you mean?

Mr. L.: You know what everyone else is going by? May 15, 1999. That's what the governors goes by, and that's what we got to go by. But everybody in this place here is going by November 30, 1988.

Dr. Kay: I see. So there are really two dates, but the real one is 1999?

Mr. L.: Yes, 1999.

Dr. Kay: You've said that this is not really a psychiatric hospital. What's the name of it?

Mr. L.: It's Broadway.

Dr. Kay: If someone wanted to write you a letter here, how exactly would he address it?

Mr. L.: Well this is not the Bronx section, it's Broadway.

Dr. Kay: And what ward are you on?

Mr. L.: 201.

Dr. Kay: That's actually not it. Want to try again?

Mr. L.: That's it, it's 201. It's a medical hospital, I told you.

Dr. Kay: We don't have a Ward 201—it doesn't go that high.

Mr. L.: In a medical hospital it's 201, but everybody else calls it Ward 18.

Dr. Kay: I see, because I know it as Ward 18. So how have you been feeling in the past week: mostly happy, mostly sad? How would you describe it?

Mr. L.: Happy.

Dr. Kay: Mostly happy?

Mr. L.: Well, happy and sad. I don't know what you'd call it. Happy because I'm alive and feel good and everything, but the fact is I'm sorry that I'm in here and all this mess is going on and everything. Can't do nothing about it, and the doctors ain't doing nothing about it.

Dr. Kay: Are you very sad or just a little bit sad?

Mr. L.: Just a little bit sad.

Dr. Kay: You haven't been upset or crying?

Mr. L.: No.

Dr. Kay: Have you been feeling worried or nervous in the past week?

Mr. L.: No, I've been fine.

Dr. Kay: Is there perhaps something that you've done in the past that you feel was wrong or feel guilty about?

Mr. L.: No, I got nothing to be guilty about.

Dr. Kay: At this point, Mr. L., I'm going to ask you to explain the similarity between two words, or what they share in common. For example, if I said the words "ball" and "orange," how would you say they're alike?

Mr. L.: Ball and orange . . . Well, I'd say they are round. That's the most I can think of.

Dr. Kay: That's a good answer. Now what about an apple and a banana: how are they alike?

Mr. L.: Well, I would say they are fruit.

Dr. Kay: All right. What about a coat and a hat?

Mr. L.: I would say they are alike.

Dr. Kay: In what way?

Mr. L.: Well, most likely in the winter you always wear a coat and a hat. But these days, you know, kids run out and the don't put no hat on.

Dr. Kay: What about an uncle and a cousin: how are they alike?

Mr. L.: You know they could be two different things, mostly just a kin, just kin people. But one could be a criminal, one could be good.

Dr. Kay: What about an axe and a saw?

Mr. L.: They both cut things.

Dr. Kay: What does the expression mean, "One man's food is another man's poison?"

Mr. L.: Never heard of that before.

Dr. Kay: But if somebody used that expression, what would you interpret it to mean?

Mr. L.: I would say it was dumb.

Dr. Kay: What about the wise old saying, "Don't judge a book by the cover." What does that one mean?

Mr. L.: You're not supposed to do that; you're supposed to read it. Just like the Holy Koran.

Dr. Kay: Have you heard the expression that "It's as plain as the nose on your face?"

Mr. L.: Oh, yeah. It means just what it says. Just like the expression could be on your nose or something like that. You know.

Dr. Kay: So it's actually about a person's nose?

Mr. L.: Yeah, it's telling you your nose carries the expression.

Dr. Kay: There's one thing that's still puzzling me. People tell you that you're in a psychiatric hospital, but you say it's a medical hospital, and then you say you have no medical illnesses. How can that be?

Mr. L.: Like I told you, I been kidnapped. They get me where they want me to be.

Dr. Kay: But with the powers you have, the special powers you described, couldn't you get out of here?

Mr. L.: That's why I'm here. There ain't nothing I can do as long as I'm here.

Dr. Kay: Well, what would you say if someone told you that you really *do* have mental problems that need treatment?

Mr. L.: I'd say they was crazy.

Rated Assessment

At this point, the trainee should perform his or her PANSS ratings, utilizing the definitions provided in Chapter 4. These can then be compared to our assessment, which was also conducted on the basis of the above interview and staff reports. Mr. L. was assigned the following PANSS ratings:

P1. *Delusions:* 6 (severe). Mr. L. demonstrated a solidly rooted network of delusions that pervaded his thoughts and may well have interfered in his social life. There was no indication, however, that in the past week he has been acting irresponsibly or dangerously as a result. The frequently bizarre character of his delusions is rated separately (item G9) and does not qualify him for an "extreme" rating on delusions.

P2. *Conceptual disorganization:* 5 (moderate severe). Difficulty in organizing thoughts was most evident in the opening remarks, i.e., during the unstructured segment of the interview. As the interview progressed, Mr. L.'s communications became briefer, possibly as a means of retaining focus. Loss of goal was frequently observed, and confabulation as well as neologisms (e.g., "infriction," "Latalian") were also present.

P3. *Hallucinatory behavior:* 1 (absent). Although there is indication of visual and probably also auditory hallucinations in Mr. L.'s past, he denied having had these experiences in the current week. His statement was not in any way contradicted by hallucinatory manifestations during the interview or by reports on his behavior from ward staff.

P4. *Excitement:* 1 (absent). No signs of excitement, such as hyper-vigilance or motor acceleration, were observed in the interview nor reported by ward staff.

P5. *Grandiosity:* 7 (extreme). An extreme rating is supported by the multiple grandiose delusions (e.g., magical powers, longevity, expert knowledge, high positions of authority); their bizarre quality (e.g., "I say the word and houses come out of the ground and food is provided"); and their dominance in his conversation.

P6. *Suspiciousness/persecution:* 5 (moderate severe). Mr. L. clearly expressed distrust and presented an array of persecutory delusions, by which he rationalized his hospitalization. At an earlier course of his illness, these had significantly influenced his interactions, for example leading to noncompliance with drug treatment. ("She can't produce [her nursing license], so I wouldn't take no medicine, and then they sent out four or five men who gave me a needle.") In the past week, however, the impact was of a more circumscribed nature, judging from his cooperativeness and adequate participation in ward life.

P7. *Hostility*: 3 (mild). Partly veiled anger seemed apparent from Mr. L.'s assertions that others are attempting to dupe him into accepting false information about the date, staff names, staff functions, hospital name and function, etc. At the close of the interview, in the directive phase, Mr. L.'s politeness shifted toward a more resentful, if not offensive, stance. At one previous point, mild hostility was directly expressed toward the interviewer who, upon asking what year it was, became briefly incorporated into Mr. L.'s web of persecutory delusions. ("I see you don't know how to read the date either.")

N1. *Blunted affect*: 3 (mild). The range of facial expression was reduced, but normal expressive gestures were retained. Overall the affect appeared to be somewhat restricted but not truly dull.

N2. *Emotional withdrawal*: 1 (absent). There was no indication from the patient or staff that Mr. L.'s emotional commitment to life's events was in any way diminished.

N3. *Poor rapport*: 4 (moderate). The conversation was characterized by a lack of genuine interpersonal connecting. Mr. L. often seemed guarded; he would not provide many of the specifics (e.g., his age, the name of the planet that he ruled); he circumvented some of the more probing questions; and he rather consistently avoided eye contact. A higher rating was ruled out, however, since the productivity of the interview was not significantly impeded as a result.

N4. *Passive/apathetic social withdrawal*: 2 (minimal). Reports on social behavior indicated no real deficit, and personal self-care was quite satisfactory. From his own description of daily activities, however, it seemed unlikely that he shows normal initiative or socializing, which would justify a "minimal" rating.

N5. *Difficulty in abstract thinking*: 5 (moderate severe). Mr. L. was successful with several of the questions on similarities but tended to recognize the functional rather than conceptual attributes. His ability to understand symbolism or derive abstract meaning from the proverbs, and even from the figurative expression ("plain as the nose on your face"), was remarkably deficient. The concrete quality of his thinking was exemplified during the interview by his answer to the question, "Do you know where you are now?"—"Sure, I'm in this room."

N6. *Lack of spontaneity and flow of conversation*: 3 (mild). Mr. L.'s communication had a somewhat uneven, halting quality, and otherwise it was characterized by fairly brief, unembellished responses.

N7. *Stereotyped thinking*:   3 (mild). A certain repetitiousness and rigidity in thinking were apparent from the recurrent themes and the tendency to foreclose discussion with a pre-established belief. One example of the latter was his insistence that he resides on Ward 201 despite assurance that no such ward number exists in the hospital.

G1. *Somatic concern*:   2 (minimal). Mr. L. early in the interview expressed some passing concern about weight gain, which he spontaneously divulged. He did not, however, appear preoccupied with this problem. No other somatic issues and no somatic delusions could be elicited.

G2. *Anxiety*:   1 (absent). No anxiety or worry was reported by Mr. L. during the structured phase of the interview. Consistent with the self-report, his appetite and sleep were unimpaired, and he did not impress the interviewer as looking worried or apprehensive.

G3. *Guilt feelings*:   1 (absent). Mr. L. likewise denied any sense of guilt, remorse, or self-blame for past misdeeds. If anything, he seemed to project a defiant, extrapunitive attitude.

G4. *Tension*:   1 (absent). Since the definition of "tension" presupposes the presence of anxiety, it too must be rated as absent.

G5. *Mannerisms and posturing*:   1 (absent). Physical observations during the interview revealed normal posture and movements, without any awkwardness, rigidity, or bizarreness.

G6. *Depression*:   3 (mild). After some initial wavering, Mr. L. acknowledged feeling "just a little bit sad." Its importance is diminished by the fact that this information did not emerge spontaneously and was not reflected in Mr. L.'s general attitude and demeanor.

G7. *Motor retardation*:   2 (minimal). As already noted, speech was halting, and yet Mr. L.'s body tone, gestures, and motor activity were in no way reduced. The highest that one can go with this rating, therefore, is to the minimal level.

G8. *Uncooperativeness*:   3 (mild). The patient was said to be cooperative on the ward, but the interview suggested that the compliance is accompanied by sarcasm and an attitude of resentment. Although he was willing to answer the interviewer's questions, he occasionally objected and took offense.

G9. *Unusual thought content*:   7 (extreme). There were numerous delusions that were patently absurd, of which quite a few had a bizarre quality; e.g., being born in the time of the Roman Empire, being ruler of another planet, being able to magically house and feed an entire population by simple powers of thinking.

G10. *Disorientation:*   2 (minimal). Mr. L. was quite aware of the correct date, his hospital ward number, and staff names and functions, even though he refused to accept these as valid. It was less clear from his answers, however, if he knew the name and address of the hospital in which he had resided for a year.

G11. *Poor attention:*   1 (absent). No manifestations of attentional deficits were witnessed during the interview.

G12. *Lack of judgment and insight:*   7 (extreme). Mr. L. not only emphatically denied having a psychiatric illness, but he denied as well having any psychiatric symptoms in the present or even in the past. Furthermore, he maintained that he was in a medical rather than psychiatric facility and gave a delusional interpretation to his hospitalization that combined persecutory and grandiose ideation.

G13. *Disturbance of volition:*   1 (absent). There was no indication of impairment in the wilful initiation, sustenance, and control of thoughts, speech, or activity.

G14. *Poor impulse control:*   3 (mild). Although the ward staff reported no distinct episodes of loss of self-control in the past week, they had noted Mr. L.'s tendency to become agitated under certain circumstances. A capacity to become easily angered and to overreact was also confirmed by his interview behavior, as already noted.

G15. *Preoccupation:*   4 (moderate). Mr. L.'s eyes were typically gazing off into space, and his facial expression was transfixed as he described his fantastic delusions, indicating significant preoccupation with autistic thoughts.

G16. *Active social avoidance:*   2 (minimal). Despite Mr. L.'s suspiciousness and hostility, these have not in the past week interfered much in his social engagements on the ward, according to the accounts by hospital staff.

SELF-TESTING OF RELIABILITY

A comparison of the trainee's ratings with those provided here can give some preliminary indication of reliability on PANSS assessment. The percent agreement may be calculated as the number of ratings within one point, divided by the total number of ratings (i.e., 30). As stated earlier, a coefficient of 0.70 is minimally acceptable, whereas one greater than 0.80 is satisfactory.

Items that produced disparity should be further reviewed. In addition, the proximity of one's summary scores to those displayed in Appendix D should be examined, and the scales that show the largest disagreement will highlight the area or areas to be targeted for further training. A deviation by more than 20 percent from any summary score is unsatisfactory. This means, for example, that the positive syndrome score should be between 23 and 33, the negative syndrome score should be between 17 and 25, and the depression cluster score should be between 7 and 9.

SCORING SUMMARY AND CLINICAL INTERPRETATION

Mr. L.'s psychopathology profile on the PANSS is summarized in Appendix D. The results indicate that he is a patient with a level of general psychopathology that is quite characteristic for schizophrenia (60th percentile), but that his symptoms are predominantly positive (90th percentile). The composite scores, denoting the polarization toward positive or negative symptoms, similarly indicated that Mr. L. is far more at the positive end of the spectrum.

The cluster scores further revealed that thought disturbance (95th percentile) and paranoid/belligerence (90th percentile) were, respectively, the most prominent areas of psychopathology, reaching the very high and high ranges of the continuum. Activation, though also a positive symptom, was contrastingly at the low end (10th percentile). Anergia was also low, while depression was in the intermediate range for a schizophrenic population.

From the foregoing, the picture of a floridly ill paranoid schizophrenic patient emerged. Profile inspection of the 30 individual PANSS symptoms revealed that Mr. L.'s most pronounced symptoms (severe or extreme) were delusions, grandiosity, unusual thought content, and lack of judgment and insight. The hallmark of his clinical presentation, thus, was abnormal ideation. Next in order, the symptoms which were rated as moderately severe were suspiciousness/persecution, conceptual disorganization, and difficulty in abstract thinking. In other words, we find that the significant symptoms of psychopathology in Mr. L.'s case all may be classified as cognitive, either involving distortions in the content or process of thinking.

Equally notable is the *absence* of certain accompanying symptoms in schizophrenia, such as hallucinations, excitement, and disturbances of attention and volition (all rated 1). This pattern supports the impression that Mr. L.'s symptoms are not associated with a hyperaroused state. Such an interpretation may, in fact, explain Mr. L.'s continued lack of response to neuroleptics, which are believed to improve symptoms via arousal regulation (Venables, 1966; Gruzelier & Hammond, 1978), and suggests the need for alternative treatment strategies. Based on our empirical studies (see Chapters 10 and 12) we have found that schizophrenic patients who manifest marked cognitive impairments but not high scores on depression tend to have a poorer prognosis. This is precisely the profile that emerged from Mr. L.'s PANSS assessment.

Standardization of the PANSS

THE PROCESS OF STANDARDIZATION

Research on positive and negative syndromes has come under fire for its reliance on measures of dubious reliability and validity (Sommers, 1985; Zubin, 1985; Kay, Fiszbein, & Opler, 1986). The divergent findings across studies and the mixed support for Crow's hypothesis (e.g., see review by Pogue-Geile & Zubin, 1988) could well be a consequence of the weak and inconsistent methods of assessment.

In the previous chapters, we stressed the importance of a well standardized instrument to delineate clinical syndromes and described, in this context, the rationale and development of the Positive and Negative Syndrome Scale (PANSS). In the current chapter we shall present the formal psychometric properties of the PANSS, as based on a series of standardization studies. From this review, three principles of test or scale development should become apparent: (a) Standardization involves many important components, some of which are highly complex; it is not limited to interrater reliability and criterion-related validity, which more typically are reported when introducing a new psychopathology rating scale (as evidenced in Table 3:1). (b) Validation is not a simple or direct procedure; it requires many studies with large samples, and like scientific research itself, it is an ever continuous process. (c) Any technique that requires some degree of human judgment for administering or scoring cannot be expected to be perfect; nevertheless, the use of sound psychometric principles in devising an instrument will pay dividends in terms of superior reliability and validity.

With this in mind, we shall proceed to describe the standardization of the PANSS, which was undertaken over the course of eight years on several cohorts that included 240 DSM–III diagnosed schizophrenic patients. These investigations helped to establish the scale's reliability, its stability, its drug sensitivity, and various facets of validity, including criterion-related, content, construct, discriminative, and predictive. Further details on the methods and results may be found in the various articles to be cited.

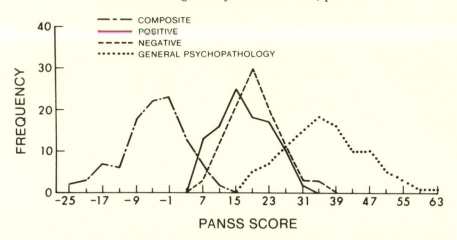

Fig. 5:1. Frequency polygon of distributions on the four scales of the PANSS for a sample of 101 chronic schizophrenic inpatients. (Reprinted from Kay, Fiszbein, & Opler, 1987). The Positive and Negative Syndrome Scale (PANSS) for schizophrenia. *Schizophrenia Bulletin* (public domain), *13*, 261–276.

DISTRIBUTION OF SCORES

The distribution characteristics of the PANSS syndrome and cluster scores, as based on the full sample of 240 medicated schizophrenic patients, are summarized in Appendix C (see Chapter 3 for description of the sample). The full spectrum of PANSS scores on the four principal scales was studied more intensively on a subset of 101 chronic schizophrenic inpatients (Kay, Fiszbein, & Opler, 1987). This group had been recruited from locked wards of an urban psychiatric hospital and selected for a DSM–III diagnosis of schizophrenia (American Psychiatric Association, 1980) and exclusion of known organic syndrome, mental retardation, affective disorder, or any additional psychiatric diagnosis. All patients were actively psychotic when studied and were undergoing neuroleptic treatment. The sample included 70 males, 31 females, 33 whites, 43 blacks, and 25 of Hispanic origin. The patients ranged in age from 20 to 68 years (mean = 36.8, SD = 11.16) and averaged 14.4 years since first psychiatric hospitalization (SD = 8.95). The distribution of their scores on the PANSS is displayed in Fig. 5:1.

It was found that all four scales exhibited the characteristic Gaussian (bell-shaped) distribution curves, without significant skewness (pile up toward the left or right tails) or kurtosis (flatness or peakedness). This observation indicates that the scores are normally distributed, and thereby it carries two important implications: (a) The PANSS is depicting continuous syndromes rather than discrete (present-absent) or co-exclusive (dichotomous) aspects of schizophrenia; (b) The scales meet the requirements for parametric statistical analysis, which is more powerful than the nonparametric (distribution-free) approaches; therefore, the chances of a type II research error (i.e., failure to detect true findings) are diminished.

The obtained range of scores in all cases was far less than the potential range. This suggests that the scales were sensitive to variations at the extremes; they were of ample breadth to avoid the restrictions of so-called "ceiling effects." The medians of the positive and negative scales were strikingly close (20 and 22, respectively), and hence the bipolar composite scale, which measures the predominance of one syndrome in relation to the other, posted a median of only −2. This indicates an almost equivalent contribution of positive and negative items to the composite score.

Because of the normality of distribution, it was possible to convert the raw scores for each of the PANSS scales into standard scores, which could then be transformed into the percentile ranks shown in Appendix C. The latter permits the examiner to interpret the protocol with reference to a medicated schizophrenic sample. The availability of an objective yardstick for interpretation carries advantages both for research and clinical applications (see Chapter 3). In terms of research, it provides empirically derived criteria for patient screening and description, as well as for quantifying the extent of improvement with treatment. For clinical purposes, it makes the psychopathology scores intelligible from a nomothetic standpoint (i.e., relative to the parent population) and also from an idiopathic one (i.e., relative to one's own test pattern). Therefore, as illustrated in the case of Mr. L. in Chapter 4, one can use the PANSS percentile ranks to characterize the clinical profile and to spotlight the most pronounced areas of abnormality and those which are relatively intact.

RELIABILITY

Reliability refers to the consistency of measurement within a scale, across time, and among raters. Corresponding to these perspectives, our standardization of the PANSS involved analyses of three separate forms of reliability: internal, longitudinal, and interrater. The results are summarized in Table 5:1 and described below.

Internal Reliability

To study the internal consistency of the PANSS and the contribution of component items, we applied Cronbach's coefficient alpha to the data from

TABLE 5:1
Summary of Reliability Studies on the PANSS

Reliability Analysis	PANSS Scales			
	Positive	Negative	Composite	General Psychopathology
Internal				
Coefficient alpha	.73***	.83***	—	.79***
Split-half	—	—	—	.80***
Longitudinal				
1 week (acute unmedicated)	.83***	.78***	—	—
3–4 months (acute medicated)	.37**	.43***	—	—
3–6 months				
(chronic medicated)	.89***	.82**	.81**	.77*
Interrater	.83***	.85***	.84***	.87***

Note: Based on Kay, Fiszbein, & Opler (1987) and Kay, Opler, & Lindenmayer (1988). See text for further explanation.
  *$p < .02$
 **$p < .01$
***$p < .001$

our sample of 101 chronic schizophrenic inpatients (Kay, Fiszbein, & Opler, 1987). As detailed in Table 5:1, each of the items included in the positive and negative scales was found to correlate strongly with the syndrome scale total ($p < 0.001$). The mean item-total correlations of 0.62 and 0.70, respectively, far exceeded the cross-correlations of 0.17 (positive items with negative scale total) and 0.18 (negative items with positive scale total). The alpha coefficients with single items removed ranged from 0.64 to 0.84, and no perceptible gain in reliability could be achieved by discarding any individual item. Overall, the internal reliability (alpha coefficient) for the positive and negative scales was 0.73 and 0.83, respectively ($p < 0.001$).

As expected, both scales correlated strongly with the composite scale, yielding coefficients of a similar magnitude ($r = 0.59$ and -0.61, respectively, $p < 0.001$). This again indicated that the two scales contribute equivalently to the composite score, which thus represents a reasonable balance between positive and negative features.

The PANSS general psychopathology scale also showed a high internal consistency, with an alpha coefficient of 0.79 ($p < 0.001$). Each of the 16 component items contributed homogeneously to the scale. As shown in Table 5:2, the alpha coefficients ranged from 0.76 to 0.79 with single items removed and correlated significantly with the total score.

The internal reliability of the 16-item general psychopathology scale could be further evaluated by the split-half method, comparing odd and

TABLE 5:2
Internal Reliability Analysis of the PANSS*

Individual Scale Items	Mean	SD	Item-Total Correlation	P	α Coefficient with Item Deleted
Positive Scale					
Delusions	3.18	1.52	.78	< .001	.64
Conceptual disorganization	3.03	1.42	.48	< .001	.73
Hallucinatory behavior	2.50	1.70	.66	< .001	.70
Excitement	2.35	1.24	.55	< .001	.71
Grandiosity	2.36	1.56	.64	< .001	.73
Suspiciousness/persecution	2.70	1.24	.61	< .001	.69
Hostility	2.10	1.14	.59	< .001	.70
Scale total	18.20	6.08	(α = .73, p < .001)		
Negative Scale					
Blunted affect	2.94	.93	.63	< .001	.81
Emotional withdrawal	3.03	1.08	.78	< .001	.78
Poor rapport	2.56	1.44	.76	< .001	.79
Passive apathetic social withdrawal	2.78	1.19	.79	< .001	.78
Difficulty in abstract thinking	3.95	1.34	.61	< .001	.82
Lack of spontaneity & flow of conversation	2.87	1.45	.86	< .001	.76
Stereotyped thinking	2.90	1.30	.50	< .001	.84
Scale total	21.01	6.17	(α = .83, p < .001)		
General Psychopathology Scale					
Somatic concern	2.39	1.21	.48	< .001	.77
Anxiety	2.43	1.20	.60	< .001	.77
Guilt feelings	1.72	1.06	.23	< .02	.79
Tension	2.35	1.19	.70	< .001	.76
Mannerisms & posturing	1.54	1.12	.33	< .001	.79
Depression	1.90	.97	.24	< .02	.79
Motor retardation	2.09	1.10	.27	< .01	.79
Uncooperativeness	2.11	1.21	.51	< .001	.78
Unusual thought content	3.42	1.49	.51	< .001	.78
Disorientation	2.09	1.14	.42	< .001	.78
Poor attention	2.45	1.28	.65	< .001	.76
Lack of judgment & insight	3.82	1.31	.35	< .001	.79
Disturbance of volition	2.10	1.30	.66	< .001	.76
Poor impulse control	2.17	1.31	.66	< .001	.76
Preoccupation	2.71	1.18	.60	< .001	.76
Active social avoidance	2.48	1.18	.43	< .001	.76
Scale total	37.74	9.49	(α = .79, p < .001)		

*Reprinted from Kay, Fiszbein, & Opler (1987). The Positive and Negative Syndrome Scale (PANSS) for Schizophrenia. *Schizophrenia Bulletin* (public domain), *13*, 261–276.

even items. Using the Spearman-Brown prophesy formula, we found the reliability coefficient in this sample of 101 patients to be 0.80 ($p < 0.001$). The general psychopathology scale correlated substantially also with the positive and negative scales ($r = 0.68$ and 0.60, respectively, $p < 0.001$), whereas its correlation with the composite scale was nonsignificant ($r = 0.07$). Accordingly, both the positive and negative symptoms were observed to be higher in the more severely ill patients, but the degree of potentiation was about the same for the two scales.

Longitudinal Reliability

From within this chronic sample, it was possible to follow for three to six months 15 unremitting patients who remained hospitalized on a research ward and, by implication, proved refractory to their ongoing neuroleptic treatment. This permitted an analysis of PANSS stability and reliability according to the test-retest method.

The initial assessment confirmed that this was a relatively ill group, with higher than average scores obtained on the positive, negative, and general psychopathology scales. It can be determined from Appendix C that their respective means of 21.2, 25.6, and 46.7 corresponded to the 60th, 73rd, and 78th percentiles. At the time of follow-up, measurable clinical gains were detected on the general psychopathology scale (mean drop of 4.74 points, $p < 0.05$), and yet the positive and negative scores were virtually unchanged (means = 21.1 and 26.3, respectively, $p > 0.40$). More importantly, the relative ordering of PANSS scores held fairly constant over the extended period between the baseline and follow-up, despite the neuroleptic intervention and the inevitable clinical fluctuations. For the positive, negative, composite, and general psychopathology scales, respectively, the test-retest reliability indexes, calculated as per Garrett (1964), ranged from 0.77 ($p < 0.02$) to 0.89 ($p < 0.001$) as estimates of their theoretically true values.

More recently we had the opportunity to assess the reliability and stability of positive and negative scores in a drug-free sample of 62 hospitalized schizophrenics who were mainly in the acute and subacute stages of schizophrenia (i.e., 0 to two years and three to five years of illness) (Kay & Singh, 1989). The study utilized a combination of the Brief Psychiatric Rating Scale (Overall & Gorham, 1962) and Psychopathology Rating Schedule (Singh & Kay, 1975a), which are the forerunners of the PANSS, and the measurement of positive and negative syndromes was derived by combining items as according to the PANSS method. The results, which will be expanded on in Chapter 10, indicated that both syndromes were unchanged during the two drug-free weeks but were significantly improved after three to four months of neuroleptic therapy ($p < 0.001$ in each case). In the drug-free baseline, the positive and negative scales were highly stable from week to week ($r = 0.83$ and 0.78, respectively, $p < 0.001$). Even after the three to four month course of treatment with chlorpromazine or haloperidol, the baseline scores were still significantly correlated with the follow-up scores ($r = 0.37$ and $r = 0.43$, respectively, $p < 0.001$). Cumulatively, therefore, these studies attested to the short-term (one week) and longer-term (three to six months) reliability and stability of the PANSS method to assess schizophrenia in different stages of the illness.

Interrater Reliability

The agreement among raters was studied in a group of young acute schizophrenic patients of average age 23.9 years and length of illness 1.45 years (Kay, Opler, & Lindenmayer, 1988). The PANSS ratings were performed independently by two psychiatrists and one psychologist on the basis of the same interview. The interrater concordance was examined both descriptively, according to percent agreement within one rating point, and statistically via Pearson correlation.

As shown in Table 5:3, a strong degree of consistency among raters was found. Agreement on individual PANSS items ranged from 0.69 (active social avoidance) to 0.94 (preoccupied behavior). The descriptive coefficient of agreement averaged between 0.78 and 0.83 for the separate scales. Statistically, the mean interrater correlations for the four scales ranged between 0.83 and 0.87 (Table 5:3), with all individual paired r's highly significant ($p < 0.0001$). These coefficients compare favorably with those reported for other negative and positive symptom scales (see Chapter 3). Furthermore, it was found that the means and standard deviations among the three rat-

TABLE 5:3
PANSS Interrater Concordance:
Coefficient of Agreement and Pearson r ($n = 31$)*

PANSS Scales	Coefficient of Agreement		Mean Pearson r	p
	Item Range	Mean		
Positive syndrome	0.73 to 0.89	0.79	0.83	< 0.0001
Negative syndrome	0.70 to 0.89	0.78	0.85	< 0.0001
Composite	—	—	0.84	< 0.0001
General psychopathology	0.69 to 0.94	0.83	0.87	< 0.0001

*Reprinted with permission from Kay, Opler, & Lindenmayer (1988). Reliability and validity of the Positive and Negative Syndrome Scale for Schizophrenics. *Psychiatry Research, 23*, 99–110.

TABLE 5:4
**PANSS Criterion-Related Validity: Means, Standard Deviations,
and Correlations with SAPS, SANS, and CGI Scales***

Area of Assessment	Rater A	PANSS Rating (n = 31) Rater B	Rater C	PANSS Correlation (r) with Corresponding Scales (n = 51)
Positive syndrome				SAPS
Mean	18.97	18.44	19.05	r = 0.77
SD	5.94	6.54	5.91	p < 0.0001
Potential range	7 to 49			
Negative syndrome				SANS
Mean	22.21	19.96	20.10	r = 0.77
SD	6.88	6.91	8.84	p < 0.0001
Potential range	7 to 49			
Composite index				
Mean	−2.69	−1.52	− 0.81	
SD	8.84	9.36	10.39	
Potential range	−42 to 42			
General Psychopathology				CGI
Mean	39.10	39.48	37.19	r = 0.52
SD	10.74	11.47	10.30	p < 0.0001
Potential range	16 to 112			

*Reprinted with permission from Kay, Opler, & Lindenmayer (1988). Reliability and validity of the Positive and Negative Syndrome Scale for schizophrenics. *Psychiatry Research*, *23*, 99–110.

Abbreviations: PANSS = Positive and Negative Syndrome Scale; SAPS = Scale for Assessing Positive Symptoms; SANS = Scales for Assessing Negative Symptoms; CGI = Clinical Global Impressions Scale.

ers were similar (Table 5:4), with no significant paired differences. Thus, independent raters were observed to be in quite close agreement when applying the PANSS.

VALIDITY

The object of validation study is to determine, from a number of vantage points, whether the instrument is measuring precisely what it purports to assess (Nunnally, 1978). To this end we have inspected several aspects of validity for the PANSS, as reviewed below. Because these studies of the instrument necessarily overlap with our research on the nature of the syndromes, we will present here only sketchy descriptions of the methods and results, reserving the fuller accounts for later chapters.

Content Validity

This facet of validity requires empirical evidence that the components of a scale or test are meaningful, relevant, and representative of the dimension being assessed. The PANSS was designed to satisfy conditions for content validity by virtue of its relatively broad selection of constituent items from a cross-section of functional spheres (see Chapter 3). The achievement of satisfactory content validity is demonstrated by the coefficient alpha analysis, described earlier in this chapter, which found that the component symptoms contributed materially to the respective scales.

Construct Validity

The object of construct validation is to ascertain that the parameters measured by a scale or test truly represent the hypothesized concepts. We attempted to maximize construct validity in development of the PANSS by selecting for the positive-negative scales only items that conform to Crow's concept and excluding those known to constitute "secondary," or derivative, negative symptoms.

As a means of analyzing the distinctiveness of the PANSS positive and negative constructs, we conducted a correlation between the two syndrome scores obtained from the sample of 101 chronic schizophrenics (Kay, Fiszbein, & Opler, 1987). A direct interrelationship of modest size was found ($r = .27$, $p < 0.01$), suggesting that the syndromes are not independent. However, their common association with general schizophrenic psychopathology, as already described, suggested that severity of illness may have mediated the covariation between two otherwise distinct scales. This proposition was supported by a partial correlation which statistically adjusted for the contribution of global illness. The result was a modest *inverse* correlation between positive and negative scales ($r = -0.23$, $p < 0.02$). This suggested that the PANSS is measuring two processes that are theoretically nonoverlapping. Because of the inevitable contribution of general psychopathology, of course, positive and negative syndromes can be expected to co-occur and covary in the same patient.

In a more recent study of 62 schizophrenic inpatients (Kay & Singh, 1989), we again found a significant direct correlation between the positive and negative scales ($r = 0.52$, $p < 0.001$). Interestingly, however, when these same patients were evaluated in the drug-free state, this correlation disappeared ($r = 0.06$, n.s.). These data suggested that under more natural conditions the positive and negative scales are unrelated and depict separate processes.

The independence of the positive and negative scales was furthermore demonstrated by their factorial distinctiveness and their association with quite separate sets of external criteria. These aspects of construct validity, referred to as factorial, convergent, and discriminant validity, will be reviewed shortly.

Criterion-Related Validity

Criterion-related validation has the purpose of determining whether the instrument covaries with another, better established measure of the same construct or, more broadly, with outside variables to which it should be expectedly related (convergent validity). Alternatively, it is equally important to establish whether the new instrument is *independent* of external criteria that are irrelevant to the construct (discriminant validity) and may be sources of contamination, or error variance. For example, a new test of intelligence should in principle correlate with a well standardized IQ scale and, to some degree, with one's grades in school and occupational achievements, but not with one's physical or personality traits, which would constitute unwanted sources of variance. First we shall review a study on the criterion-related validity of the PANSS and, next, we shall look at a series of investigations that reflect on its convergent and discriminant validity.

To examine criterion-related validity, we compared the PANSS against the Scale for Assessing Positive Symptoms (SAPS) and Scale for Assessing Negative Symptoms (SANS) of Andreasen and Olsen (1982). These scales were selected as comparative measures since, despite their limitations (see Chapter 3), they have served as the standard bearer in the United States. Subjects were 51 chronic schizophrenic inpatients, all meeting DSM–III diagnostic criteria, who averaged 33.1 years old and had a history of up to 29 years since first hospital admission (mean = 11.1, SD = 6.55). The PANSS ratings were assigned by one or more trained research fellows in psychiatry, who rated consensually as a team. The same raters performed assessments also on the SAPS, SANS, and Clinical Global Impressions Scale (CGI) (Guy, 1976), a holistic seven-point clinical scale that provided for comparison with the PANSS general psychopathology scale. The database in all cases covered a one-week period and included information from patient interview, direct ward observation, and nursing reports, as specified by the particular scales.

Evidence of criterion-related validity was found from the close correspondence between the PANSS and Andreasen rating methods (Kay, Opler, & Lindenmayer, 1988). The PANSS positive scale was significantly correlated with the SAPS ($r = 0.77$, $p < 0.0001$); the PANSS negative scale with the SANS ($r = 0.77$, $p < 0.0001$); and the PANSS general psychopathology scale with the CGI ($r = 0.52$, $p < 0.0001$). A direct correlation between positive and negative scores was insubstantial for the PANSS ($r = 0.25$, n.s.)

but quite strong for the Andreasen scales ($r = 0.42$, $p < 0.005$), suggesting that the latter method is perhaps less successful in discriminating the positive and negative constructs.

A more recent study of 30 hospitalized schizophrenics (Ramirez, 1989), which also compared the PANSS with the SAPS/SANS scales, confirmed the significant correlations between the methods on the positive ($r = 0.62$, $p < 0.001$), negative ($r = 0.60$, $p < 0.001$), and composite scales ($r = 0.74$, $p < 0.0001$). In addition, this study reported low and nonsignificant cross-correlations between theoretically unrelated scales: PANSS positive with SANS, $r = 0.00$, and PANSS negative with SAPS, $r = -0.01$. Thus, the criterion-related validity of the PANSS was supported and replicated in a separate study.

Convergent and Discriminant Validity

These facets of validation for the PANSS were examined by correlations with a series of clinical, genealogical, psychometric, and historical assessments on the sample of 101 chronic schizophrenic inpatients (Kay, Opler, & Fiszbein, 1986). First, in terms of discriminant validity, the results indicated that the PANSS ratings were not influenced by extraneous or contaminating variables, such as race, cultural group, chronicity of illness, self-reported depression, sad affective tone, and general intelligence.

On the other hand, analysis of the convergent validity revealed several fundamental parameters that distinguished the positive and negative scales. The PANSS positive score was uniquely and significantly associated with sociopathy in first degree relatives, more frequent episodes of hospitalization, and a clinical profile that included anger, labile affect, preoccupation, disorientation, and bizarre thoughts. Conversely, the PANSS negative scale was uniquely characterized by presence of schizophrenia and absence of affective illness in first degree relatives, prevalence among males, lesser education, dysfunction on a series of cognitive developmental and information processing tests, and a clinical profile that included affective deficits, slowed motorium, and impoverished thinking (see Chapter 9 for details). The general psychopathology scale, by comparison, yielded fewer external correlations and a nonspecific profile that encompassed both positive and negative clinical features.

Accordingly, the convergent validity of the PANSS was supported by specific positive-negative distinctions along familial, historical, and concurrent assessments. The nature of the difference was such that the negative scale as applied to chronic schizophrenia connoted a more pernicious disease process, one devolving from genealogical and ontogenetic sources (Kay,

Opler, & Fiszbein, 1985; Opler & Kay, 1985; Opler, Kay, & Fiszbein, 1987).

In keeping with the distinctiveness shown by the correlational analyses, a stepwise multiple regression revealed no overlap among the variables that best accounted for the positive and negative scales. The positive syndrome score, with 74 percent of its variance explained ($p < 0.001$), was predicted by a family history of sociopathy, bizarre ideation, and global psychopathology. The negative syndrome score, with 81 percent of its variance explained ($p < 0.001$), was instead predicted by a family history of schizophrenia, affective deficits, impaired cognitive development, impoverished thinking, poor judgment and insight, and active social avoidance. These analyses, therefore, indicated that the two scales reflect quite different historical, genealogical, and clinical profiles.

Further support for the discriminant validity of the PANSS was derived from separate studies of neurological signs and information processing disorders. To a sample of 28 chronic schizophrenic patients, we independently administered the PANSS and a multi-item neurological signs inventory (Merriam et al., in press). The latter has yielded five statistically independent scores associated with prefrontal, praxis, parietal, fine motor, and nonlocalizing signs of neuropathology. Whereas the PANSS positive scale was unrelated to all five scores, the negative scale was distinguished by its significant correlation with prefrontal signs ($r = 0.49$, $p < 0.01$) but with none of the other neurological parameters.

In another study on 30 chronic schizophrenic inpatients, we obtained measurements from the Span of Attention (SOA) (Kay & Singh, 1974), which provides a behavioral work sample of concentration on a rote motor task, and from the Memory Organization Test (MOT) (Kay, Murrill, & Opler, 1989). The MOT, as a test of verbal encoding and memory functions, assesses the gains in free recall attributable to category clustering; it utilizes triads of different word composition as a strategy to measure one's success in registering the conceptual, affective, and phonemic properties of words. In relation to the PANSS, it was found that the negative scale alone was significantly associated with a specific deficiency in encoding the affective cues. This deficit could not be explained by poorer functioning in terms of sustained attention (SOA) or general memory (MOT), which in this study was not associated with the positive or negative scale (Kay, Murrill, & Opler, 1989).

Discriminative Validity

This form of validation, which is actually a particular variant of criterion-related validity, refers to the ability of an instrument to differentiate between two groups that are, in principle, expected to test differently. The discriminative validity of the PANSS was assessed in a study (Lindenmayer, Kay, & van Praag, 1989) that compared 21 schizophrenic with 21 schizoaffective patients, all of whom were so diagnosed by Research Diagnostic Criteria (Spitzer, Endicott, & Robins, 1977) as well as by the DSM-III (American Psychiatric Association, 1980). The groups were recruited from the same psychiatric hospital and matched for age, age at onset of illness, and total years since first psychiatric hospitalization in order to ensure that any clinical differences could not be attributable to differences in sampling characteristics.

We found that the two diagnostic groups, as expected, scored comparably high on severity of general psychopathology and on the positive scale of the PANSS (means = 43.5 and 23.7 for schizophrenics vs. 41.3 and 21.8 for schizoaffectives). They were significantly distinguished, however, on the PANSS negative scale and PANSS depression cluster. Consistent with the diagnostic definitions, the schizoaffective patients had substantially lower negative scores (mean of 19.4 vs. 23.8 for schizophrenics, $p < 0.02$) but higher scores on depression (13.3 vs. 9.3, $p < 0.05$).

This finding, in addition to lending evidence of discriminative validity, demonstrated the distinctiveness of the PANSS negative scale from depression (construct validity). More support for the independence of the PANSS negative and depression scales, to be discussed later, accrues from their differential prediction of outcome in chronic schizophrenia (Chapter 10) and their orthogonal relationship as identified by principal component factor analysis (Chapter 2). Thus, despite the similar manifestations of negative and depressed states that could contaminate research (cf. Carpenter, Heinrichs, & Alphs, 1985), these are teased apart on the PANSS. The findings also carry obvious implications for the clinical use of the PANSS in differentiating negative from depressive syndromes and schizophrenic from schizoaffective disorders.

Factorial Validity

Another form of validation involves demonstration that the test or scale is composed of the same factors that it purports to measure. To analyze the factorial validity of the PANSS, we conducted a principal component analysis with equimax rotation on the full sample of 240 schizophrenic inpatients (Kay, 1989; Kay & Sevy, in press). As described in Chapter 12, the findings were complex and of considerable theoretical interest, revealing that more than two factors are needed to explain schizophrenic phenomenology.

The factorial validity of the PANSS was supported by analysis of the 30 symptoms, which found that the two main components to emerge were, respectively, the negative and positive syndromes. These factors were very robust (eigenvalues of 7.08 and 3.74, respectively) and together accounted for the main share of the total variance in symptomatology (36.1 percent). In addition, as will be later seen, five other significant psychopathology components were revealed: excitement, depression, cognitive dysfunction, suspiciousness/persecution, and stereotyped thinking. These factors rounded out the description of schizophrenia, increased the total variance explained to 64.7 percent, confirmed the independence of the negative scale from depression, and provided contrasting dimensions to the positive and negative syndromes. At the same time, the principal component analysis suggested alternative, empirically derived ways of measuring positive, negative, and other symptom complexes in schizophrenia.

Typological Validity

The PANSS has been applied also as a method of classifying patients as having a predominantly positive vs. negative syndrome. To study the validity of this typological application, we categorized patients who scored "moderate" or higher (i.e., ratings of 4 to 7) on at least three of the seven positive items as "positive-type schizophrenia," and those with the reverse pattern ("moderate" or higher on at least three of the seven negative items) as "negative-type schizophrenia." Those who qualified for both groups were labeled as "mixed type," while those who met criteria for neither one were labeled as such. This system was tested in separate studies involving 37 acute (less than two years of illness) and 47 chronic schizophrenic inpatients (more than two years), all with a confirmed DSM–III diagnosis (Lindenmayer, Kay, & Opler, 1984; Opler et al., 1984).

The results supported the validity of the PANSS for isolating groups that differ on both antecedent and concurrent variables. When excluding patients who met criteria for neither positive nor negative type, a significant inverse relationship was found between positive and negative symptoms in the acute sample ($r = -0.62$, $p < 0.001$) as well as in the chronic ($r = -0.55$, $p < 0.01$).

In acute schizophrenia, those classified as negative differed from positive-type patients as having significantly less education, poorer premorbid work adjustment, and a host of deficit symptoms that encompassed the cognitive, social, affective, and motor spheres (Lindenmayer, Kay, & Opler, 1984). The chronic study also found the negative type to have less education and, generally, a worse premorbid status (Opler et al., 1984). They were characterized by an earlier onset of illness and a more primitive cognitive style on the developmentally-based Cognitive Diagnostic Battery (Kay,

1982), despite similar intelligence test scores. In both studies, no group differences were obtained on control variables such as sex, race, ethnic background, years of illness, and severity of general psychopathology.

A more recent study of information processing (Weiner et al., in press) further expanded on the cognitive differences between PANSS positive and negative types. We recruited a sample of 45 hospitalized schizophrenics who, based on the PANSS composite scale, could be classified empirically as predominantly positive in symptoms (> 75th percentile in relation to our norms for schizophrenia, $n = 15$) vs. negative (< 25th percentile on the composite scale, $n = 15$) and a mixed group who fell in between ($n = 15$). For all patients as well as a healthy control group ($n = 15$), we assessed the speed of visual information processing using the backward masking technique of Braff and Saccuzzo (1985). A psychologist who was kept blind to patient classification very briefly exposed to subjects one letter on a tachistoscope, and this was immediately replaced by another letter that could mask the perception of the first. The results indicated that negative-type schizophrenics were significantly slower in processing visual information as compared to all other patient and normal groups.

Typological validity was also supported in a double-blind study of clinical response to anticholinergic antiparkinsonian agents, either benztropine or trihexyphenidyl (Singh, Kay, & Opler, 1987). These medications, which are routinely prescribed to treat the adverse extrapyramidal reactions induced by neuroleptics, were systematically introduced in our study for two to four weeks during the course of neuroleptic therapy. From baseline drug-free assessments, 47 schizophrenic patients were prospectively classified as predominantly positive ($n = 25$) or negative type ($n = 22$) according to the valence of the PANSS composite scale score (< 0 and > 0, respectively). It was found that positive schizophrenics showed significant clinical worsening when the anticholinergic agents were subsequently introduced ($p < 0.02$), whereas the negative group was unaffected.

Predictive Validity

The predictive validity of the PANSS, i.e., its ability to anticipate one's future clinical course, was supported in the above study of response to anticholinergics. It was further demonstrated in an entirely unrelated Portuguese study of drug-induced psychosis (Simoes, 1989). The investigator found that a shift in schizophrenic symptoms precipitated by cannabis was predicted by an improvement on productive psychotic symptoms, measured by the PANSS, that had occurred within the first week of inpatient treatment.

Predictive validity was examined more systematically by our group in three separate longitudinal follow-up studies. These involved a total of 157 schizophrenic patients who were in different stages of the illness (see Chapter 10 for details). In all three studies, PANSS assessments were conducted prospectively, and a follow-up was undertaken 2 to 3 years later by an investigator who was blinded to the baseline ratings.

First, in a sample of 37 young acute schizophrenics (mean age = 23.6 years) with up to two years history of psychiatric disorder (mean = 1.42 years), the PANSS negative scale proved to be a reliable prognosticator. A high negative score in the baseline predicted favorable outcome in terms of less hospitalization, less severe symptomatology, better social and occupational adjustment, experience of a fuller life, and an overall higher functional level. A positive syndrome, by contrast, was not associated with any of these outcome variables (Lindenmayer, Kay, & Friedman, 1986; Kay & Lindenmayer, 1987).

The second investigation, which focused on the somewhat later subacute period (up to five years of illness, mean = 2.90 years), assessed 62 schizophrenic patients in a drug-free baseline and then followed them for a period of three years (Kay & Singh, 1989). At this stage of the illness, a baseline negative syndrome was no longer of major prognostic consequence, whereas a positive syndrome reliably predicted poorer treatment outcome ($r = -0.32$, $p < 0.02$) and earlier relapse ($r = -0.37$, $p < 0.01$).

The third longitudinal study prospectively followed for 2.7 years a cohort of 58 schizophrenic patients who were in the chronic stage of illness and averaged 11.8 years since first hospitalization (Kay & Murrill, in press). As in the previous study, we found that a baseline PANSS positive syndrome was a significant predictor of poorer outcome, which was measured by days of subsequent hospitalization as well as by occupational functioning and fullness of life (see details in Chapter 10). The PANSS depression cluster, alternatively, predicted a favorable outcome. By contrast, neither the negative scale nor the general psychopathology scale were of predictive consequence for this chronic schizophrenic group.

Accordingly, although the significance of the syndromes depended on the stage of illness, the predictive validity of the PANSS was established in each of these longitudinal studies, hence for the acute, subacute, and chronic conditions. The exact formulas for optimal prediction of outcome have been derived in each case by multiple regression analysis and are reported in the above-cited publications.

Pharmacological Validity

The ability of the PANSS scales to monitor drug-related changes and to reflect syndromal differences in response to psychotropic drugs was demonstrated in several independent studies which, all together, involved nine different medications. Since the details will be presented in Chapter 11, at this point we shall merely summarize the findings as they pertain to validation of the PANSS.

First, in an experimental study of 47 neuroleptic-treated schizophrenics, we found that only the positive syndrome scale was adversely influenced by the introduction of anticholinergic drugs (benztropine or trihexyphenidyl) that normally are used to guard against or treat extrapyramidal symptoms (Singh, Kay, & Opler, 1987). Indeed, a longitudinal correlation showed that the positive and negative scales did not covary in their response to anticholinergics but rather they responded differentially.

Second, we subjected 62 schizophrenic inpatients to a 14-to-18-week double-blind trial on standard neuroleptics, either chlorpromazine or haloperidol (Kay & Singh, 1989). As compared to the drug-free baseline, we found significant improvements after neuroleptic treatment for both positive syndrome (51.5 percent, $p < 0.001$) and negative syndrome (35.0 percent, $p < 0.001$). The degree of change in the positive scale, however, was marginally greater than that obtained for the negative scale ($p = 0.06$), consistent with Crow's hypothesis and other psychopharmacological investigations (Breier et al., 1987; Johnstone et al., 1987).

Third, we explored the possibility that a drug which augments rather than blocks dopamine transmission may help to improve the negative syndrome which, as we have noted, was less responsive to neuroleptic therapy. Specifically, we studied the clinical effects of L-dopa, a dopamine precursor, when prescribed adjunctively with neuroleptics (Kay & Opler, 1985). Using a 27-week double-blind single-subject experimental design, we compared an eight-week course on L-dopa plus haloperidol combination against the preceding and following four-week periods on placebo and haloperidol. Significant improvement was seen along the PANSS negative scale ($p < 0.05$) as well as on two of the individual negative items (difficulty in abstract thinking, $p < 0.025$, and passive/apathetic social withdrawal, $p < 0.05$). By comparison, neither the positive scale nor any of its component symptoms showed improvement or worsening with L-dopa ($p > 0.50$).

Fourth, we assessed changes on the PANSS associated with pimozide (Feinberg et al., 1988), a neuroleptic marketed in the United States only for treating Gilles de la Tourette's syndrome (a neurological disorder characterized by violent, uncontrollable tics and verbalizations). Our interest in the application of this drug to schizophrenia was prompted by some European reports (Pinder et al., 1976; Falloon, Watt, & Shepherd, 1978) which had suggested that it may particularly address certain enduring social and functional deficits.

We thus selected 10 neuroleptic refractory schizophrenic inpatients and treated them with pimozide after a two week baseline on a standard neuroleptic. Significant improvement was observed on the PANSS negative scale after four weeks of the new drug and continuing through the six week trial ($p < 0.001$). The positive scale, meanwhile, remained unchanged by pimozide. Together with the other studies described in this section, the pimozide findings upheld the pharmacological validity of the PANSS in reflecting differential syndromal responses to medications.

Fifth, a recent study from an independent group in Belgium (Peuskins et al., 1989) utilized the PANSS to assess the therapeutic action of risperidone, a new drug for schizophrenia that is a potent combined serotonin ($5HT_2$) and dopamine (D_2) antagonist (Gelders et al., 1989). Based on its chemical profile that intervenes in two neurotransmitter systems, risperidone was expected to ameliorate both positive and negative symptoms. The medication was tested on 42 treatment-nonresponsive chronic schizophrenic patients in a 12-week double-blind comparison with haloperidol, a standard dopamine blocking agent. The investigators reported that the PANSS showed high interrater reliability and was sensitive in reflecting the rapid and significant improvements with risperidone on the positive, negative, depressive, and general psychopathology scales. The changes with risperidone were, in fact, more pronounced than those obtained with haloperidol, again supporting the pharmacological validity of the instrument.

The PANSS has since been utilized as the key clinical efficacy parameter in an international multicenter study of risperidone (Janssen Research Foundation, 1989). The double-blind protocol begins with a three-week placebo washout and drug-free baseline. This is followed by six weeks on either risperidone, administered in one of five fixed doses, or haloperidol as the reference drug. Those who successfully complete the double-blind trial on risperidone are, on a voluntary basis, admitted to a long-term open evaluation of this experimental drug. Thus far, several independent reports from Europe have described findings from the inpatient phase of study (De Buck, Hoffman, & De Smet, 1989; De Cuyper, 1989; Jansen & Boom, 1989; Reilly et al., 1989; Turner, Lowe, & Hammond, 1989). The results confirm the pharmacological validity of the PANSS positive and negative scales in terms of sensitivity to drug-induced changes and ability to reflect the relatively greater potency of risperidone, as compared to classical neuroleptics, for improving the negative spectrum of symptoms.

Sixth, Paunović et al. (1988) in Yugoslavia found the PANSS to be sensitive in reflecting changes on the negative syndrome across brief trials with pimozide and clozapine. They observed significant reduction of negative syndrome ratings within ten days and a significant difference between these two medications that was discernible also by Day 10 of drug treatment.

They concluded that "The PANSS ratings yielded data far more detailed [than the Brief Psychiatric Rating Scale] for quantitative and qualitative analysis; therefore, the PANSS is highly commendable for clinical studies of drug treatment."

Finally, two additional psychopharmacological studies with the PANSS have been conducted in our research program, one involving the atypical neuroleptic, clozapine (Lindenmayer et al., 1989), and the other low-dose treatment with bromocriptine (Marangell, Kay, & Lindenmayer, 1989). Both supported the sensitivity of the PANSS in monitoring medication-related clinical changes. These latter studies will be reviewed in some detail in Chapter 11.

CONCLUSIONS

In aggregate, this series of studies provided evidence of suitable psychometric properties of the PANSS for typological, dimensional, and longitudinal assessment of distinct syndromes in schizophrenia. The scales proved to be normally distributed and internally consistent, and they demonstrated stability and high reliability when assessed by coefficient alpha, split-half method, interrater concordance, and test-retest index. The validation of the PANSS was supported in terms of construct, criterion-related, convergent, discriminant, predictive, discriminative, factorial, and pharmacological validity. The PANSS positive and negative scales consistently showed different sets of associations with historical, genealogical, phenomenological, psychometric, and clinical outcome. They were found to be sensitive in reflecting drug-related therapeutic changes and to show differential response to specific medications.

It is likely that the principles by which the PANSS was developed, especially the operational criteria for the interview and ratings, contributed to its strength as a psychometric instrument and its promise for measuring distinct syndromes in schizophrenia. Our hope is that its use will reduce error variance in future studies of positive and negative dimensions, enabling a clearer focus on the significance of these parameters for schizophrenia.

PART III

New Directions in Assessment

6

Spanish Adaptation of the PANSS (PANSS-S)

REQUIREMENTS FOR TRANSLATION

In the previous chapter we argued the importance of a psychometrically sound method for assessing syndromes of schizophrenia, one that adheres to the *Standards for Educational and Psychological Tests* of the American Psychological Association (1985). With this in mind, we described the development and standardization of our Positive and Negative Syndrome Scale (PANSS). Briefly stated, it aimed to provide detailed operational criteria to enhance the objectivity and psychometric qualities in measuring positive, negative, and other symptoms of schizophrenia.

Since its introduction, the PANSS has been applied in various non-English speaking countries in Europe, Asia, and South America in connection with independent studies as well as industry-sponsored multinational studies on new medications for schizophrenia.* At present the PANSS Rating Manual has been translated into 13 languages (see Appendix B for an index of translators): Spanish, Portuguese, French, German, Italian, Dutch, Swedish, Hungarian, Serbo-Croatian, Japanese, Chinese, Korean, and Turkish.

The adaptation of the PANSS to different languages and cultures raised for us the question of whether the psychometric properties established for the English version are upheld. Clearly, to the extent that the text is inevitably altered by translation, we cannot presume that the new version is equally well standardized. Research on reliability and validity are therefore required. However, instead of repeating for each language all the studies described in Chapter 5, one can reevaluate the reliability of the translated

---

*These new medications include risperidone by Janssen Pharmaceutica, Belgium; amperozide by Sandoz Pharmaceuticals, U.S.A.; remoxipride by Astra Pharma, Canada; seboxapine by Ciba-Geigy Pharmaceuticals, U.S.A.; ondansetron by Glazo, Canada; and new drugs being developed by Akzo (Organon) in the Netherlands, Lilly Research in Great Britain, and Squibb in Canada.

version and then standardize it against the original, a process known as criterion validation. The assumption here is that if the new instrument is shown to be reliable and statistically comparable to the well standardized one, then it too shares the established psychometric properties.

We present in this chapter data on reliability and criterion validity of a Spanish language translation of the PANSS, known as the PANSS-S.* Its translation into Spanish was undertaken by the Chilean psychiatrist, Luis Silva Fuentes, M.D., and the Argentinian-American psychiatrist, Abraham Fiszbein, M.D., who also had been a collaborator on the English version. The object of this effort was to serve the following needs: (a) to develop and standardize an edition of the PANSS for use in Spanish speaking countries; (b) to facilitate cross-cultural psychiatric studies by making available comparable scales in different languages; and (c) to provide for use in the United States as well, where Spanish is the most commonly spoken language after English.

An official translation that promotes uniformity across languages is truly a difficult task. The new instrument must maintain not only a literary equivalence but also must be idiomatically and psychometrically equivalent (Flaherty et al., 1988). Because of this difficulty, attempts at official translation and restandardization have often been inadequate or altogether ignored. Even for the major psychological tests and large-scale surveys, the translations for linguistic minorities and international use have led to unsatisfactory results (Berkanovic, 1980; Olmedo, 1981). For example, the Spanish edition of the Wechsler Adult Intelligence Scale (Green & Martinez, 1968) has been seriously criticized for its incomparability with the well standardized English test, as revealed by wide differences in mean IQ scores (Davis & Rodriguez, 1979).

For a psychiatric rating scale, suitable translation requires strict care that the operational criteria not be altered. Thus, the definition of items, their anchoring in levels of severity, and the distance between rating points must be the same in both languages. Secondly, it requires that the standard interview process and the structured questions for eliciting psychopathology by equivalent. In particular, items that depend mainly on verbal report, such as the assessment of depression and abstract reasoning ability, must be comparable in the new language and also congenial to the different culture (Fabrega, 1974). Finally, studies are needed to determine that the reliability established in the original language is not compromised with the translation and that the two instruments are statistically interchangeable. These endeavors were the object of the current work.

---

*The text of the PANSS-S is available on request from the authors.

PSYCHOMETRIC STUDY

This project began with the translation into Spanish of the full PANSS Rating Manual (Kay, Opler, & Fiszbein, 1987), which includes formal interview guidelines as well as the foregoing definitions and criteria for symptom ratings. The translation, which was prepared by two South American psychiatrists, was in the official Spanish language that is used internationally and approved by the Real Academia Española (Royal Academy of Spain).

Our next step was to study the reliability of the PANSS-S and its equivalence to the original PANSS (Kay et al., in press). The research design involved the assessment of three groups of psychiatric inpatients by three bilingual psychiatrists, whose mother tongue was Spanish. These psychiatrists rated conjointly but independently in pairs after the specified 35–45 minute patient interview, which was performed alternately by one of the two examiners.

One group of 20 patients, of whom four were bilingual and of Hispanic origin, was interviewed and assessed in English, using the standard PANSS. A second group of 20 patients, all of whom spoke Spanish as their primary language, was interviewed and rated in Spanish with the PANSS-S. These two conditions permitted a comparison of the reliability of the PANSS-S vs. the PANSS in terms of consistency across raters. A third group of 17 patients, which included five bilingual Hispanic Americans, was interviewed in English and assessed simultaneously in both languages. For this purpose, one examiner rated in English and one in Spanish, and they systematically alternated in their assignment to the English vs. Spanish PANSS in order to achieve counterbalance across the full group. This condition provided for assessment of criterion validity of the PANSS-S in relation to the PANSS, i.e., the degree of correspondence between the two versions as revealed by their interrelatedness and their similarity in mean scores and variances.

The details on sample characteristics are reported in Table 6:1. All subjects were inpatients from a state psychiatric hospital in New York City. They were predominantly unmarried males with an extensive history of psychiatric illness. The majority was currently diagnosed as schizophrenic by DSM–III–R criteria (American Psychiatric Association, 1987) and was receiving neuroleptic treatment. Overall, the patients ranged in age from 18 to 56 years and in chronicity of illness, based on duration since first hospital admission, from 0 to 39 years. As shown in Table 6:1, the three sets of patients were similar in age, diagnostic composition, medication status, chronicity of illness, and other demographic characteristics, with no significant differences except, of course, in ethnic background.

TABLE 6:1
Sample Characteristics in Standardization Study of the PANSS-S

	Assessment Group		
Variable	PANSS	PANSS-S	PANSS/ PANSS-S
N	20	20	17
Sex (male:female)	17:3	15:5	16:1
Marital status (unmarried:married)	18:2	17:3	17:0
Hispanic ethnic origin (%)	20	100	29
Diagnosis of schizophrenia* (%)	85	75	82
Medicated with neuroleptic (%)	95	95	94
Medicated with anticholinergic (%)	40	45	65
Age (mean ± SD)	33.1 ± 9.28	38.2 ± 8.77	34.8 ± 10.74
Chronicity of illness** (mean ± SD)	12.5 ± 8.01	12.8 ± 10.12	12.6 ± 9.56
Years of education (mean ± SD)	8.8 ± 3.63	7.2 ± 3.14	10.0 ± 2.53

Note: Reprinted with permission from Kay et al. (in press). The Positive and Negative Syndrome Scale, Spanish adaptation (PANSS-S). *Journal of Nervous and Mental Disease.* Copyright © by Williams & Wilkins.
    *Determined by DSM-III-R criteria (American Psychiatric Association, 1987).
    **Determined by years since first psychiatric hospital admission.

PANSS-S STANDARDIZATION

Reliability and Comparability

The interrater correlations for the PANSS-S ratings and the comparative values for the PANSS are summarized in Table 6:2. Significant Pearson correlations were obtained for the four principal scales of the PANSS-S, and these coefficients were highly similar to those of the PANSS as applied by the same raters on a separate sample. Comparison of the PANSS with the PANSS-S (using Fisher's z) indicated no differences between any of the reliability coefficients. Analysis of the interrater reliabilities by intraclass r yielded correlational values on a par with those obtained by Pearson r, with coefficients ranging from .66 to .98 (mean = .81).

Table 6:2 also lists the means and standard deviations for the PANSS-S and PANSS after averaging the observations of the two raters. The scale scores were highly similar, with no significant differences between the corresponding PANSS and PANSS-S means. Conversion of scores into percentile ranks, based on norms from a sample of 101 drug-treated chronic schizophrenic inpatients (Kay, Fiszbein, & Opler, 1987), are additionally shown in Table 6:2. These percentiles underscore the similarity of results with the PANSS and PANSS-S and the generally mid-range placement of the current cohort in relation to a standardization sample of like age

TABLE 6:2

Interrater Reliability, Means, Standard Deviations, and Percentile Ranks for PANSS and PANSS-S

Psychopathology Scale

Statistic	Positive Syndrome		Negative Syndrome		Composite Index		General Psychopathology	
	PANSS	PANSS-S	PANSS	PANSS-S	PANSS	PANSS-S	PANSS	PANSS-S
N	20	20	20	20	20	20	20	20
Scoring range	7 to 49		7 to 49		−42 to +42		16 to 112	
Pearson r	.87***	.93***	.84***	.74**	.72**	.65*	.89***	.83***
Fisher's z	.95		.79		.39		.68	
Mean	19.10	19.08	23.50	23.70	−4.40	−4.62	39.88	38.90
SD	4.52	3.87	4.95	4.17	4.35	4.17	8.70	7.96
Student t	.02		.14		.16		.37	
Percentile****	51	51	63	64	43	44	57	55

Note: Reprinted with permission from Kay et al. (in press). The Positive and Negative Syndrome Scale, Spanish adaptation (PANSS-S). *Journal of Nervous and Mental Disease.* Copyright © by Williams & Wilkins.

*p < .002
**p < .001
****p < .0001
****Percentiles derived from Kay, Fiszbein, & Opler (1987).

(mean = 36.8 years), length of illness (mean = 14.4 years), and sex ratio (70% male).

Criterion-related Validity

This was studied by the statistical comparability of the PANSS-S with the PANSS when assessed by different raters in the same patient sample. The results (Table 6:3) indicated no differences between any of the corresponding means and standard deviations. In addition, the correlations between the PANSS and PANSS-S scales were all significant, with the two principal scales significant beyond $p < 0.0001$: positive, $r = 0.92$; negative, $r = 0.83$.

Table 6:4 reports the cross-correlations for the individual items comprising the positive and negative scales and for the five psychopathology cluster scores. The item correlations extended from 0.64 (passive/apathetic social withdrawal) to 0.97 (grandiosity), and all were significant at $p < 0.01$ or better. Each of the symptom clusters also showed substantial correlations that ranged from 0.81 (anergia) to 0.93 (thought disturbance), with $p < 0.0001$ in all cases.

CONCLUSIONS

The present research considered whether the basic psychometric qualities determined for the standardized PANSS are upheld in a Spanish adaptation. The results indicated that the PANSS-S ratings were consistent across judges and interchangeable with those of the PANSS. Thus, the scale yielded sound interrater reliabilities, which were on a par with those from the PANSS in the present as well as previous samples (Kay, Fiszbein, & Opler, 1987; Kay, Opler, & Lindenmayer, 1988). With regard to criterion validity, the correspondence of the PANSS-S with the PANSS was supported by lack of significant differences between the means and standard deviations, suggesting similarity in the rating points and distribution characteristics. We also found significant crosscorrelations for the positive and negative scales, their component symptoms, and the five psychopathology clusters. The latter finding supports the use of the PANSS-S for assessing symptom complexes other than positive and negative; the benefit of this application is in providing a broader-range symptomatic profile as well as reference points for interpreting the positive and negative syndrome scores. Because of its scope of assessment, the PANSS or PANSS-S may serve as a reasonable alternative to the Brief Psychiatric Rating Scale and other psychiatric rating instruments.

TABLE 6:3
Analysis of the Correspondence Between PANSS and PANSS-S Ratings

| | Scale Scores | | | | Mean Difference Between Scales | Statistical Tests | | |
| | PANSS | | PANSS-S | | | Differences Between | | Rater Agreement (Pearson r) |
Scale	Mean	(SD)	Mean	(SD)		Means (Paired t)	Variance (t)	
Positive syndrome	21.29	(4.81)	20.77	(5.16)	0.52	1.09	0.69	0.92**
Negative syndrome	21.71	(4.89)	21.47	(4.78)	0.24	0.34	0.16	0.83**
Composite index	−0.41	(5.71)	−0.71	(6.31)	0.30	0.50	0.99	0.92**
General psychopathology	43.17	(6.89)	41.53	(5.20)	1.64	1.09	1.34	0.57*

Note: Reprinted with permission from Kay et al. (in press). The Positive and Negative Scale, Spanish adaptation (PANSS-S). *Journal of Nervous and Mental Disease.* Copyright © by Williams & Wilkins.

Data are from a single group in which each patient was assesed by different raters with both methods. See text for further explanation.

*p < .02
**p < .0001

TABLE 6:4

Cross-Correlations Between the PANSS and PANSS-S on Positive Symptoms, Negative Symptoms, and Psychopathology Clusters (n = 17)*

Symptom/Cluster	Pearson r	p
Positive symptoms		
P1. Delusions	0.79	< 0.0002
P2. Conceptual disorganization	0.84	< 0.0001
P3. Hallucinatory behavior	0.78	< 0.0002
P4. Excitement	0.85	< 0.0001
P5. Grandiosity	0.97	< 0.0001
P6. Suspiciousness/persecution	0.75	< 0.001
P7. Hostility	0.78	< 0.0002
Negative symptoms		
N1. Blunted affect	0.66	< 0.005
N2. Emotional withdrawal	0.73	< 0.001
N3. Poor rapport	0.90	< 0.0001
N4. Passive/apathetic social withdrawal	0.64	< 0.01
N5. Difficulty in abstract thinking	0.83	< 0.0001
N6. Lack of spontaneity and flow of conversation	0.76	< 0.0005
N7. Stereotyped thinking	0.67	< 0.005
Psychopathology cluster		
Anergia	0.81	< 0.0001
Thought disturbance	0.93	< 0.0001
Activation	0.89	< 0.0001
Paranoid belligerence	0.86	< 0.0001
Anxiety/depression	0.82	< 0.0001

*Reprinted with permission from Kay et al. (in press). The Positive and Negative Syndrome Scale, Spanish adaptation (PANSS-S). *Journal of Nervous and Mental Disease.* Copyright © by Williams & Wilkins.

The availability of a Spanish language psychopathology scale that is standardized against the English provides for its use in Spanish-speaking populations and may set the stage for crosscultural studies with an equivalent yardstick. In fact, little is yet known about the comparative prevalence of positive and negative syndromes in different regions of the world. Crosscultural research of this kind may reflect on the societal influences on symptomatic expression or, conversely, on its universality. Still unexplored is the elementary question of whether the cognitive, neurobiological, family history, and other covariates of positive and negative syndromes are constant across cultures. For example, if there is merit to Crow's (1980a) hypothesis that a negative presentation signifies structural brain abnormality, one might expect this to transcend geographic and societal bounds. The validity of such a comparison, of course, depends on measures that are psychometrically equivalent and culturally compatible (Berry, 1969; Flaherty et al., 1988).

Further research is clearly needed on the application of the PANSS-S in other Spanish cultures and subcultures, particularly to the extent that the spoken language varies from the standard Spanish used in our translation. The current study, however, represents a first effort at standardization of positive-negative symptom assessment across languages. The results are encouraging and suggest that psychopathology can be measured reliably and comparably in different languages.

7

Structured Clinical Interview for the PANSS (SCI-PANSS)

AIMS OF THE SCI-PANSS

The Positive and Negative Syndrome Scale (PANSS) is a 30-item, seven-point rating instrument for assessing positive, negative, and other symptoms in schizophrenia (Kay, Fiszbein, & Opler, 1987; Kay, Opler, & Lindenmayer, 1988). The component scales are operationalized by provision of detailed definitions for each symptom at all levels of severity. The sources of information for ratings vary from item to item and are specified in the item definition. As a whole, the information derives partly from primary care staff or family, but mainly from a 30–45 minute formalized clinical interview. As outlined in PANSS Rating Manual (Kay, Opler, & Fiszbein, 1987), this interview includes a nondirective, semistructured, structured, and directive phase in order to evaluate functional impairments under different conditions of examination.

To optimize the scale's objectivity and standardization, however, a tightly structured interview is important. For this reason we have developed the Structured Clinical Interview for the PANSS (SCI-PANSS), which is patterned after other structured interview methods (Burdock & Hardesty, 1973; Spitzer, Williams, Gibbon, & First, 1988). The current procedure attempts to generate a productive flow of conversation while systematically eliciting information on various realms of psychopathology. Symptoms that are not directly probed by the verbal transaction are assessed on the basis of behavioral observation from the interview (e.g., motor retardation and uncooperativeness) or from daily life, as reported by primary care staff or the family (e.g., poor impulse control and passive/apathetic social withdrawal).

The object of the SCI-PANSS is to secure reliable information for ascertaining first the presence, and next the severity, of an array of symptoms in Schizophrenia. To this end, the method includes both yes-no and open-ended questions that allow the examiner to establish the existence, nature, and impact of clinical manifestations. The interview applies a decision-tree sequence, such that the follow-up question often depends on the previous answer. For example, in the portion that assesses a patient's judgment and insight into illness, the examiner asks, "Did you have a problem that needed treatment?" If the patient responds affirmatively, the question is followed by one that seeks to determine whether the patient perceives the stated problem as a psychiatric one. If the patient has answered in the negative, however, the examiner proceeds to the next question: "In your opinion, do you need to be taking medicine?" The full interview usually will require between 30 and 40 minutes.

The interview should start, as previously mentioned, with a nondirective phase serving to establish rapport and a "warm up" for both patient and interviewer. It is followed by the structured phase as outlined below. It is during this phase that the listed items should be covered. While the outlined interview follows a specific format, interviewers can establish their own sequence to accommodate the particular patient situation as long as all items are covered systematically as indicated.

The general rules for the rating of the degree of severity have been outlined in the manual. They are based on the following principle: Scores from 0 to 3 establish the degree of presence of the psychopathological manifestation. Scores from 4 to 7 establish the degree of severity by which the particular manifestation interferes in the patients' day-to-day functioning:

4: Moderate interference
5: Distinct impact with moderate to severe interference
6: Very frequent interference
7: Continuous interference in almost all life functions.

It is expected that the SCI-PANSS will be helpful toward facilitating and standardizing the PANSS training. Equally important, it is likely to enhance the comparability of its application in different research settings. The SCI-PANSS is to be used, of course, in concert with the PANSS Rating Manual (Kay, Opler, & Fiszbein, 1987), which provides the operational criteria for performing the rating as well as information on scoring.

The full text of the SCI-PANSS interview, developed in collaboration with Drs. Lewis A. Opler, Jean-Pierre Lindenmayer, and Abraham Fiszbein, is presented in the following section.

STRUCTURED CLINICAL INTERVIEW
FOR THE POSITIVE AND NEGATIVE SYNDROME SCALE
(SCI-PANSS)*

Data on "Lack of Spontaneity and Flow of Conversation," "Poor Rapport," and "Conceptual Disorganization"

Hi, I'm. . . . We're going to be spending the next 30 or 40 minutes talking about yourself and your reasons for being here. Maybe you can start out by telling me something about yourself and your background? (Instruction to interviewer:
Allow at lest 5 minutes for a non-directive phase serving to establish rapport in the context of an overview before proceeding to the specific questions listed below.)

Data on "Anxiety"

Have you been feeling worried or nervous in the past week?
IF NO:
Would you say that you're usually calm and relaxed?
IF YES:
What's been making you feel nervous (worried, uncalm, unrelaxed)?
Just how nervous (worried, etc.) have you been feeling?
Have you been shaking at times, or has your heart been racing?
Do you get into a state of panic?
Has your sleep, eating, or participation in activities been affected?

Data on "Delusions (General)" and "Unusual Thought Content"

Have things been going well for you?
Has anything been bothering you lately?
Can you tell me something about your thoughts on life and its purpose?
Do you follow a particular philosophy?
Some people tell me they believe in the Devil; what do you think?
Can you read other people's minds?
IF YES:
How does that work?
Can others read your mind?
IF YES:

---

*Reprinted with permission from Multi-Health Systems, Inc., Toronto, Canada.

How can they do that?
Is there any reason that someone would want to read your mind?
Who controls your thoughts?

Data on "Suspiciousness/Persecution," "Passive/Apathetic Social Withdrawal," "Active Social Avoidance," and "Poor Impulse Control"

How do you spend your time these days?
Do you prefer to be alone?
Do you join in activities with others?
> IF NO:
> Why not? . . . Are you afraid of people, or do you dislike them?
>> IF YES:
>> Can you explain?
> IF YES:
> Tell me about it.
Do you have many friends?
> IF NO:
> Just a few?
>> IF NO:
>> Any? . . . Why?
>> IF YES:
>> Why just a few friends?
> IF YES:
> Close friends?
>> IF NO:
>> Why not?
Do you feel that you can trust most people?
> IF NO:
> Why not?
Are there some people in particular that you don't trust?
> IF YES:
> Can you tell me who they are?
> Why don't you trust people (or name specific person)?
>> IF "DON'T KNOW" OR "DON'T WANT TO SAY":
>> Do you have a good reason not to trust. . .?
> Is there some thing that . . . did to you?
> Perhaps might do to you now?
>> IF YES:
>> Can you explain to me?
Do you get along well with others?

IF NO:
What's the problem?
Do you have a quick temper?
Do you get into fights?
  IF YES:
  How do these fights start?
  Tell me about these fights.
  How often does this happen?
Do you sometimes lose control of yourself?
Do you like most people?
  IF NO:
  Why not?
Are there perhaps some people who don't like you?
  IF YES:
  For what reason?
Do others talk about you behind your back?
  IF YES:
  What do they say about you?
  Why?
Does anyone ever spy on you or plot against you?
Do you sometimes feel in danger?
  IF YES:
  Would you say that your life is in danger?
  Is someone thinking of harming you or even perhaps thinking of killing you?
  Have you gone to the police for help?
  Do you sometimes take matters into your own hands or take action on those who might harm you?
    IF YES:
    What have you done?

Data on "Hallucinatory Behavior" and associated delusions

Do you once in a while have strange or unusual experiences?
Sometimes people tell me that they can hear noises or voices inside their head that others can't hear. What about you?
  IF NO:
  Do you sometimes receive personal communications from the radio or TV?
    IF NO:
    From God or the Devil?

IF YES:

What do you hear?

Are these as clear and loud as my voice?

How often do you hear these voices (noises, messages, etc.)?

Does this happen at a particular time of day or all the time?

IF HEARING VOICES:

Can you recognize whose voices these are?

What do the voices say?

Are the voices good or bad?

Pleasant or unpleasant?

Do the voices interrupt your thinking or your activities?

Do they sometimes give you orders or instructions?

    IF YES:

    For example?

    Do you usually obey these orders (instructions)?

What do you make of these voices (or noises): where do they really come from?

Why do you have these experiences?

Are these normal experiences?

Do ordinary things sometimes look strange or distorted to you?

Do you sometimes have "visions" or see things that others can't see?

IF YES:

For example?

Do these visions seem very real or life-like?

How often do you have these experiences?

Do you sometimes smell things that are unusual or that others don't smell?

IF YES:

Please explain.

Do you get any strange or unusual sensations from inside your body?

IF YES:

Tell me about this.

Data on "Somatic Concern"

How have you been feeling in terms of your health?

IF OTHER THAN "GOOD":

What has been troubling you?

IF "GOOD":

Do you consider yourself to be in top health?

IF NO:
What has been troubling you?
Do you have any medical illness or disease?
Has any part of your body been troubling you?
  IF NO:
  How is your head? Your heart? Stomach? The rest of your body?
  IF YES:
  Could you explain?
Has your head or body changed in shape or size?
  IF YES:
  Please explain.
  What is causing these changes?

Data on "Depression"

How has your mood been in the past week: mostly good, mostly bad?
  IF "MOSTLY GOOD":
  Have there been times in the past week that you were feeling sad or unhappy?
    IF YES:
  IF "MOSTLY BAD":
  Is there something in particular that is making you sad?
  How often do you feel sad?
  Jut how sad have you been feeling?
  Have you been crying lately?
  Has your mood in any way affected your sleep?
  Has it affected your appetite?
  Do you participate less in activities on account of your mood?
  Have you had any thoughts of harming yourself?
    IF YES:
    Any thoughts about ending your life?
      IF YES:
      Have you attempted suicide?

Data on "Guilt Feelings" and "Grandiosity"

If you were to compare yourself to the average person, how would you come out: a little better, maybe a little worse, or about the same?
  IF WORSE:
  Worse in what ways?

Just how do you feel about yourself?
IF BETTER:
Better in what ways?
IF ABOUT THE SAME:
Are you special in some ways?
   IF YES:
   In what ways?
Would you consider yourself gifted?
Do you have talents or abilities that most people don't have?
   IF YES:
   Please explain.
Do you have any special powers?
   IF YES:
   What are these?
   Where do these powers come from?
Do you have extrasensory perception (ESP), or can you read other people's minds?
Are you very wealthy?
   IF YES:
   Explain please.
Can you be considered to be very bright?
   IF YES:
   Why would you say so?
   Would you describe yourself as famous?
   Would some people recognize you from TV, radio, or the newspapers?
   IF YES:
   Can you tell me about it?
Are you a religious person?
   IF YES:
   Are you close to God?
      IF YES:
      Did God assign you some special role or purpose?
      Can you be one of God's messengers or angels?
         IF YES:
         What special powers do you have as God's messenger (angel)?
      Do you perhaps consider yourself to be God?
Do you have some special mission in life?
   IF YES:
   What is your mission?
   Who assigned you to that mission?

Did you ever do something wrong—something you feel bad or guilty about?

IF YES:

Just how much does that bother you now?

Do you feel that you deserve punishment for that?

   IF YES:

   What kind of punishment would you deserve?

   Have you at times thought of punishing yourself?

      IF YES:

      Have you ever acted on those thoughts of punishing yourself?

Data on Disorientation

Can you tell me what is today's date (i.e., the day, month, and year)?

What is the name of the place that you are in now?

(If hospitalized:) What ward are you on?

What is the address of where you now stay?

If someone had to reach you by phone, what number would that person call?

What is the name of the doctor who is treating you?

(If hospitalized:) Can you tell me who else is on the staff and what they do?

Do you know who is now the President?

Who is our Governor?

What is the Mayor (town Supervisor) of this city (town, etc.)?

Data on "Difficulty in Abstract Thinking"

I'm going to now say a pair of words, and I'd like you to tell me in what important way they're alike. Let's start, for example, with the words "apple" and "banana." How are they alike—what do they have in common?

   IF "THEY'RE BOTH FRUIT":

Good. Now what about. . .? [SELECT THREE OTHER ITEMS FROM THE SIMILARITIES LIST AT VARYING LEVELS OF DIFFICULTY: SEE APPENDIX A.]

IF ANSWER THAT IS CONCRETE, TANGENTIAL, OR IDIOSYN-CRATIC, E.G., "THEY BOTH HAVE SKINS," "YOU CAN EAT THEM," "THEY'RE SMALL," or "MONKEYS LIKE THEM":

O.K., but they're both fruit. Now how about . . . and . . .: how are these

alike? [SELECT THREE OTHER ITEMS FROM THE SIMILARITIES LIST AT VARYING LEVELS OF DIFFICULTY; SEE APPENDIX A.]
You've probably heard the expression, "Carrying a chip on the shoulder." What does that really mean?
What about when people say, "It's as plain as the nose on your face": what do they mean?
There's a very old saying, "Don't judge a book by its cover." What is the deeper meaning of this proverb?
[SELECT THREE OTHER PROVERBS FROM THE LIST IN APPENDIX B AT VARYING LEVELS OF DIFFICULTY]

Data on "Lack of Judgment and Insight"

How long have you been in the hospital (clinic, etc.)?
Why did you come to the hospital (clinic, etc.)?
Did you need to be in a hospital (clinic, etc.)?
  IF NO:
  Did you have a problem that needed treatment?
    IF YES:
    Would you say that you had a psychiatric or mental problem?
  IF YES:
  Why? . . . Would you say that you had a psychiatric or mental problem?
    IF YES:
    Can you tell me about it and what it consists of?
    IF YES:
    In your own opinion, do you need to be taking medicine?
  IF NO:
  (If medicated:) Why then are you taking medicines?
  (If unmedicated:) Why are you still in the hospital (clinic, etc.)?
  IF YES:
  Why? . . . Does the medicine help you in any way?
Do you at this time have any psychiatric or mental problems?
  IF NO:
  For what reason are you still in the hospital (clinic, etc.)?
  IF YES:
  Please explain.
  Just how serious are these problems?
  (If hospitalized:)
    Are you ready yet for discharge from the hospital?

Do you think you'll be taking medicine for your problems after discharge?

What are your future plans?

What about your longer-range goals?

Well, that's about all I have to ask of you now. Are there any questions that you might like to ask of me?

Thank you for your cooperation.

APPENDIX A: Items for assessing SIMILARITIES in the evaluation of "Difficulty in Abstract Thinking"*

1. How are a ball and orange alike?
2. Apple and banana?
3. Pencil and pen?
4. Nickel and dime?
5. Table and chair?
6. Tiger and elephant?
7. Hat and shirt?
8. Bus and train?
9. Arm and leg?
10. Rose and tulip?
11. Uncle and cousin?
12. The sun and the moon?
13. Painting and poem?
14. Hilltop and valley?
15. Air and water?
16. Peace and prosperity?

---

*From: Kay, S. R., Opler, L. A., & Fiszbein, A. (1987). *Positive and Negative Syndrome Scale (PANSS) Rating Manual.* San Rafael, Calif.: Social and Behavioral Sciences Documents.

NOTE: Similarities are generally assessed by sampling four of the above items at different levels of difficulty (i.e., one item selected from each quarter of the full set). When using the PANSS longitudinally, items should be systematically alternated with successive interviews so as to provide different selections from the various levels of difficulty and thus minimize repetition.

APPENDIX B. Items for assessing PROVERB INTERPRETATION in the evaluation of "Difficulty in Abstract Thinking"*

What does the saying mean:

1. "Plain as the nose on your face"
2. "Carrying a chip on your shoulder"
3. "Two heads are better than one"
4. "Too many cooks spoil the broth"
5. "Don't judge a book by its cover"

6. "One man's food is another man's poison"
7. "All that glitters is not gold"
8. "Don't cross the bridge until you come to it"
9. "What's good for the goose is good for the gander"
10. "The grass always looks greener on the other side"
11. "Don't keep all your eggs in one basket"
12. "One swallow does not make a summer"
13. "A stitch in time saves nine"
14. "A rolling stone gathers no moss"
15. "The acorn never falls far from the tree"
16. "People who live in glass houses should not throw stones at others"

---

*From: Kay, S. R., Opler, L. A., & Fiszbein, A. (1987). *Positive and Negative Syndrome Scale (PANSS) Rating Manual*. San Rafael, Calif.: Social and Behavioral Sciences Documents.

NOTE: Proverb interpretation is generally assessed by sampling four of the above items at different levels of difficulty (i.e., one item selected from each quarter of the full set). When using the PANSS longitudinally, items should be systematically alternated with successive interviews so as to provide different selections from the various levels of difficulty and thus minimize repetition.

8

Diagnostic Edition of the PANSS (SCID-PANSS)

NEW CONCEPT ON DIAGNOSIS

Researchers today are in general agreement that schizophrenia comprises more than one disease process. The data from separate perspectives, such as premorbid history, genetic study, neurological findings, and drug response, are constantly reminding us that we are witnessing in schizophrenia quite distinct syndromes, ones that have different origins and will require different treatments. Central to the delineation of these syndromes, as we shall see in the forthcoming chapters, is the presenting profile of symptoms, and in particular the predominance of positive and negative features.

To date, however, the prevalent diagnostic system in psychiatry (American Psychiatric Association, 1987) has not incorporated the positive-negative distinction. The subclassification of schizophrenia is still undertaken as according to Kraepelin (1919), using a conceptualization that was developed over 70 years ago out of informal clinical observation, without the benefit of broad-based research and the technological innovations available in our time. This system of subclassification recognizes three principal subtypes of schizophrenia: paranoid (characterized mainly by delusions, especially of a persecutory type), disorganized or hebephrenic (characterized mainly by affective impairment and cognitive disorganization), and catatonic (characterized mainly by motor excitement, reduction, or stupor). Despite the value of the Kraepelinian model in highlighting the importance of different symptom complexes, it has not contributed materially to clarifying the diversity in the pathogenesis of schizophrenia, nor to specific treatment strategies. All three subtypes, for example, tend to be medicated in the same fashion, without the subdiagnosis providing an instructive lead. Later, in Chapter 12, we shall present evidence that these subtypes are not fundamental facets of schizophrenia but, rather, derive from the interplay of purer dimensions, including positive and negative syndromes.

It is our view, therefore, that the diagnostic subtyping of schizophrenia is in need of major updating. A newer nosology must recognize syndromes that represent meaningful distinctions in schizophrenia and carry direct implications about the causes, the specific treatment, and the probable outcome. Furthermore, a revised classification needs to take into account the likelihood that different syndromes are not mutually exclusive but, in fact, may typically coexist in the same patient (see Chapter 12). It is clear that we do not usually encounter pure "types" in schizophrenia; most patients constitute a mix of different dimensions that prevail to varying degrees.

The result of this mix may, in principle, be either addictive or interactive. In other words, the co-occurrence of two or more syndromes may be understood as the sum of its components, or yet it may alter the presentation in ways that are not readily predictable. In either case, the multiplicity of syndromes in a single patient suggests that the clinical picture is more accurately depicted dimensionally, according to a profile assessment, rather than by a simple, discrete categorization.

Twenty-five years ago, van Praag and Leijnse (1965) pointed out the sterility of a categorical approach to diagnosis, one that serves primarily a nosological purpose. Aside from its limitations in depicting the clinical processes, it is inadequate from the standpoint of biological psychiatry: psychopharmacological treatments address a patient's symptoms, behaviors, and functioning, not disease types (van Praag et al., 1987). Therefore, van Praag has advocated a "denosologization" in favor of assessment of functional psychopathology. This implies the need for a two-tier diagnostic system, whereby we first classify the general disorder (e.g., via DSM–III–R criteria) and then proceed to characterize the precise functional disturbances of the individual. This latter dimensional evaluation will permit a more faithful and detailed account of the patient's psychopathology, and one that has far greater relevance for treatment decisions as well as for research (Katz, 1968; van Praag et al., 1987).

In light of these principles and the importance of the positive-negative distinction, our group has originated and standardized the Positive and Negative Syndrome Scale (PANSS) as a method for assessing these and other facets of schizophrenic symptomatology (Chapter 3). Our next step was to integrate the PANSS into the diagnostic system of the American Psychiatric Association (1987) so as to provide for a two-tier "nosological-dimensional" diagnostic assessment. This involved the development of a structured clinical interview that, in combined fashion, gathers information for both the general diagnostic criteria to classify psychotic disorders (Spitzer et al., 1988) and the specific rating criteria to assess various symptoms and syndromes of schizophrenia (Kay & Opler, 1990; see Chapter 7). The result was a new and more comprehensive document, referred to as the Structured Clinical Interview for the DSM–III–R, PANSS Edition (SCID-PANSS) (Kay et al., 1989, 1990). Its value is in providing a highly structured and thorough description of psychopathology that may augment the diagnostic, clinical, and research evaluation of schizophrenia.

INSTRUCTIONS FOR THE SCID-PANSS

The SCID-PANSS consists of a precise text, or script, for securing pertinent clinical data in a rigorous and standard manner. There are two distinct segments, one pertaining to the patient's observed daily behavior (the "pre-interview") and one dependent on direct patient interview. The first segment entails a brief review of patient functioning over the past week from the primary care staff or, if not hospitalized, from the family. This is followed by a systematic patient interview that provides data to assess the presence and severity of 30 psychiatric symptoms over the course of the prior week. To this end, the method involves both yes-no and open-ended questions that allow the examiner to establish the existence, nature, and seriousness of the clinical manifestations.

The interview responses are entered and codified according to the key presented in the right hand column of the interview text. Ratings that directly apply toward the diagnostic evaluation as according to the Structured Clinical Interview for the DSM–III–R (SCID) (Spitzer et al., 1988) are highlighted by bold type. Items for symptom assessment are defined and scored as according to the PANSS. These definitions and the anchoring for symptom severity appear at the point of interview in which the principal information for that item is obtained. SCID and PANSS ratings are thus conducted as the interview progresses by encircling the appropriate level of symptom severity along the 1–3 or 1–7 point range. For purpose of alignment of the three-point SCID and seven-point PANSS items, we regard a rating of 1 on the SCID ("absent or false") as equivalent to a 1 on the PANSS ("absent"), a 2 on the SCID ("subthreshold") to equal a 2 on the PANSS ("minimal"), and a 3 on the SCID ("threshold") to encompass ratings between 3 and 7 on the PANSS ("mild" to "extreme").

The structured interview applies a decision-tree sequence, such that the follow-up questions often depend on the previous answer. Thus, there are many "skip-outs," and the full SCID-PANSS text is never used for an individual patient. The interview can ordinarily be performed in less than an hour.

The comprehensive SCID-PANSS text, of course, is intended to systematically divulge and elucidate areas of psychopathology and to anticipate the various possible responses to interview questions. In assessing somatic delusions, for example, one begins with a general inquiry on *"How have you been feeling in terms of your health?"* If the response indicates "other than good," the probing interviewer asks, *"Do you have any medical illness or disease?"* . . . *"Has any part of your body been troubling you?"*. . .etc. If the answers are affirmative, the ensuing line of inquiry explores the extent of somatic concern, thoughts, and possible delusions. On the other hand, if the opening general question had failed to disclose somatic themes, the interviewer follows up with an even broader question—*"Do you consider yourself in top health?"*—in a continued effort to open the door to possible abnormal ideation. Depending on the patient's answer, the interviewer continues with *"What has been troubling you?"* or else proceeds to the next area of inquiry.

Not all ratings, however, are determined by the content of answers. For example, the assessment of thought processes, affect, rapport, and communication are derived largely by observation of interview behavior, and several items such as emotional withdrawal and social avoidance are judged primarily from the pre-interview data. The observational items are necessarily rated at the end of the session, whereas the items from the pre-interview are rated earlier but may need to be revised by the close of the patient interview if new information is elicited.

Diagnostic assessment is performed by reference to the bold-type items from the SCID, using the method described by Spitzer et al. (1988) that adheres to the criteria of the DSM–III–R (American Psychiatric Association, 1987). For PANSS assessment, the symptom ratings are transferred from within the interview booklet to the summary rating form (Appendix D). Scoring is done as described for the PANSS in Chapter 3. Positive and negative scores that equal or exceed a threshold of 24 and 26, respectively, are considered to signify a severe syndrome, since they surpass the 75th percentile of our provisional norms for schizophrenic inpatients (Appendix C). Also according to these criteria, a composite index of greater than 2 or less than −6 indicates, respectively, polarization toward the positive or negative end of the continuum (i.e., $\geq$ 75th percentile or $\leq$ 25th percentile). Use of the normative table in Appendix C will allow for a fuller breadth of interpretation of scores on the four PANSS syndromes and five symptom clusters

Field testing of the SCID-PANSS by five psychitrists on a sample of 34 psychotic inpatients has revealed strong interrater correlations (0.85 to 0.97 for the summary scales, $p < 0.0001$) (Kay et al., 1990). These data support the reliability of the new instrument for clinical and research applications.

In the remainder of this chapter, we present the text of the SCID-PANSS, developed in collaboration with Drs. Lewis A. Opler, Robert L. Spitzer, Janet B. W. Williams, Miriam Gibbon, and Michael B. First from Columbia University and the New York State Psychiatric Institute.

SCID-PANSS PRE-INTERVIEW

The pre-interview provides information on the patient's characteristic functioning over the course of the preceding week. It consists of a brief inquiry (approximately five minutes) from the patient's primary care clinician (e.g., primary therapist, case manager, nurse), if hospitalized, or else from a family member or caretaker.

- I'm going to be asking you a few questions that pertain to the patient's behavior on the ward [*or* your son's (daughter's, etc.) behavior at home] during the past week. How does he/she typically spend the day?

  1. sociable
  2. retiring
  3. isolated/withdrawn

- Has he/she been regularly participating in activities in the past week?

  1. yes
  2. no

  IF YES:
  Does he/she show real interest and initiative?

  1. yes
  2. no

  IF NO:
  How involved is he/she with peers and with the social life around him/her?

  1. involved
  2. minimally involved
  3. not at all involved

  Does he/she participate in activities if asked?

  1. yes
  2. no

  IF YES:
  Is the participation passive or "mechanical," that is, without real interest?

  1. no
  2. yes

  Does the patient [your son, daughter, etc.] avoid activities because of disinterest or, rather, because of fear, hostility, or distrust?

  1. disinterest
  2. fear
  3. hostility
  4. distrust

- Does the patient [your son, daughter, etc.] have any problems with activities of daily living, such as sleeping, eating, dressing, or personal hygiene?

  1. none   4. dressing
  2. sleeping 5. personal
  3. eating   hygiene
              6. other

  How serious is the problem?

  1. not very serious
  2. serious

  What seems to be causing this problem? _____

[PERFORM PANSS RATINGS ON: *N4. PASSIVE-APATHETIC SOCIAL*
WITHDRAWAL
G16. ACTIVE SCIAL AVOIDANCE]

- Does the patient [your son, daughter, etc.] show   1. yes
  interest in life's events?   2. no
- Is he/she involved emotionally in daily plans and   1. yes
  events? Please explain.   2. no

[PERFORM PANSS RATING ON: *N2. EMOTIONAL WITHDRAWAL*

- Does the patient [your son, daughter, etc.]   1. no problem
  represent a management problem on account of   2. hostile
  being hostile, impulsive, or aggressive?   3. impulsive
                                                          4. aggressive

  IF YES:
                                                          1. rarely (once or twice)
  How often do these incidences occur?   2. occasionally
                                                          3. often

  Is special supervision, seclusion, or use
  of restraining device necessary?   1. no 2. yes
- Does he/she tend to be irritable or sarcastic?   1. no 2. yes
- Is he/she usually cooperative with others?   1. yes 2. no

[PERFORM PANSS RATINGS ON: *P7. HOSTILITY*
G14. POOR IMPULSE CONTROL
G8. UNCOOPERATIVENESS]

- Is he/she sometimes observed talking, muttering,   1. no
  or mumbling to himself/herself?   2. yes
  IF YES:
  Please describe. _____
  _____

- Does he/she sometimes seem to respond to voices   1. no
  or things that are not present?   2. yes
  IF YES:
  Please describe. _____
  _____

- Is he/she usually too slow or too fast in his/her   1. no
  movements?   2. too slow
                                                          3. too fast

  IF EITHER:
  What is the evidence of this? _____
  _____

  How serious a problem is this?   1. not very serious
                                                          2. serious

[PERFORM PANSS RATINGS ON: *P4. EXCITEMENT*
G7. *MOTOR RETARDATION*]

- Are his/her movements and posture natural or,   1. natural
  instead, are they stiff, disorganized, or   2. stiff
  bizarre?   3. disorganized
                                                      4. bizarre

- Does the patient sometimes display rituals,   1. no
  stereotypic movements, or an unnatural, fixed   2. rituals
  posture?   3. stereotypic movements
                                                      4. unnatural fixed posture

[PERFORM PANSS RATING ON: *G5. MANNERISMS AND POSTURING*]

- When the patient [your son, daughter, etc.]   ? **no information**
  experienced symptoms, was he/she taking drugs,   **1. no**
  drinking a lot, or physically ill?   **2. yes**

SCID-PANSS Patient Interview

- Hello, I'm ___. We're going to be spending some
  time talking about yourself and [IF HOSPITALIZED] . . .
  your reasons for being here. How long have you
  now been in the hospital? _____
  [IF NOT HOSPITALIZED] . . . whatever problems you may
  have had. Have you previously been in a hospital   1. no
  or received treatment?   2. yes
- Why did you come to the hospital (clinic, etc., or   1. realistic appraisal
  receive treatment)?   2. unrealistic appraisal
                                                       3. delusional appraisal

- Did you need to be in a hospital (clinic, under   1. yes
  treatment, etc.)?   2. no
    IF NO:
    Did you have a problem that needed treatment?   1. yes
                                                       2. no

    IF YES:
    Would you say that you had a psychiatric or   1. yes
    mental problem?   2. no
    IF YES:
    Just how serious was it?   1. serious
                                                       2. not serious

    Can you tell me about it and what it   1. realistic appraisal
    consisted of?   2. unrealistic appraisal
                                                       3. delusional appraisal

  IF YES:
  Why did you need to be in a hospital (clinic,   1. mental disorder
  under treatment, etc.)?   2. other explanation

Would you say that you had a psychiatric or
mental problem?

    1. yes
    2. no

IF YES:

Just how serious was it?

    1. serious
    2. not serious

Can you tell me about it and what it
consisted of?

    1. realistic appraisal
    2. unrealistic appraisal
    3. delusional appraisal

• In your opinion, do you need to be taking medicine?

    1. yes
    2. no

IF YES:

Why?

    1. for psychiatric reasons
    2. other explanation

Does the medicine help you in some way?

    1. yes
    2. no

IF NO:

[IF MEDICATED] Why then are you taking the
medicine?

    1. for psychiatric reasons
    2. other explanation

[IF UNMEDICATED] Why are you still in the
hospital (clinic, under treatment, etc.)?

    1. for psychiatric reasons
    2. other explanation

• Do you at this time have any psychiatric or mental
problems?

    1. yes
    2. no

IF NO:

For what reason are you still in the hospital
(clinic, under treatment, etc.)?

    1. plausible explanation
    2. delusional explanation

IF YES:

Please explain.

    1. ample understanding
       of symptoms
    2. poor understanding
       of symptoms

Just how serious are these problems?

    1. serious
    2. not serious

• Are you ready yet for discharge from the hospital
(termination of treatment, etc.)?

    1. no
    2. yes

• Do you think you'll be taking medicine for your
problems after discharge (termination of treatment,
etc.)?

    1. yes
    2. no

• What are your future plans?

    1. realistic
    2. unrealistic

• What about your longer range goals?

    1. realistic
    2. unrealistic

[PERFORM PANSS RATING ON: *G12. LACK OF JUDGMENT AND INSIGHT*]

• How do you spend your time these days?

    1. socially active
    2. mostly isolated

- Do you prefer to be alone?   1. no
                                                      2. yes

- Do you join in activities with others?   1. yes
                                                      2. no

    IF NO:
    Why not? . . . Are you afraid of people, or do   1. fear
    you maybe dislike them? Please explain.   2. dislike
                                                      3. other explanation

    IF YES:
    All activities?   1. yes
                                                      2. no

    IF NO TO EITHER OF THE ABOVE:
    Why not? . . . Are you afraid of some people,   1. fear
    or perhaps don't like certain people?   2. dislike
                                                      3. other explanation

- Do you have many friends?   1. yes
                                                      2. no

    IF NO:
    Do you have any or just a few?   1. just a few
                                                      2. none

    Why?   1. apathy
                                                      2. ideas of suspicion
                                                         or persecution
                                                      3. other explanation

    IF YES:
    Are these close friends?   1. yes
                                                      2. no

    Why not?   1. apathy
                                                      2. ideas of suspicion
                                                         or persecution
                                                      3. other explanation

[REVIEW/REVISE RATING ON N4. PASSIVE/APATHETIC SOCIAL
                     WITHDRAWAL]

- Do you feel that you can trust most people?   1. yes
                                                      2. no

    IF NO:
    Why not?   1. suspiciousness
                                                      2. persecutory ideation
                                                      3. other explanation

- Are there some people in particular that you don't 1. no
  trust?   2. yes
    IF YES:
    Can you tell me who they are?   1. specific group
                                                      2. particular individual(s)
                                                      3. unwilling to divulge

Why don't you trust people [or name specific group or person]?

1. suspiciousness
2. persecutory ideation
3. other explanation

IF "DON'T KNOW" OR "DON'T WANT TO SAY":
Do you have a good reason not to trust people [or name specific group or person]?

1. suspiciousness
2. persecutory ideation
3. other explanation

Is there something that . . . did to you or might do to you now?

1. suspiciousness
2. persecutory ideation
3. other explanation

• Do you get along well with others?

1. yes
2. no

IF NO:
What's the problem?

1. apathy/disinterest
2. hostility
3. impulsivity
4. suspiciousness
5. persecutory ideation
6. other

• Do you have a quick temper?

1. no
2. yes

• Do you get into fights?

1. no
2. yes

IF YES TO EITHER OF THE ABOVE:
How do these fights [How does this loss of temper] start?

1. with clear provocation
2. with minimal or no provocation

Tell me about these fights [this loss of temper].
How often does this happen?

1. not serious problem
2. serious problem
1. not in past week
2. rarely (once or twice)
3. occasionally
4. often

• Do you sometimes lose control of yourself?

1. not in past week
2. rarely (once or twice)
3. occasionally
4. often

[REVIEW/REVISE RATINGS ON *P7. HOSTILITY* AND *G14. POOR IMPULSE CONTROL*]

• Do you like most people?

1. yes
2. no

IF NO:
Why not?

1. suspiciousness
2. persecutory ideation

• Are there perhaps some people who don't like you?

IF YES:
For what reason?

• Did it ever seem that people were talking about you or taking special notice of you?

• What about receiving special messages from the TV, radio, or newspaper?

IF YES TO EITHER OF THE ABOVE:
What do they say [or think] about you?

Why?

• Does anyone ever spy on you or plot against you?
[IF YES: Tell me about it.]
• Do you sometimes feel in danger?

IF YES:
Would you say that your life is in danger?
[IF YES: Please explain.]
Is someone thinking of harming you or perhaps thinking of killing you?
Have you gone to the police for help or notified some other authorities?
Do you sometimes take matters into your own hands or take action on those who might harm you?

IF YES:
What have you done?

3. other explanation
1. no
2. yes

1. suspiciousness
2. persecutory ideation
3. other explanation

Delusions of reference: personal significance is falsely attributed to objects or events in environment

? inadequate information
1. absent
2. subthreshold
3. threshold
1. good comments/thoughts
2. bad comments/thoughts

1. no delusional explanation
2. persecutory ideation
3. other delusion

1. no
2. yes
1. no
2. yes

1. no
2. yes
1. no
2. yes
1. no
2. yes
1. no
2. yes

1. restrained action (e.g., social avoidance, verbal confrontation, etc.)
2. consequential action (e.g., physical brawl, telephone police, etc.)

[REVIEW/REVISE RATING ON *G16. ACTIVE SOCIAL AVOIDANCE*]

Persecutory delusions: false belief of being attacked, harassed, cheated,

persecuted, or conspired against
? inadequate information
1. absent
2. subthreshold
3. threshold

• If you were to compare yourself to the average person, how would you come out: a little better, maybe a little worse, or about the same?

1. same
2. worse
3. better

IF WORSE:
Worse in what ways?

1. guilt feelings
2. depression
3. other

Just how do you feel about yourself?

1. guilt feelings
2. depression
3. other

IF BETTER OR ABOUT THE SAME:
Better in what ways?

1. realistic appraisal
2. expansive
3. delusional

Are you special in some ways?

1. no
2. yes

IF YES:
In what ways?

1. realistic
2. expansive
3. delusional

Would you consider yourself gifted?

1. no
2. yes

Do you have talents or abilities that most people don't have?

1. no
2. yes

IF YES TO EITHER OF THE ABOVE:
Please explain.

1. realistic
2. expansive
3. delusional

Do you have any special powers?

1. no
2. yes

IF YES:
What are these?

1. nonsystematized delusions

Where do these powers come from?
Do you have extrasensory perception (ESP), or can you read other people's mind?

2. systematized delusions
1. no
2. yes

Are you very wealthy? [IF YES: Please explain.]

1. no
2. yes

Can you be considered to be very intelligent? [IF YES: Why would you say so?]

1. no
2. yes

Would you describe yourself as famous?	1. no
[IF YES: Please explain.]	2. yes
Would some people recognize you from TV,	1. no
radio, or the newspapers?	2. yes
IF YES:	
Can you tell me about it?	1. nonsystematized delusions
	2. systematized delusions
• Are you a religious person?	1. no
	2. yes
IF YES:	
Are you close to God?	1. no
	2. yes
IF YES:	
Did God assign you some special role or purpose?	1. no
	2. yes
Can you be considered to be one of God's	1. no
messengers or angels?	2. yes
IF YES TO EITHER OF THE ABOVE:	
Please explain . . . . What special powers do	1. none
you have from God?	2. some
	3. exceptional powers
Do you perhaps consider yourself to be god?	1. no
	2. yes
• Do you have some special mission in life?	1. no
	2. yes
IF YES:	
What is your mission?	1. no delusional ideation
	2. nonsystematized delusions
	3. systemized delusions
Who assigned you to that mission?	1. no delusional ideation
	2. nonsystematized delusions
	3. systematized delusions

Grandiose delusions: content involves expanded power, knowledge, or importance

? inadequate information
1. absent
2. subthreshold
3. threshold

[PERFORM PANSS RATING ON: *P5. Grandiosity*]

• Did you ever do something wrong—something you	1. no

may feel bad or guilty about?	2. yes
IF YES:	
Just how much does that bother you now?	1. not at all
	2. slightly
	3. considerably
Do you feel that you deserve punishment for that?	1. no
	2. yes
IF YES:	
What kind of punishment would you deserve?	1. mild punishment
	2. severe punishment
Have you at times thought of punishing yourself?	1. no
	2. yes
IF YES:	
Have you ever acted on those thoughts of punishing yourself? [IF YES: What did you do?]	1. no
	2. yes

[PERFORM PANSS RATING ON: *G3. GUILT FEELINGS*]

• Has anything been bothering you lately?	1. no delusional ideation
	2. nonsystematized delusions
	3. systematized delusions
• Can you tell me something about your thoughts on life and its purpose?	1. no delusional ideation
	2. nonsystematized delusions
	3. systematized delusions
• Do you follow a particular philosophy?	1. no delusional ideation
	2. nonsystematized delusions
	3. systematized delusions
• Some people say they believe in the devil: what do you think?	1. no delusional ideation
	2. nonsystematized delusions
	3. systematized delusions
• Can other people read your mind?	1. no
	2. yes
IF YES:	
How can they do that?	1. delusions not elicited
	2. delusions elicited
Is there any reason that someone would want to read your mind?	1. delusions not elicited
	2. delusions elicited
	Other delusions
	? **inadequate information**
	1. **absent**
	2. **subthreshold**
	3. **threshold**

- Do you sometimes feel that someone or something outside yourself controls your thoughts or actions against your will?

Delusions of being controlled by external forces

    ?   inadequate information
    1. absent
    2. subthreshold
    3. threshold

- Are thoughts that were not your own ever put into your head or maybe taken out of your head?
- Do you sometimes feel as if your thoughts were being broadcast out loud so that other people could actually hear what you were thinking?

Thought broadcasting: delusions that one's thoughts are audible to others

    ?   inadequate information
    1. absent
    2. subthreshold
    3. threshold

- How have you been feeling in terms of your health?

    1. good
    2. other than good

    IF "OTHER THAN GOOD"
    What has been troubling you?

    1. no somatic concern
    2. somatic concern
    3. somatic delusion

    IF "GOOD":
    Do you consider yourself to be in top health?

    1. yes
    2. no

      IF NO:
      What has been troubling you?

    1. no somatic concern
    2. somatic concern
    3. somatic delusion

- Do you have any medical illness or disease?

    1. no somatic concern
    2. somatic concern
    3. somatic delusion

- Has any part of your body been troubling you?

    1. no somatic concern
    2. somatic concern
    3. somatic delusion

    IF NO:
    How is your head? Your heart? Stomach? The rest of your body?

    1. no somatic concern
    2. somatic concern
    3. somatic delusion

    IF YES:
    Could you explain?

    1. somatic concern
    2. somatic delusion

- Has your head or body changed in shape or size?

    1. no
    2. yes

    IF YES:

Please explain . . . . What is causing these changes?

1. no delusional ideation
2. nonsystematized delusions
3. systematized delusions

Somatic delusions: content involving change or disturbance in body functioning

? inadequate information
1. absent
2. subthreshold
3. threshold

Systematized delusions: single delusion with multiple elaborations or group of delusions all related to a single event or theme

? inadequate information
1. absent
2. subthreshold
3. threshold

Bizarre delusions: content regarded by one's subculture as totally implausible

? inadequate information
1. absent
2. subthreshold
3. threshold

[PERFORM PANSS RATING ON: G1. SOMATIC CONCERN]

- Do you once in a while have strange or unusual experiences? [IF YES: Tell me about it.]

  1. no
  2. yes

- Sometimes people say that they can hear noises or voices inside their head that others can't hear. What about you?

  1. no
  2. yes

  IF NO:

  Do you sometimes receive personal communications from the radio or TV?

  1. no
  2. yes

  IF NO:

  From God or the devil?

  1. no
  2. yes

  IF YES TO ANY OF THE ABOVE:

  What do you hear?

  1. vague sounds
  2. clear-cut voices

  Are these as clear and loud as my voice?

  1. no
  2. yes

How often do you hear these voices (noises, messages, etc.)?

1. not in past week
2. rarely (once or twice)
3. occasionally
4. often

Does this happen at a particular time of day or all the time?

1. particular time
2. several times
3. continuously

IF HEARING VOICES:

How many voices do you hear?

Do they talk to each other?

Two or more voices conversing with each other
   ? inadequate information
   1. absent
   2. subthreshold
   3. threshold

Can you recognize whose voices these are?

1. no
2. yes

What do the voices say? _____

_____

Are the voices good or bad?

1. good
2. bad

Are they pleasant or unpleasant?

1. pleasant
2. unpleasant

More than two words heard more than twice, unrelated to depression or elation
   ? inadequate information
   1. absent
   2. subthreshold
   3. threshold

Do the voices interrupt your thinking or your activities?

1. no
2. yes

Do they sometimes criticize or comment on what you're doing or thinking?

Voices keeping running commentary on one's behavior or thoughts as they occur
   ? inadequate information
   1. absent
   2. subthreshold
   3. threshold

Do they sometimes give you orders or instructions?

1. no
2. yes

  IF YES:
  For example? Do you usually obey these orders (instructions)?

1. no
2. yes

What do you make of these voices (or noises): where do they really come from?

1. realistic appraisal
2. delusional interpretation

Why do you have these experiences?

1. realistic appraisal
3. delusional interpretation

Are these normal experiences?

1. realistic appraisal
2. delusional interpretation

Auditory hallucinations: auditory perception without external sensory stimulation when fully awake

? **inadequate information**
1. **absent**
2. **subthreshold**
3. **threshold**

- Do ordinary things sometimes look strange or distorted to you?
  IF YES:
  Please explain. _____

1. no
2. yes

- Do you sometimes have "visions" or see things that others can't see?
  IF YES:
  For example? Do these visions seem very real or life-like?
  How often do you have these experiences?

1. no
2. yes

1. no
2. yes

1. not in past week
2. rarely (once or twice)
3. occasionally
4. often

Visual hallucinations: visual perception without external sensory stimulation when fully awake

? **inadequate information**
1. **absent**
2. **subthreshold**
3. **threshold**

- Do you sometimes smell things that are unusual or that others don't smell?
  IF YES:
  Please explain. . . . How often?

1. no
2. yes

1. not in past week
2. rarely (once or twice)
3. occasionally
4. often

- Do you get any strange or unusual sensations from inside your body?
  IF YES:
  Tell me about this. . . . How often?

1. no
2. yes

1. not in past week
2. rarely (once or twice)
3. occasionally

4. often
Tactile hallucinations
? **inadequate information**
1. **absent**
2. **subthreshold**
3. **threshold**
Other hallucinations
? **inadequate information**
1. **absent**
2. **subthreshold**
3. **threshold**

[PERFORM PANSS RATINGS ON: *P3. HALLUCINATORY BEHAVIOR*
P1. DELUSIONS
G9. UNUSUAL THOUGHT CONTENT
G15. PREOCCUPATION]

• How has your mood been in the past week:
mostly good, mostly bad?
    IF "MOSTLY GOOD":
    Have there been times in the past week
    that you were feeling sad or unhappy?
    IF "MOSTLY BAD" OR "YES" TO THE ABOVE:
    Is there something in particular that is
    making you sad?
    How often do you feel sad?

    Just how sad have you been feeling?

    Have you been crying lately? How often?

    Has your mood in any way affected your sleep?
    Please explain.
    Has it affected your appetite? How?

• Do you participate less in activities on
account of your mood?
• Have you had any thoughts of harming yourself?

    IF YES:
    Any thoughts about ending your life?

      IF YES:

1. mostly good
2. mostly bad

1. no
2. yes

1. no
2. yes
1. rarely (once or twice)
2. occasionally
3. often
1. somewhat
2. quite a bit
3. extremely
1. no
2. sometimes
3. frequently
1. no
2. yes
1. no
2. yes
1. no
2. yes
1. no
2. yes

1. no
2. yes

Have you attempted suicide?

1. no
2. yes

[PERFORM PANSS RATING ON: G6. *DEPRESSION*]

- Have you been feeling worried or nervous
in the past week? [IF YES: How often?]

1. no
2. sometimes
3. frequently

IF NO:
Would you say that you're usually calm
and relaxed?

1. yes
2. no

  IF NO:
IF "SOMETIMES" OR "FREQUENTLY" WORRIED/NERVOUS:
What's been making you feel nervous
(worried, anxious, unrelaxed)? _____
_____

Just how nervous (worried, etc.) have you
been feeling?

1. somewhat
2. quite a bit
3. extremely

Have you been shaking at times, or has your
heart been racing?

1. no
2. yes

Do you get into a state of panic?

1. no
2. yes

Has your sleep, eating, or participation in
activities been affected?

1. no
2. activities affected
3. sleep affected
4. eating affected

[PERFORM PANSS RATINGS ON: G2. *ANXIETY*
G4. *TENSION*]

- In view of the problems and experiences that
we've discussed so far, would you say that you
have had a serious psychiatric illness, a mild
one, or none at all?

1. serious
2. mild
3. none

[REVIEW/REVISE RATING ON *G12. LACK OF JUDGMENT AND INSIGHT*]

- Just a few more direct questions, and we'll be
through. First, can you tell me what is today's
date (i.e., the day, month, and year)?

1. correct answer
2. minor error
3. major error

- What is the name of the place that you are
in now?

1. correct answer
2. minor error
3. major error

- [IF HOSPITALIZED] What ward are you on?

1. correct answer
2. minor error
3. major error

- What is the address of where you now stay?

1. correct answer

- If someone had to reach you by phone, what number would that person call?

  2. minor error
  3. major error
  1. correct answer
  2. minor error
  3. major error

- What is the name of the doctor who is treating you?

  1. correct answer
  2. minor error
  3. major error

- [IF HOSPITALIZED] Can you tell me who else is on the staff and what they do?

  1. correct answer
  2. minor error
  3. major error

- Would you know who is now the President of this country? Our Governor? The Mayor (Town Supervisor) of this city (town, etc.)?

  1. correct answer
  2. minor error
  3. major error

[PERFORM PANSS RATING ON: *G10. DISORIENTATION*]

- I'm going to now say a pair of words, and I'd like you to tell me in what important way they're alike. Let's start, for example, with the words *apple* and *banana*. How are they alike—what do they have in common?

  IF "THEY'RE BOTH FRUIT":

  Good. Now what about . . . ? *[Select three other items from the similarities list at varying levels of difficulty; see Appendix A.]*

  IF ANSWER THAT IS TANGENTIAL, CONCRETE, OR IDIOSYNCRATIC, E.G., "THEY BOTH HAVE SKINS," "YOU CAN EAT THEM," "THEY'RE SMALL," OR "MONKEYS LIKE THEM":

  O. K., but they're both fruit. Now how about . . . and . . . : how are these alike? *[Select three other items from the similarities list at varying levels of difficulty; see Appendix A.]*

  Item A:
  1. abstract
  2. tangential
  3. concrete
  4. idiosyncratic/bizarre

  Item B:
  1. abstract
  2. tangential
  3. concrete
  4. idiosyncratic/bizarre

  Item C:
  1. abstract
  2. tangential
  3. concrete
  4. idiosyncratic/bizarre

  Item D:
  1. abstract
  2. tangential
  3. concrete
  4. idiosyncratic/bizarre

  Metaphor:
  1. abstract
  2. tangential
  3. concrete
  4. idiosyncratic/bizarre

  Simile:
  1. abstract
  2. tangential

- You've probably heard the expression, "Carrying a chip on the shoulder." What does that really mean?

- What about when people say, "It's as plain as the nose on your face": what do they mean?

- There's a very old saying: "Don't judge a book by its cover." What is the deeper meaning of this proverb?

[Select three other proverbs at varying levels of difficulty from the list in Appendix A.]

3. concrete
4. idiosyncratic/bizarre
Proverb A:
1. abstract
2. tangential
3. concrete
4. idiosyncratic/bizarre
Proverb B:
1. abstract
2. tangential
3. concrete
4. idiosyncratic/bizarre
Proverb C:
1. abstract
2. tangential
3. concrete
4. idiosyncratic/bizarre
Proverb D:
1. abstract
2. tangential
3. concrete
4. idiosyncratic/bizarre

- Thank you for your cooperation. I'm going to ask you now to please sit quietly for a few minutes while I make some notes.

[PERFORM PANSS RATING ON: *N5. DIFFICULTY IN ABSTRACT THINKING*]

Catatonic behavior: marked motor anomalies, including apparent purposeless excitement, negativism, rigidity, posturing, stupor, and waxy flexibility
    ? inadequate information
    1. absent
    2. subthreshold
    3. threshold
Grossly inappropriate affect: affect clearly discordant with content of speech or ideation
    ? inadequate information
    1. absent
    2. subthreshold
    3. threshold
Incoherence: speech mostly not understandable because of either:

lack of logical or meaningful connection; excessive use of incomplete sentences, excessive irrelevancies, or abrupt changes in subject matter; or idiosyncratic word usage

? inadequate information
1. absent
2. subthreshold
3. threshold

Marked loosening of associations: thinking characterized by speech in which ideas shift from one subject to another that is completely or only obliquely related, without the speaker's awareness that the topics are unconnected (Exclude abrupt shifts associated with a nearly continuous flow of accelerated speech, e.g., flight of ideas.)

? inadequate information
1. absent
2. subthreshold
3. threshold

Emotional turmoil: rapid shifts from one intense affect to another, or overwhelming perplexity of confusion, not due to a Mood Disorder.

? inadequate information
1. absent
2. subthreshold
3. threshold

[REVIEW/REVISE RATINGS ON: N2. EMOTIONAL WITHDRAWAL
G8. UNCOOPERATIVENESS
P4. EXCITEMENT
G7. MOTOR RETARDATION
G5. MANNERISMS AND POSTURING]

[PERFORM PANSS RATINGS ON: P2. CONCEPTUAL DISORGANIZATION
N1. BLUNTED AFFECT
N3. POOR RAPPORT
N6. LACK OF SPONTANEITY AND FLOW OF CONVERSATION
N7. STEREOTYPED THINKING

G11. POOR ATTENTION
G13. DISTURBANCE OF VOLITION]

- O. K., we're just about finished. Before you
leave, are there any questions that you would
like to ask of me? . . . Thank you for participating.

PART IV

Research and Significance

9

Significance of Positive and Negative Syndromes

PROGRAMMATIC STUDY

Research in psychiatry is largely dominated by "one shot" studies, in which the investigators report an isolated finding and then move on to an unrelated avenue of inquiry. It is well known, however, that there are few decisive studies in science, and that valuable contributions typically require a series of related investigations to systematically clarify a new area. This was our intention in pursuing the significance of positive and negative syndromes in schizophrenia. In recognition of the complexity of schizophrenia and its resistance to traditional study methods, we adopted the following research strategies (Kay, in press-c):

(a) *Psychometric advancement.* As already emphasized, we began our work with the development of a better operationalized and more comprehensive instrument to evaluate psychopathology, since this would enable greater power and precision of study.

(b) *Delineating syndromes.* Because of the heterogeneity of schizophrenia, which might reflect on distinct underlying processes, we chose *not* to search for uniformity that characterizes the illness. Instead, our aim was to identify the consistent and meaningful *differences* within schizophrenia and to understand their import for the disease processes.

(c) *Multidimensional approach.* Rather than to lock ourselves into a narrow or premature hypothesis, we thought it wiser to canvass a variety of potentially important variables, and in this way to more fully characterize the different syndromes of schizophrenia.

(d) *Longitudinal study.* Since schizophrenia is not a static condition, there is little that we can learn from a static perspective. In particular, the attempt to understand its origins, course, and treatment outcome requires a prospective, longitudinal design that spans a period of years.

131

Having devised our method for measuring positive, negative, and other facets of psychopathology, we next set out to study their meaning and their sufficiency in evolving a model of schizophrenia (Kay, in press-d).

TYPOLOGICAL STUDY

It will be recalled that Andreasen (1982; Andreasen et al., 1982) originally regarded the positive-negative distinction in schizophrenia as typological, i.e., representing co-exclusive subtypes of schizophrenia that differ on cognitive and neurological variables. As was noted in Chapter 2, however, her study methods had serious limitations, and her report of an inverse correlation between the syndromes has not since been replicated. In terms of the instrumentation, Andreasen's ratings of psychopathology derived from the Scale for Assessing Negative Symptoms and the Scale for Assessing Positive Symptoms (see critique in Chapter 3), and cognitive processes were evaluated with a "mini-mental status" interview rather than with standardized tests (Andreasen & Olsen, 1982). With regard to sampling, a large unclassifiable or "mixed" group was defined, and the negative patients had far more extensive experience with electroconvulsive treatment, which might have biased the cognitive and neurological findings. Andreasen's most notable observation, which linked negative symptoms to enlarged cerebral ventricles (Andreasen et al., 1982), was based on data that largely failed to achieve the acceptable standards of statistical significance (see Chapter 2). Except for an association of bizarre behavior with *smaller* ventricles ($p = 0.035$), none of the positive or negative symptoms varied with ventricular size (p's ranging from 0.11 for anhedonia to 0.79 for affective flattening). Subsequent research, indeed, has failed to confirm the association between negative syndrome and dilated ventricles (e.g., Peuskins et al., 1989).

In our initial studies with the Positive and Negative Syndrome Scale (PANSS), therefore, we set out to examine the viability of a positive-negative classification. Typological studies were performed separately on samples of 47 chronic schizophrenic inpatients, who had more than two years of illness since first hospitalization (Opler et al., 1984), and 37 acute schizophrenic inpatients, who had up to two years of illness (Lindenmayer, Kay, & Opler, 1984). The diagnosis of schizophrenia in both cases was established according to DSM–III criteria (American Psychiatric Association, 1980). For purposes of subtyping, patients who rated a 4 ("moderate psychopathology") or higher on at least three items from the PANSS positive or negative scale alone were classified as "positive" or "negative" accordingly.

Chronic Schizophrenia

From the total of 47 patients in the chronic study (Opler et al., 1984), we found that 10 fulfilled the criteria for positive subtype and 8 for negative subtype, leaving a large group of 29 patients (61.7 percent) indeterminate. Of this latter group, however, only four (8.5 percent) showed a mixed picture, i.e., met criteria for both positive and negative syndrome, while the remaining 25 exhibited too few pronounced symptoms for assignment to either category.

Comparison of the positive and negative subtypes on the PANSS defining items affirmed the internal reliability of this typological strategy. As expected, the positive group scored significantly higher on all seven positive symptoms, while the negative group showed more severe pathology on five of the seven negative items.

Since impaired affect has been considered one of the most important aspects of negative psychopathology in schizophrenia (Crow, 1985), but also perhaps the most inscrutable, it was subjected to multiaxial study using a 15-item Manifest Affect Rating Scale (Lindenmayer & Kay, 1987, 1989) that was modified from the procedure of Alpert and Rush (1983). A consistent pattern of subtype differences emerged, indicating far greater emotional deficits among patients with a negative syndrome. They had more serious difficulty in facial, motoric, and communicative expression in the service of relating emotionally. Specifically, they displayed a more "wooden" expression ($p < 0.05$), lacked expressive gestures ($p < 0.01$) and vocal emphasis ($p < 0.05$), were slower in their speech rate ($p < 0.02$) and latency of response ($p < 0.05$), used a lower voice level ($p < 0.002$), and impressed the raters as being more distant emotionally ($p < 0.01$), slower motorically ($p < 0.01$), and less spontaneous in their affective display ($p < 0.001$). Incongruity of affect, on the other hand, did not prove to be a distinguishing feature.

A series of psychometric tests was applied to address the hypothesis that negative schizophrenics present more severe cognitive and neurological dysfunctions. Intelligence was assessed with the Ammons and Ammons (1962) Quick Test, a recognition vocabulary measure that correlates strongly with the conventional IQ scales. The Memory For Designs Test (MFD) (Graham & Kendall, 1960) provided a standardized global measure of neurological soft signs based on impaired perception of configurations and defective short-term visual memory.

To obtain a developmentally-based assessment of cognitive processes, four tests from our Cognitive Diagnostic Battery (Kay, 1982) were administered. This Battery, devised as a means of clarifying the nature of disordered cognition, uses a Piagetian framework to delineate developmental impairments and distinguish these from other intellectual deficits and abnormalities particular to schizophrenia. The tests have been standardized with schizophrenic and normal subjects and have shown various facets of reliability and validity (Kay, 1977, 1982, 1986, 1989).

The Color-Form Preference Test (CFP) (Kay & Singh, 1975a) is a 20-item similarity judgment test from the Battery that examines primitive bases for perceiving relationships and gauges prerepresentational modes of thinking. The task involves matching to a standard one of three cards similar in color, form, or neither cue. The response strategy is analyzed and translated according to the earlier stages of conceptual development, characterized by purposeless perseveration, random responding, reliance on salient concepts (color), or use of a more abstract mode (form).

The Color Form Representation Test (CFR) (Kay, Singh, & Smith, 1975) extends the CFP to focus on the later verbal-symbolic stages of conceptual growth. It introduces the further option of matching cards by figural representation, a maturer conceptual basis than either color or form.

The Egocentricity of Thought Test (EOT) (Kay & Singh, 1975a) depicts four major phases of development identified by Piaget (1952) as crucial to cognitive and social growth: preconceptual (up to age 5), egocentric (ages 5 to 8), socialized (ages 8 to 11), and objective (ages 11 to adult).

Disturbance of attention is quantified using the Span of Attention Test (SOA) (Kay & Singh, 1974), which samples the average duration that one concentrates on a routine motor task (i.e., encircling X's on a page) before showing signs of distractibility. It also yields a measure of spontaneous psychomotor rate, which is calculated as the ratio of test items completed to time elapsed.

The psychometric assessment (Table 9:1) revealed no subtype differences in IQ, visual memory, or temporal attention but suggested, instead, that the negative schizophrenics are distinguished by a developmentally more primitive conceptual mode and slower spontaneous psychomotor pace. Specifically, verbal IQ on the Quick Test and mental ages from the CFP and CFR were not significantly different, nor were the MFD neuropathology scores. The two groups, therefore, were not distinguished on global measures of functional intelligence and organic impairment. Likewise there was no disparity in average length of concentration on the SOA, contrary to the premises of Andreasen and Olsen (1982), but the negative patients proved significantly slower than the positive type on the SOA measure of psychomotor rate.

Clearly the most striking test distinction was on the conceptual style assessed by the CFP. The modal response strategy for the positive syndrome patient was form dominance, embracing 62.5% of this group, whereas none exhibited color dominance. By sharp contrast, a clear majority of patients

TABLE 9:1

Cognitive Test Performance by Positive and Negative-Type Schizophrenics*

Cognitive Test	Area of Assessment	Schizophrenics ($\bar{x}$ or %)		Statistical Analysis	P
		Positive Type	Negative Type		
Quick Test (Ammons & Ammons, 1962)	Verbal intelligence	53.88	51.33	$t = 0.25$	
Memory for Designs Test (Graham & Kendall, 1960)					
	Perceptual recall	17.38	15.08	$t = 0.57$	
	Organic impairment	87.5%	83.0%	$\chi^2 = 0.05$	
Cognitive Diagnostic Battery (Kay, 1982)	Developmentally based measures				
CFP mental age	Mental age (years)	7.49	4.99	$t = 1.48$	
CFR mental age	Mental age (years)	7.27	4.86	$t = 1.00$	
SOA attention span	Span of concentration (min.)	2.17	3.50	$t = 0.97$	
SOA psychomotor rate	Spontaneous motor pace	0.91	0.50	$t = 2.15$	$< .05$
CFR representational thinking	Later cognitive development	12.00	10.00	$t = 1.00$	
EOT socialized thinking	Later cognitive development	2.14	2.00	$t = 0.13$	
CFP Color-Form Scale:	Early cognitive development				
Perserverative or random response	Lack of goal directedness	37.5%	25.0%	$\chi^2 = 0.29$	
Color dominance	Primitive conceptual mode guided by perceptual salience (age 4–6 yr.)	0%	62.5%	$\chi^2 = 7.27$	$< .01$
Form dominance	Maturer conceptual mode guided by conceptual relevance (age 7–11 yr.)	62.5%	12.5%	$\chi^2 = 4.27$	$< .05$

*Reprinted from Kay & Opler (1987). The positive-negative dimension in schizophrenia: Its validity and significance. Psychiatric Developments, 5, 79–103. Reprinted by permission of Oxford University Press.

with a negative syndrome was color responsive ($p < 0.01$), whereas only one showed the more mature form dominance ($p < 0.05$). On the CFR and EOT, which depict higher-level conceptual operations, the differences were not significant.

From the psychometric analyses, therefore, it appeared that negative schizophrenics were characterized not by a lesser general cognitive ability nor by a specific disorder of visual memory, but rather by cognitive deficits relating to the early years of conceptual growth. Accordingly, their intellectual impairment was uniquely traceable to failures in cognitive maturation instead of mental subnormality or global neuropathology.

On demographic variables, the two patient types were not distinguished in terms of sex, race, or marital status. The chronicity of illness, as defined by duration since first hospital admission, also proved comparable for the positive and negative types (means = 18.6 and 20.9, respectively, $t = 0.39$, not significant). However, there was a significant difference in season of birth ($\chi^2 = 6.43$, $p < 0.02$), with 50 percent of the negative patients born in winter (Opler & Kay, 1985). Other researchers who have found winter birth more common for schizophrenics as a whole have attributed this pattern to a greater risk of intrauterine viral infection (Watson et al., 1984), which as a biological stressor may play an etiological role in at least some cases. The present results suggest that the negative schizophrenic patient is perhaps especially vulnerable to this risk factor.

Other demographic comparisons also suggested differences antedating the overt onset of illness. The negative type was significantly less educated, having discontinued school after only the sixth grade on average, some four years earlier than the other group ($p < 0.02$). They began their hospital career at a significantly later age (mean = 27.8 vs. 19.6, $p < 0.02$) and currently were older. Over the past year, the negative group was prescribed only half the daily neuroleptic dosages as for positive schizophrenics ($p < 0.05$), very likely reflecting the greater amount of medication perceived necessary to control more florid manifestations.

Finally, the two discrete subtypes were compared on drug-related side effects using the Abnormal Involuntary Movement Scale (National Institute of Mental Health, 1974), which assesses choreoathetoid disorder involving but not limited to tardive dyskinesia, and the Extrapyramidal Rating Scale (Alpert et al., 1978), which assesses natural as well as drug-induced parkinsonian symptoms. Both schizophrenic groups presented few instances of serious extrapyramidal symptoms, and no reliable differences were found on any of the individual scales. Accordingly, we felt confident that the principal findings could not be ascribed to artifacts of drug-induced motor symptoms.

To summarize, the results supported the positive-negative dimension as a means of delineating more homogeneous schizophrenic subtypes. Key differences emerged on historical and cognitive developmental measures, suggesting that subtype distinctions may have in fact *antedated* the overt psychosis. Meanwhile, there were no group differences on major control variables, such as age, ethnicity, IQ, chronicity of illness, and drug-induced motor side effects.

Acute Schizophrenia

Using a parallel research design, we conducted a second positive-negative typological study involving acute, rather than chronic, schizophrenic patients (Lindenmayer, Kay, & Opler, 1984). Thirty-seven DSM–III confirmed schizophrenics (22 males, 15 females) with up to two years of illness were assessed on the PANSS and various other clinical, historical, and demographic variables. They ranged in age from 18 to 34 years (mean = 23.6), and all had been recently admitted for inpatient hospital care.

In brief, we found that the negative syndrome in this acute group was as prominent as the positive syndrome, and thus not, as sometimes postulated (e.g., Crow, 1980a), the end product of an extended illness or prolonged institutionalization. Indeed, the mean positive and negative ratings were similar to those obtained in the chronic study, and in both the acute and chronic samples the duration of illness from onset was the same for the positive and negative types. Also our data again showed no relationship of positive-negative characterization to race, sex, marital status, neuroleptic dose, or extrapyramidal symptoms.

The negative type was distinguished, however, by significantly less schooling ($p < 0.02$) and a somewhat poorer premorbid work adjustment ($p < 0.10$), which confirms the importance of premorbid differences reported elsewhere by Andreasen and Olsen (1982) as well as Pogue-Geile and Harrow (1984). In terms of the Kraepelinian subtypes of schizophrenia, the negative patients tended to be diagnosed as undifferentiated (63 percent); none of the positive schizophrenics were so classified, whereas 78 percent had been diagnosed as paranoid subtype ($\chi^2 = 6.56$, $p < 0.02$) (Lindenmayer, Kay, & Opler, 1984).

The typological strategy thus yielded a number of intriguing findings. Nevertheless, we observed that (a) only a minority of acute or chronic schizophrenics could be categorized as predominantly positive (24 percent and 21 percent, respectively) or negative (22 percent and 17 percent, respectively), and (b), as discussed in Chapter 5, the positive and negative scores were independent rather than co-exclusive. This would suggest that the constructs are better conceptualized as separate yet co-occurring dimensions, and not as distinct subtypes.

DIMENSIONAL STUDIES

To proceed beyond the limitations imposed by a typological framework, therefore, we adopted a dimensional approach, which enabled inclusion of the full sample while making no *a priori* assumptions about a positive-negative dichotomy (Kay, Opler, & Fiszbein, 1986).

The PANSS was now applied as a continuous scale for assessing syndromes, rather than as an instrument for subtyping patients. Positive and negative syndrome scores were calculated as the sum of the seven symptoms in the respective scales, with each symptom rated individually from 1 to 7, and general psychopathology was scored as the sum of the remaining 16 nonaligned items. In addition, we utilized the composite index from the positive minus negative scale scores, which provided a measure of polarization toward either syndrome (see scoring details in Chapter 3).

Subjects for the present study were selected from five long-term psychiatric units of an urban psychiatric hospital. They were recruited by consecutive survey and interviews to ascertain fulfillment of DSM–III criteria for schizophrenia (American Psychiatric Association, 1980). The final cohort consisted of 101 subjects (70 males and 31 females) who ranged in age from 20 to 68 years (mean = 36.8) and averaged 14.4 years since onset of illness. In addition to the enlarged sample size, this study assessed a broader range of predictor variables than before, encompassing demographic, historical, genealogical, clinical, psychometric, extrapyramidal, and outcome measures (Kay, Opler, & Fiszbein, 1986).

The external covariates of these syndromes were examined, using simple correlations and second-order partial correlations to root out the influence of age and drug-induced extrapyramidal symptoms, which in the present study were modestly associated with a negative presentation. We found the two syndromes distinguished by a particular pattern of premorbid, familial, cognitive, and phenomenological deficits, with the negative syndrome connoting a more pernicious disease process, one that apparently devolves from genealogical and ontogenetic sources. The results are summarized in Table 9:2.

On demographic and historical parameters, the positive-negative dimension once again was observed to be unrelated to such control variables as race, cultural group, marital status, age first hospitalized, and the chronicity of illness (years since first hospitalization). On the other hand, the negative pole was distinguished by its association with significantly less education. Prognostically, the positive scale alone anticipated a longer duration of inpatient care in the ensuing 30 months. More details about the prognostic import of the syndromes will be discussed in the next chapter on longitudinal course.

TABLE 9:2
Significant Nonoverlapping External Covariates of the PANSS*

Variable	Simple Correlation			Partial Correlation		
	Pos.	Neg.	Comp.	Pos.	Neg.	Comp.
Demographic/catamnestic						
Male gender					.21	
Years of education			.27		−.29	.33
No. of hospital admission				.20		
Days in hospital, follow-up	.25					
Family history of illness						
Sociopathy	.22			.21		
Major affective disorder					−.21	
Probable schizophrenia		.30			.29	
Cognitive/psychometric						
QT verbal intelligence		−.23				
Random number fluency			.31		−.33	.39
SOA psychomotor rate		−.27	.25			
CFP multi-level concepts		−.33	.34			.27
CFR conceptual maturation			.23			
EOT cognitive-social level		−.35	.23		−.34	.24
Affective (MARS impairment)						
Facial expression (wooden)		.62	−.45		.54	−.40
Expressive gestures (lacking)		.54	−.43		.41	−.37
Vocal emphasis (monotone)		.61	−.44		.49	−.40
Global relatedness (constricted)		.62	−.46		.50	−.42
Speech rate (retarded)		.42	−.44	−.27	.25	−.39
Response latency (slow)		.58	−.38		.47	−.36
Voice level (soft)		.40	−.34		.32	−.30
Global mobility (sluggish)		.55	−.47		.43	−.43
Impoverished thought content		.54	−.51		.52	−.49
Noncommunicative movements	.24					
Affective lability	.33			.31		
Angry affective tone	.47	.23		.46		.23
MARS total		.74	−.45		.64	−.41
Clinical (PANSS)						
Somatic concern	.22					.20
Anxiety	.41		.29	.38		.33
Mannerisms and posturing		.25				
Motor retardation		.41	−.35		.22	−.28
Unusual thought content	.73	.21	.42	.73		.50

*Reprinted with permission from Kay, Opler, & Fiszbein (1986). Significance of positive and negative syndromes in chronic schizophrenia. *British Journal of Psychiatry, 149*, 439–448.

As regards genealogical variables, which were elicited by interviews and chart review, the positive scale alone was correlated with sociopathy in the patient's first-degree relatives. This finding directly contrasted the significant correlation of the negative scale alone with a family history of "probable schizophrenia," i.e., with major psychosis that required hospitalization.

On the objective psychometric tests, the negative but not positive scale correlated with lower verbal IQ on the Quick Test (Ammons & Ammons, 1962) and with a poorer rendition on three tests from the Cognitive Diagnostic Battery (Kay, 1982) that assess cognitive developmental impairments (i.e., the CFP, CFR, and EOT). In face of these findings, of special note was the *absence* of significant associations involving the MFD (Graham & Kendall, 1960) and the Progressive Figure Drawing Test (Kay, 1980), both of which assess visual-motor deficits and, by inference, a general neuropsychological impairment.

In terms of affective symptoms, the negative scale and the negative pole of the composite scale uniquely posted high correlations with serious affective deficits on nine of the 15 MARS items as well as with the scale total, an index of global dysfunction on this realm. Other clinical ratings suggested that the positive syndrome is aligned with unusual thought content, anxiety, and somatic delusions, while the negative syndrome embraces motor retardation and peculiar mannerisms or posturing (Table 9:2).

The statistical partialing out of age and extrapyramidal symptom ratings generally had little effect on the correlations, suggesting that the observed relationships were not artifacts of these covariates. The association of negative syndrome with familial psychosis, cognitive developmental failure, and affective deficits was upheld. New findings to emerge from the partial correlations included an association of the positive scale with a greater number of previous hospitalizations, indicating an episodic course with apparent remissions and relapses. We now also discerned an association of the negative scale with male gender, which is more characteristic of schizophrenic patients who are regressed and neuroleptic nonresponsive (Todd, 1989); with impaired performance on a random number fluency test of adaptive cognitive flexibility; and with *absence* of a family history of affective illness (Kay, Opler, & Fiszbein, 1986). Therefore, chronic patients with a marked negative syndrome appeared to resemble insidious onset, poor outcome schizophrenics, such as the process, simple, or nuclear subtypes, in their demographic, historical, genealogical, as well as phenomenological profiles.

As a means of distilling the critical variables from this mass of data, the significant covariates were subjected to multiple regression analysis to identify which ones are most important in accounting for the positive and negative dimensions. As shown in Table 9:3, we found that the positive

TABLE 9:3
Multiple Regression Analysis of Positive, Negative, and Composite Scales*

Variable	R^2	Cumulative variance Increase in R^2	P	Cumulative R
Positive Scale (R^2 = .74)				
Unusual thought content	.57	.57	< .0001	.75
General psychopathology	.70	.13	< .0001	.84
Angry affective tone	.72	.02	< .001	.85
Sociopathy in family history	.74	.02	< .05	.86
Negative Scale (R^2 = .81)				
MARS total	.59	.59	< .0001	.77
Lack of judgment and insight	.71	.12	< .0001	.84
Psychosis in family history	.76	.05	< .0001	.87
EOT cognitive-social level	.79	.03	< .001	.89
Active social avoidance	.80	.01	< .05	.89
Impoverished thought content	.81	.01	< .05	.90
Composite Scale (R^2 = .71)				
MARS emotional unrelatedness	.30	.30	< .0001	.55
Unusual thought content	.56	.26	< .0001	.75
CFR conceptual maturation	.63	.07	< .01	.79
Years of education	.67	.04	< .01	.82
Impoverished thought content	.69	.02	< .05	.83
Age	.71	.02	< .05	.84

*Reprinted with permission from Kay, Opler, & Fiszbein (1986). Significance of positive and negative syndromes in chronic schizophrenia. *British Journal of Psychiatry, 149,* 439–448.

syndrome could be explained generally by wealth of psychopathology and, specifically, by productive features evident in the cognitive and affective domains, namely, bizarre thinking and angry emotional tone. A family history of sociopathy also was a major covariate of the positive syndrome. The negative syndrome, in sharp contrast, was explained by impoverished cognitive and affective processes as well as by deficits in social functioning and in the developmental underpinnings of cognitive and social growth. In terms of genealogy, a family history of psychosis, rather than sociopathy, was a significant aspect of this syndrome.

On the bipolar composite scale, unusual thought content emerged as the chief indicator of a uniquely positive syndrome. A negative syndrome, conversely, was explained by emotional unrelatedness, older age, and cognitive deficits reflected in flawed conceptual development, earlier arrest in education, and impoverished thinking.

The results, summarized in Table 9:4, thus corroborated and extended the findings from our typological approach. Early premorbid failure in cognitive development, including premature termination of schooling, was

TABLE 9:4
Distinguishing Features of Positive and Negative Syndromes in Chronic Schizophrenia*

Variable	Syndrome	
	Positive	*Negative*
Family history	Positive for sociopathy	Positive for major psychosis (probable schizophrenia) Negative for major affective illness
Premorbid history	Relatively unremarkable	Greater cognitive developmental deficits Lesser education Poorer social and occupational adjustment
Demographics	More hospital admissions Greater amount of psychotropic dose	Older Male Later onset of illness
Clinical	Florid presentation Bizarre thinking Affective lability and anger Symptoms of hyperarousal	Multimodal deficits Failures in adaptive cognitive flexibility Affective dulling Motor retardation

*Reprinted from Kay & Opler (1987). The positive-negative dimension in schizophrenia: Its validity and significance. *Psychiatric Developments, 5,* 79–103. Reprinted by permission of Oxford University Press.

again implicated in the negative syndrome. In addition, we now detected an association between a chronic negative presentation and an ominous genealogical loading, one characterized by presence of major psychosis and absence of affective illness in first-degree relatives.

In regard to Crow's (1980a, 1980b) hypothesis, however, no direct evidence was obtained to support a neurobiological basis for the negative syndrome. Psychological tests of visual-motor impairment and organic integrity disclosed no significant differences. Instead, our findings suggested that the negative syndrome may issue from genetic vulnerability to early stress, culminating in developmental failures, premorbid dysfunctions, and a clinical picture dominated by multimodal deficits (Kay, Opler, & Fiszbein, 1985, 1986).

NEUROCOGNITIVE STUDY

The findings thus far revealed cognitive impairment to be a key distinguishing feature between positive and negative syndromes. However, since the negative assessment included in its definition certain cognitive items, such as "difficulty in abstract thinking," it was necessary to examine the cognitive processes in greater detail to ensure that our observations were not purely tautological. In addition, although the work reviewed so far found no special neuropsychological liability associated with a negative syndrome, it remained possible that a more localizing or specialized battery would reflect the structural deficits postulated by Crow (1980a). In subsequent studies, therefore, we examined positive and negative syndromes in relation to specific neurological signs, possible neurochemical basis, and information processing disorders.

Neurological Signs

First, 28 chronic schizophrenic patients were assessed independently on the PANSS and on a multi-item neurological battery that had been assembled to help localize areas of neurological deficit (Merriam et al., in press). This inventory was found to produce, by combination of subtest items, five statistically independent scores: prefrontal, praxis, parietal, fine motor, and nonlocalizing. Upon correlating the PANSS with the neurological inventory, we found that the positive syndrome was unrelated to all five scores, suggesting absence of neurological mediation. The negative syndrome, however, was distinguished by its significant and specific correlation with prefrontal signs ($r = 0.49$, $p < 0.01$) but none of the other neurological variables. Thus, although our previous study had shown no association of negative syndrome with global neuropsychological measures, a more localizing battery suggested its relationship to prefrontal deficit in particular. The implications for the pathophysiology of schizophrenia will be described in Chapter 13.

Neurochemistry

To further study the neurochemical basis for the negative syndrome, which would carry direct implications for pharmacotherapy, we examined negative symptoms in relation to the glabellar tap reflex (Sandyk, & Kay, in press-d). This procedure consists of 10 repeated taps on the glabella, which in a normal subject produces a blinking response that ceases after the first few taps. In patients with Parkinson's disease, however, there is virtually no reduction in the blinking reflex (Hall, 1945; Pearce, Hassan, &

Gallagher, 1968), and this failure in habituation is interpreted as direct evidence of decreased cerebral dopaminergic functions (Karson, 1983). Thus, our interest in this procedure was as a means of assessing the possibility that negative symptoms reflect a dopamine deficiency, as per MacKay (1980) and van Kammen et al. (1986), which could explain its responsiveness to L-dopa and amphetamines (Alpert & Rush, 1983; Friedhoff, 1983; Kay & Opler, 1985).

The sample comprised 78 DSM–III diagnosed chronic schizophrenic patients under treatment in a psychiatric hospital in Rome, Italy. Two research psychiatrists rated the patients on the three negative features described by Johnstone et al. (1978a), namely flat affect, poverty of speech, and motor retardation, and a neurologist who was blind to these ratings administered the glabellar tap test. Failure to habituate (i.e., glabellar tap positive) was detected in 12 patients, who did not differ from the others in age, chronicity of illness, duration of neuroleptic treatment, and current treatment with neuroleptic or anticholinergic agents. This group, however, displayed significantly higher ratings on all three negative symptoms, supporting the hypothesis that a negative profile involves diminished cerebral dopaminergic functions. Further evidence from psychopharmacological studies will be presented in Chapter 11, and discussion of the theoretical import will be reserved for Chapter 13.

Information Processing Disorder

Our next studies, which aimed to examine disorders of information processing, utilized techniques that derive from experimental psychology. First, in a sample of 45 schizophrenic patients, we assessed speed of visual processing using the Braff and Saccuzzo (1985) backward masking paradigm with tachistoscopic exposure (Weiner et al., in press). Second, in 30 schizophrenic patients we obtained measurements from the Span of Attention Test (SOA) (Kay & Singh, 1974), described earlier in this chapter, which provides a behavioral sampling of concentration on a routine motor task. The verbal encoding of these patients was also assessed using the Memory Organization Test (MOT) (Kay, Murrill, & Opler, 1989); this procedure uses category clustering in free recall as a vehicle to determine whether the conceptual, affective, or phonemic properties of words are registered.

The results indicated that schizophrenics with a pronounced negative syndrome (i.e., > 75th percentile in relation to PANSS norms for schizophrenia) were significantly slower in information processing ($p < 0.025$) than other patients and normal controls (Weiner et al., in press). The negative schizophrenics had the longest visual identification threshold and the lowest number of correct stimulus detections, followed respectively by the mixed and positive type of schizophrenics and a group of normal controls ($n = 15$ each). These visual information processing measures, meanwhile, were uncorrelated with demographic characteristics, IQ, and all other cognitive and psychiatric variables under study. The results supported the findings of Green and Walker (1984, 1986) indicating an association between negative symptoms and impaired information processing. These data suggested that negative schizophrenic patients have deficits that involve the earliest stage of sensory registration.

Our work in this area furthermore revealed that not only the speed of information processing, but the selectivity of stimuli as well, seems to be deviant. Although a negative syndrome did not entail poorer scores on attention span (SOA), general recall (MOT), and conceptual or phonemic encoding, it was significantly associated with a deficiency in encoding the specific affective connotation of words (Kay, Murrill, & Opler, 1989). This suggests that the affective deficits which characterize the negative presentation, beyond their well known impact on emotional expression (i.e., output), also impact more fundamentally on the very process of registering affective cues from the milieu (i.e., input).

CONCLUSIONS

Across these studies, therefore, we observed that a chronic negative syndrome was related to measures of prefrontal deficit, reduced dopaminergic functions, cognitive developmental failure, slower information processing, and poorer encoding of affective attributes. Cumulatively, the results support the validity of the positive-negative distinction and imply that the schizophrenic disease process which is manifested as a negative syndrome devolves from an early malignant neurodevelopmental pathology, one that may have a genetic basis (Kay, Fiszbein, & Opler, 1985). The consequence for the patient is impaired cognitive maturation that interferes with fundamental cognitive operations and contributes to multimodal deficits in functioning. In the next two chapters we shall consider the impact on the patient's course of illness and response to psychotropic drugs.

---10---

Longitudinal Course
of the Syndromes

In the previous chapter, we described the covariates of positive and negative syndromes, which cast light on the significance of these attributes in schizophrenia. However, since schizophrenia is not a static or immutable condition, a fuller understanding of its components requires a longitudinal perspective as well. For this reason, our studies have looked at positive and negative syndromes not only cross-sectionally—as a snapshot, frozen momentarily in time—but also longitudinally, as a motion picture that provides an ongoing chronicle. Only with a research design of this kind can one adequately address the important issues about the stability of syndromes, their changes over time, their comparative response to different medications, and their prognostic meaning.

Our research on these issues will be reviewed in the present chapter. We shall describe the results from separate prospective investigations of schizophrenia that analyzed positive and negative syndromes in relation to subsequent functioning, response to classical neuroleptics, as well as their significance in the drug-free state. It will be seen that the import of the syndromes indeed varies according to the stage of the illness and that the pessimism which is usually attached to a negative syndrome seems to apply only to an established chronic condition.

PROSPECTIVE FOLLOW-UP STUDY

To examine the stability, course, and prognosis of the syndromes, we undertook separate long-term prospective follow-up studies on acute, subacute, and chronic schizophrenic samples (Kay, in press-a).

146

Stability and Course of the Syndromes

First, the Positive and Negative Syndrome Scale (PANSS) was applied to 37 young acute schizophrenics, ages 18 to 34, who had been newly admitted to an intake unit of an urban psychiatric hospital (Lindenmayer, Kay, & Opler, 1984). All patients had two or fewer episodes of illness since first psychiatric admission (mean = 1.42), and approximately 60 percent had no or only one prior hospitalization. The baseline data indicated that negative symptoms were as prevalent as positive symptoms and were not secondary to prolonged institutionalization, severity of illness, neuroleptic dose, or drug side effects (see further details in Chapter 9).

It was possible to follow 19 patients from this sample for an average period of 2.2 years, which reflected on the progression from the acute into the early chronic phase of schizophrenia (Lindenmayer, Kay, & Friedman, 1986). The follow-up evaluations were conducted by investigators who were blind to the positive-negative ratings at index admission. A comparison of this group with dropouts (*n* = 19) found them to be similar, with no significant differences in age, sex, ethnic group, marital status, education, premorbid adjustment ratings, age first hospitalized, or baseline severity of illness (*p*'s ranging from 0.15 to 0.90).

When we examined the longitudinal course of the negative and positive syndromes over two years, we detected no measurable increase or decrease in the mean ratings, and the autocorrelations from baseline to follow-up were not significant (see Table 10:1). On an individual basis, some patients worsened over time, some improved, and some were unchanged, thus confirming the three-directional pattern of outcome described for newly treated schizophrenic patients (Torrey, 1983). It appeared, therefore, that these young acute patients were, clinically, still in a state of flux.

The observations on acute schizophrenia sharply contrasted those from patients in the subacute (Kay & Singh, 1989) and chronic phases (Kay, Fiszbein, & Opler, 1987; Kay & Murrill, 1990), confirming an impression of greater instability during the early period of illness. For the subacute group of 62 patients (two to five years of illness), which will be described later in this chapter, the correlations from before to after a three to four month course of neuroleptic therapy were significant for both the positive ($r = 0.37$, $p < 0.005$) and negative syndrome ($r = 0.43$, $p < 0.001$).

The chronic group (more than five years of illness) also showed stability in these syndromes (Kay, Fiszbein, & Opler, 1987). We followed for three to six months a cohort of 15 unremitting schizophrenics who remained hospitalized on our research unit, proving refractory to ongoing neuroleptic treatment. Their initial PANSS assessment revealed higher than average

TABLE 10:1
Stability of Positive and Negative Syndromes in the Acute and Chronic Stages of Schizophrenia*

Pre/Post Data	PANSS Scales		
	Positive Syndrome	Negative Syndrome	General Psychopathology
Acute Group (n = 19)			
Baseline score	17.3	21.1	39.1
Retest score (2 years)	18.4	21.2	38.6
Pre-post change	1.1	−0.9	−0.5
Significance (Paired *t*)	n.s.	n.s.	n.s.
Test-retest *r*	0.24	−0.13	−0.18
Significance (*r*)	n.s.	n.s.	n.s.
Chronic Group (n = 15)			
Baseline score	21.1	25.6	46.7
Retest score (3–6 mo.)	21.1	26.3	42.0
Pre-post change	0.0	0.7	−4.7
Significance (Paired *t*)	n.s.	n.s.	$p < 0.05$
Test-retest *r*	0.80	0.68	0.60
Significance(*r*)	$p < 0.001$	$p < 0.01$	$p < 0.02$

*Based on Kay, Fiszbein, & Opler (1987) and Lindenmayer, Kay, & Opler (1986).

scores on the positive, negative, and general psychopathology scales (Table 10:1). Measurable clinical improvement was indicated by a small but statistically significant reduction in general psychopathology (4.74 points, $p < 0.05$). The positive and negative scores, however, were not significantly changed over time. Of special note, the longitudinal correlations were quite high ($r = 0.80$, $p < 0.001$, and $r = 0.68$, $p < 0.01$, respectively), revealing stability of these syndromes during the chronic phase.

Prognosis in Acute Schizophrenia

In early schizophrenia, however, not only were the syndromes unstable, but their prognostic meaning seemed to differ from that which later develops. Our two-year follow-up of the young acute schizophrenic patients (Lindenmayer, Kay, & Friedman, 1986; Kay & Lindenmayer, 1987) revealed that, contrary to popular belief, the negative syndrome at index admission predicted not worse, but *better* subsequent functioning (Table 10:2). This was indicated by significant correlations with follow-up assessments on the nine-item Strauss and Carpenter (1972) Multidimensional Outcome Scale, which probes social, occupational, and psychiatric adjustment. Some of the predictive correlations were remarkably high, e.g., a Pearson *r* of 0.73 ($p < 0.001$) between baseline negative syndrome and follow-up quantity of useful work. A positive syndrome, meanwhile, carried no prognostic significance. Interestingly, when the syndromes were reassessed two years later, as the patients traversed into a chronic phase of illness, *both* kinds of manifestations reflected greater severity of the concurrent illness (see Table 10:2).

Although these data supported the predictive validity of a negative syndrome in acute schizophrenia, they of course do not imply that this clinical variable fully or uniquely explains outcome. Good premorbid adjustment, which is a long-established prognosticator for schizophrenia (Phillips, 1953), also as expected showed sizable correlations with overall level of functioning ($r = 0.47$, $p < 0.05$) and lower general psychopathology ($r = 0.54$, $p < 0.02$) at two-year follow-up. The premorbid functioning, however, was found to be unrelated to negative syndrome ($r = -0.25$). Because of their independence, these two predictors combined to produce significantly stronger multiple correlations with the two outcome measures ($R = 0.77$, $p < 0.001$, and $R = 0.70$, $p < 0.005$, respectively) (Kay & Lindenmayer, 1987).

We concluded, therefore, that the stability and unfavorable portent of a negative syndrome apply only after the acute phase, at which point it may signify an intransigent, residual deficit picture. In the early course of schizophrenia, a negative syndrome in fact correlated with two harbingers of good outcome: depressive features (Kay & Lindenmayer, 1987) and atypical catatonic symptoms (Kanofsky et al., 1987; Kay et al., 1987). Either of these phenomena can produce impairments that are usually characterized as negative or deficit, namely constriction of one's social activity, movements, and range of affect (Rifkin, Quitkin, & Klein, 1975).

Prognosis in Chronic Schizophrenia

To provide for a direct comparison with acute schizophrenia, we next undertook a parallel longitudinal study on a sample of 58 chronic schizophrenic patients (Kay & Murrill, 1990). This group was drawn from long-term units of the same psychiatric hospital as the acute sample. It was possible to relocate 46 of the patients (79.3 percent) for follow-up after a period that averaged 2.7 years. This group was almost 10 years older than the acute patients (mean = 33.1 years) and had a mean of 11.8 years of illness since onset. The dropouts from follow-up in this study did not differ significantly from those relocated in terms of any of the demographic or baseline clinical variables.

The follow-up assessments, again conducted blindly with respect to baseline data, yielded contrasting conclusions about prognosis as compared to

TABLE 10:2
Negative and Positive Syndromes in Acute Schizophrenia: Predictive and Contemporaneous Significance

Outcome Criteria	Baseline (predictive r)			Follow-up (contemporaneous r)		
	Negative Score	Positive Score	Negative-Positive Difference	Negative Score	Positive Score	Negative-Positive Difference
Multidimensional Outcome Scale						
Duration of nonhospitalization	.53*	-.13	p < .10	-.20	-.30	
Frequency of social contacts	.39	.04		-.36	-.52*	
Quality of social relations	.48*	.02	p < .10	-.45	-.67***	
Quantity of useful work	.73****	.26	p < .05	-.56**	-.60***	
Quality of useful work	.61***	-.09	p < .01	-.67***	-.68***	
Absence of symptoms	.48*	-.08	p < .05	-.61***	-.83****	
Ability to meet own basic needs	.29	.17		-.53*	-.05	
Fullness of life	.59***	.05	p < .02	-.71****	-.53*	p < .05
Overall level of functioning	.47*	.04	p < .10	-.69***	-.69***	
PANSS General Psychopathology	-.30	.01		.70*****	.65***	

Note: Reprinted with permission from Lindenmayer, Kay, & Friedman (1986). Negative and positive schizophrenic syndromes after the acute phase: A prospective follow-up. *Comprehensive Psychiatry, 27,* 276–286.

*p < .05
**p < .02
***p < .01
****p < .001

TABLE 10:3
Predictors of Outcome in Chronic Schizophrenia: A 2.7 Year Follow-Up
(Pearson *r*, *n* = 46)

| | Baseline PANSS Score | | | |
Outcome Measure	Positive	Negative	General Psychopathology	Depression
Number of days in hospital subsequently	.35**	.04	.17	−.21
Strauss-Carpenter Scale:				
Continuously hospitalized	.37***	−.02	.16	−.24
Minimal quantity of work	.30*	.28	.20	−.33**
Global emptiness of life	.33**	.09	.18	−.48****

Note: Based on Kay & Murrill (1990).
  *$p < .05$
 **$p < .025$
***$p < .01$
****$p < .001$

acute schizophrenia (see Table 10:3). The PANSS negative syndrome in the chronic phase did not significantly predict better or poorer outcome on any of the follow-up measures. The positive syndrome, however, now carried ominous implications for subsequent functioning on three parameters from the Multidimensional Outcome Scale: length of continued hospital care ($p < 0.01$), quantity of useful work ($p < 0.05$), and fullness of life ($p < 0.025$). In addition to the rated assessment, the positive syndrome predicted a greater number of days of actual inpatient hospitalization during the follow-up term ($p < 0.025$). General psychopathology, like the negative scale, did not significantly predict any of the ten outcome variables in the 2.7 year followup. Depression, conversely, emerged as a reliable predictor of good outcome in our chronic sample, revealing an especially strong relationship with fullness of life ($p < 0.001$). In this respect it clearly stood apart from the negative, positive, and other facets of psychopathology.

Multiple regression analysis was performed to identify the optimal sets of predictors for the several outcome measures employed in this study (Kay & Murrill, 1990). The findings revealed that nine of the 10 outcome criteria could be significantly predicted by combination of PANSS clusters with demographic and historical variables, namely age, years of illness, and family psychiatric history. The multiple *R*'s ranged from 0.49, $p < 0.01$ (for "days subsequently hospitalized") to 0.61, $p < 0.0002$ (for "fullness of life" and "ability to meet own basic needs"). Of the various symptom clusters mea-

sured by the PANSS, thought disturbance stood out as the single most robust predictor of poor outcome in chronic schizophrenia, subsuming most
of the predictive variance from the positive syndrome. Alternatively, the
depression cluster was the only clinical variable to forecast good outcome,
and it also accounted for a large share of the general predictive variance. In
predicting "duration of nonhospitalization" and "fullness of life," for example, thought disturbance accounted for 15.0 percent and 13.7 percent of
the variance, respectively, and depression for 11.2 percent and 21.4 percent,
while neither positive nor negative syndrome contributed further to their
predictions.

The present observations are consistent with recent findings that disorganized thinking may constitute a component that is separate from the positive syndrome (Bilder et al., 1985; Liddle, 1987; Kay, 1989b) and portends
a poorer functional recovery (Liddle, 1987). Likewise, this analysis confirmed that depression in schizophrenia is clearly distinguishable from the
negative syndrome and suggested that depression may form an opposing
pole with thought disturbance along the prognostic axis (see also Chapter
12).

Of particular interest was the indication from the multiple regression
analysis that different aspects of outcome were predicted by different baseline parameters (Kay & Murrill, 1990). Overall, the variables that consti-
tuted positive symptoms were more relevant for predicting poor subsequent
social rehabilitation and continued need for hospital care. Those associated
with negative symptoms, in contrast, were more relevant for predicting
poor *occupational* rehabilitation. Our observations concur with reports on
the Scottish follow-up study of acute schizophrenia (Todd, 1989) and re-
mind us that restoration of one's mental health involves several distinct
components. We have seen, therefore, that different symptoms may impact
on separate facets of outcome.

PHASIC STUDIES OF THE SYNDROMES

Despite the methodological strengths of the longitudinal research design,
two shortcomings are characteristic: (a) attrition of subjects, which may affect both the sample size and its representation, and (b) limited length of
follow-up that is feasible. For these reasons, we also pursued a cross-sectional approach for large-scale phasic study of positive and negative syndromes (Kay et al., 1986). The investigation involved 134 schizophrenic
inpatients, ages 18 to 68 years (mean = 33.5) who, as per the convention of
Brown (1960) and others, were classified according to three stages of the illness: acute (up to two years since first hospital admission; mean = 0.61,

TABLE 10:4
Comparison of Negative and Positive Syndrome Scores in Acute, Chronic, and Long-Term Chronic Schizophrenic Inpatients*

| | | PANSS Syndrome Scale | |
| | | Negative | Positive |
Schizophrenic Group	(n)	Mean ± SD	Mean± SD
Acute	(33)	21.42 ± 7.16	18.76±5.98
Chronic	(38)	21.22 ± 5.47	19.71±6.64
Long-term chronic	(63)	21.27 ± 6.19	17.98±5.50
ANOVA: F		< 1	1.00
p		.99	.37

*Based on Kay et al. (1986).

$n = 33$), chronic (three to 10 years; mean $= 6.13$, $n = 38$), and long-term chronic (more than 10 years; mean $= 19.78$, $n = 63$).

In this study, again we found no difference in the magnitude of syndrome scores as a function of chronicity, which suggests that, contrary to popular assumption, there is no evolution toward a greater negative presentation. As shown in Table 10:4, both the negative and positive syndrome scores on the PANSS were strikingly similar for the three schizophrenic populations.

Also in keeping with our longitudinal data, the present study found that the significance of the syndromes was stage-specific (see Table 10:5). In acute schizophrenia, a negative score correlated with familial and clinical indicators of good prognosis, i.e., with absence of familial psychosis and presence of various atypical and catatonic phenomena, such as expressive immobility, motor retardation, disorientation, and mannerisms and posturing. Quite the reverse profile—one that bodes a poor prognosis—was found for a positive syndrome in the acute stage and, likewise, for a negative syndrome in the chronic stage. Patients of these kinds had a family history of either less affective disorder or more psychosis. They also had poorer premorbid functioning, as suggested by a curtailed education and failure to marry.

Although the interpretation of any particular correlation coefficient must be tempered due to the multiple analyses conducted, the overall differences in pattern far exceeded chance level. In brief, the negative and positive symptoms were found to be equally pronounced across decades of illness, and yet their import seemed to differ systematically in correspondence with the evolving illness.

The results of the negative syndrome in chronic schizophrenia were consistent with our previous typological (Opler et al, 1984) and dimensional studies (Kay, Opler, & Fiszbein, 1986), which found it associated with

TABLE 10:5
Covariates of Negative and Positive Syndromes According to Chronicity
of Illness, and Tests of Significance of the Differences

Variables	Partial Correlation (r)			Difference Between rs (z)		
	Acute	Chronic	LTC	Acute-Chronic	Acute-LTC	Chronic-LTC
Negative Syndrome With:						
Familial psychosis	−.30	.09	.40****		3.07***	
Years of education	−.24	−.13	−.29*			
Guilt feelings	−.17	−.44***	−.05			1.98*
Mannerisms & posturing	.25	−.25	.12	1.98*		
Disorientation	.55***	.24	.14		2.10*	
Poor impulse control	.06	.35*	.40****			
Preoccupation	.47***	−.10	.34***	2.37**		2.12*
Expressive immobility	.75****	.42***	.51****	2.04*		
Psychomotor retardation	.47***	.00	.28*	1.97*		
Positive Syndrome With:						
Familial affective disorder	−.49***	−.18	−.06		1.99*	
Familial sociopathy	.29	.40**	.06			
Years of education	−.25	.33	.05	2.26*		
Marital status	.06	.27	−.26			2.54**
Sex (male)	−.33	−.23	.35***		3.07***	2.81***
Guilt feelings	.13	−.29	.20			2.35**
Tension	.06	.46***	.48****		2.01*	
Uncooperativeness	−.20	.48***	.24	2.82***		
Poor attention	.09	.42***	.27*			
Disturbance of volition	.00	.18	.46****		2.15*	
Inappropriate affect	.19	.53****	.42****			
Severity of illness	.39*	.73****	.61****	2.01*		

Note: Reprinted with permission from Kay et al. (1986). Positive and negative syndromes in schizophrenia as a function of chronicity. *Acta Psychiatrica Scandinavica*, n4, 507–518. Copyright © 1986 by Munksgaard International Publishers Ltd., Denmark.
　*p < .05
　**p < .02
　***p < .01
　****p < .001

lesser education, a more primitive conceptual development, and a family history of "probable schizophrenia," i.e., schizophrenia or unspecified psychosis that required inpatient treatment. These data on the chronic negative syndrome were in agreement also with findings from independent groups which noted similar relationships between negative symptoms and premorbid deficits (Andreasen & Olsen, 1982; Pogue-Geile & Harrow, 1984), cognitive impairment (Andreasen & Olsen, 1982; Green & Walker, 1984, 1986), and genetic liability (Dworkin & Lenzenweger, 1984).

COMPATIBILITY WITH CROW'S MODEL

Despite the convergent sources of validation of the positive-negative distinction, our findings were *not* in full harmony with Crow's or Andreasen's hypotheses. The data challenge the very premises of the stability of the syndromes in the early stages of illness; the constancy of their import across the course of illness; the tendency of the negative syndrome to worsen over time; and its connotation of poor prognosis, which instead seemed dictated primarily by thought disorganization and premorbid factors. As we shall see in the next chapter, there is also reason to discard the assumption that the negative syndrome is unresponsive to neuroleptic medications.

Given the current findings that the syndromes are stage specific and that clinical outcome has multiple determinants, there are grounds to question whether positive and negative syndromes constitute monolithic constructs and ones that have clear-cut and intrinsic prognostic value. Only in the chronic negative condition did it appear that a negative presentation may reflect an intransigent residual deficit picture; it may be for these patients alone that Crow's (1980a, 1985) hypothesis on negative schizophrenia applies. In early schizophrenia, a negative syndrome was just as prominent as the positive, but it carried the opposite implications for prognosis and was associated with a more benign family history and symptom constellation.

One could reasonably argue from the foregoing that the type of negative syndrome which signifies a stable deficit syndrome, as described by Carpenter, Heinrichs, and Wagman (1988), arises only in the chronic phase. Such a view would regard the chronic negative profile as a marker of an enduring and pernicious form of schizophrenia. Alternatively, it is conceivable that the chronic negative picture is simply the visible symptom residue in treatment nonresponders. A related possibility is that we are witnessing in these patients an iatrogenic end state rather than a genuine deficit. To tease apart these explanations clearly requires a prospective, drug-free design with long-term longitudinal follow-up. Such methodological controls are necessary to guard against contamination by neuroleptic effects that can be expected to alter the nature and course of the illness.

PROSPECTIVE DRUG-FREE STUDY

Methods

With this aim, we pooled data from four earlier inpatient psychopharmacological studies (Singh & Kay, 1975a, 1975b, 1976; Singh & Smith, 1973). The combined sample included 62 schizophrenic patients who were generally young (mean = 25.2 years), in the subacute phase (mean = 2.9 years since first hospital admission), and balanced in gender, ethnic composition, and diagnostic subtype. Combined analysis was possible because all four studies had used comparable assessments, similar populations, and a within-subjects research design, whereby patients served as their own controls.

The studies consisted of a one- to two-week drug washout, followed by two to three weeks on a drug-free placebo baseline. Patients then received, in double-blind fashion, an individually titrated therapeutic dose of a prototypic neuroleptic drug, either chlorpromazine or haloperidol, which averaged 15 mg daily in haloperidol equivalence. This drug phase lasted 14 to 18 weeks, after which the patients were transferred to another unit or, if possible, discharged to the community. Fifty-four patients (87 percent) could be followed for three years to determine at what point, if at all, they had to be rehospitalized.

Symptoms were assessed prospectively in the placebo baseline and again after the neuroleptic phase, using the Brief Psychiatric Rating Scale (Overall & Gorham, 1962) and the Psychopathology Rating Schedule (Singh & Kay, 1975a). Since these scales were the precursors of the PANSS (see Chapter 3), we were able to calculate positive and negative scores post hoc, applying the same item combinations as for the PANSS. The sum of 32 individual symptoms provided a measure of total psychopathology.

Four outcome criteria were applied: (a) neuroleptic response was gauged as the degree of improvement in total psychopathology from placebo baseline to final neuroleptic week; (b) residual disorder was the total psychopathology score at the final neuroleptic week; (c) functional reconstitution was judged after the neuroleptic phase by the five-point Therapy Outcome Rating Scale (Singh & Kay, 1979a), which measures final disposition in terms of how fully the patient is restored to premorbid levels of social and emotional adjustment; and (d) sustained recovery was quantified as the number of months after treatment until hospital readmission, with a range from 0 (never discharged) to 36 (still in the community after 36 months).

Stability in the Drug-Free State

These prospective drug-free data were applied to assess the longitudinal stability, independence, and prognostic significance of negative and positive syndromes in schizophrenia (Kay & Singh, 1989). First we examined the short-term stability during the two-week drug-free baseline (Table 10:6). High correlations from the end of placebo weeks one to two were found for both the negative ($r = 0.78$, $p < 0.0001$) and positive syndrome ($r = 0.83$,

TABLE 10:6

Stability and Changes in Syndromal and Total Psychopathology Scales During Drug-Free Baseline and After 14–18 Weeks on Neuroleptics*

	Spectrum of Psychopathology		
Basis for Comparison	Negative	Positive	Total (Item Mean)
Drug-Free Baseline (n = 27)			
Week 1 mean ± SD	20.9 ± 10.85	17.7 ± 6.01	2.05 ± .61
Week 2 mean ± SD	21.3 ± 9.35	16.7 ± 6.68	2.06 ± .52
Change: mean/percent	.4/ + 1.9%	−1.0/− 5.6%	.01/+ .5%
Significance: paired *t*	.34	.70	.32
p	n.s.	n.s.	n.s.
Correlation: Pearson *r*	.78	.83	.72
p	< .0001	< .0001	< .0001
Drug-Free vs. Final Neuroleptic Week (n = 62)			
Week 1 mean ± SD	22.6 ± 8.97	20.0 ± 6.66	2.36 ± .74
Final week mean ± SD	14.7 ± 7.82	9.7 ± 7.22	1.28 ± .78
Change: mean/percent	−7.9/−35.0%	− 10.3/−51.5%	−1.08/−45.8%
Significance: paired *t*	6.85	10.34	9.34
p	< .0001	< .0001	< .0001
Correlation: Pearson *r*	.43	.37	.27
p	< .001	< .005	< .05

*Reprinted with permission from Kay & Singh (1989). The positive-negative distinction in drug-free schizophrenic patients: Stability, response to neuroleptics, and prognostic significance. *Archives of General Psychiatry*, 46, 711–718. Copyright © 1989 by the American Medical Association.

$p < 0.0001$). Paired t tests revealed no significant changes during this brief time.

To examine the longer-range stability, we compared the initial drug-free week with the final neuroleptic week, three to four months later. As indicated in Table 10:6, the longitudinal correlations for the two syndromes were still significant despite the longer interval and despite the neuroleptic intervention. The 35 percent improvement in negative syndrome with neuroleptic treatment was highly significant ($p < 0.0001$), but not as impressive as the gains in positive syndrome (52 percent) or total psychopathology (46 percent). The difference between reduction in negative vs. positive scores was in the marginal zone ($p = 0.06$), which tends to support the relative, but not the absolute, nonresponsiveness of the negative syndrome to these medications.

Independence of the Syndromes

To assess the independence or relatedness of the syndromes, we performed intercorrelations (Pearson r) during both the drug-free and final neuroleptic week. The finding of note was that the negative and positive scores were initially unrelated ($r = 0.06$), but they were strongly intercorrelated after the neuroleptic stabilization ($r = 0.52$, $p < 0.001$). This interrelation in drug stabilized patients may be explained by the shared benefits from neuroleptic treatment, which promotes a longitudinal covariance between the syndromes. Other analyses during the drug-free state revealed, once again, that chronicity of illness (years since first hospital admission) was not associated with negative ($r = 0.13$) or positive syndrome ($r = 0.08$).

Prognostic Significance

Finally, we analyzed the drug-free baseline data in relation to the four separate outcome criteria in order to study short-term and longer-range prognosis (Table 10:7). We found, first, that higher drug-free negative and positive syndromes *both* predicted a better short-term outcome, as measured by reduction in total psychopathology after three to four months of neuroleptic treatment. This observation could simply reflect the principle of "regression to the mean," whereby those patients with a severer initial illness have the greater opportunity for improvement. In keeping with this argument, we found that higher scores on both syndromes also were associated with a greater degree of remaining symptoms after treatment, indicating poorer outcome.

On the other hand, the two syndromes differed clearly in regard to func-

TABLE 10:7
Prognostic Significance (Pearson *r*) of Drug-Free Negative and Positive Syndromes in Acute Schizophrenia*

Outcome Criteria	Observation Period	n	Drug-Free Baseline Measure		
			Negative Syndrome	Positive Syndrome	Total Psycho-pathology
Neuroleptic response	3–4 months	62	.28*	.25*	.55****
Residual disorder	3–4 months	62	.26*	.28*	.27*
Functional reconstitution	3–4 months	62	−.14	−.32**	−.28**
Months to relapse	36 months	54	−.08	−.37***	−.35***

Note: Reprinted with permission from Kay & Singh (1989). The positive-negative distinction in drug-free schizophrenic patients: Stability, response to neuroleptics, and prognostic significance. *Archives of General Psychiatry*, 46, 711–718. Copyright © 1989 by the American Medical Association.
   *$p < .05$
  **$p < .02$
 ***$p < .01$
****$p < .005$

tional reconstitution and sustained recovery. These results were consistent with our other prognostic studies on acute schizophrenia (op. cit.) but ran counter to prevailing expectations on the positive-negative distinction. As shown in Table 10:7, we found that the drug-free positive syndrome predicted significantly *poorer* outcome as judged by more substantial and longer-range criteria. It alone correlated with less complete functional reconstitution after neuroleptic treatment and also with an earlier relapse across the three-year follow-up. Severity of total psychopathology yielded a similar prognostic pattern as the positive syndrome. These findings suggest that a positive syndrome may *seem* to convey a better outlook because it responds better to neuroleptics. Over the long course, however, we consistently found it to bear a worse prognosis for subacute (Kay & Singh, 1989) and chronic schizophrenics (Kay & Murrill, 1990).

SUMMARY OF FINDINGS

A number of conclusions and implications can be generated from the several studies that we have so far described, but we will reserve these for Chapters 13 and 14. At this juncture, however, let us summarize some of the more salient findings:

(a) Positive and negative syndromes differ in relation to a variety of fundamental parameters, including premorbid history, family history of psychiatric illness, cognitive development, information processing, neurological soft signs, and present functioning.

(b) Although positive and negative syndromes frequently occur together, they are theoretically independent. This means that they represent unrelated processes and are not co-exclusive.

(c) The syndromes are equally prominent in all phases of schizophrenia but appear to be in a state of flux during the first two years. After the acute phase, they show considerable stability over long periods of time.

(d) Whereas negative symptoms tend to be less responsive than positive symptoms to standard neuroleptics, they do improve significantly.

(e) The patient's positive-negative profile, nevertheless, seems to be essentially unaltered by neuroleptic treatment: those who initiate drug-treatment with a predominance of one syndrome or the other appear to retain this pattern.

(f) A marked positive or negative presentation bodes a poor outlook for the short term; the two syndromes, however, carry quite contrasting implications for the long-term outcome and general prognosis.

(g) The significance of the syndromes varies directly as a function of the stage of the illness. In acute schizophrenia, a negative syndrome seems to represent a benign course, while its reputation for signaling poor outcomes seems warranted only in the chronic stage.

(h) Positive and negative syndromes are comprised of distinct and internally consistent symptom constellations. This does not imply, however, that they constitute unitary constructs. Within the positive syndrome, for example, thought disorganization seems to stand apart as an aspect that most clearly connotes an unfavorable prognosis.

(i) The predictive validity of positive and negative syndromes is sharpened when used in combination with other established prognosticators, such as premorbid adjustment, and when utilizing different outcome criteria. For example, after the acute phase a positive syndrome predicts poorer long-term course and impaired social rehabilitation, whereas a negative syndrome predicts poorer drug response and impaired occupational rehabilitation.

(j) Overall the findings consistently support the validity and importance of the positive-negative distinction in schizophrenia. Its meaning, however, does not fit the models proposed by Crow (1980a) or Andreasen (1982, 1985), since the data contradicted the following assumptions about a negative syndrome: that it constitutes a subtype which is co-exclusive of the positive syndrome (as per Andreasen, 1982); that it is stable in the early phase; that it worsens as the disease progresses; that its import is the same at all stages of schizophrenia; that it is unimproved by neuroleptic treatment; and that it necessarily conveys a worse long-term outcome than a positive syndrome.

In the next chapter we shall further pursue the issue of the psychopharmacological validity of the positive-negative distinction in schizophrenia and its ramifications for newer treatment strategies. Then in Chapter 12 we shall proceed to challenge the view, which is implicit in most discussions of the positive-negative model, that this distinction is sufficient to describe the phenomenology of schizophrenia. In so doing we shall describe a more encompassing "pyramidical model" and thereafter, in Chapter 13, theorize about what these syndromes may be indicating about the pathophysiology of schizophrenia.

11

Response to Psychotropic Medications

TARGETING THE SYNDROMES FOR TREATMENT

Across the various research perspectives that we pursued, we have seen that the results supported the distinctiveness of positive and negative syndromes in terms of basic premorbid, developmental, neuropsychological, family history, and prognostic variables. A number of investigators have provided evidence of a psychopharmacological differentiation as well, generally reporting less responsiveness of the negative syndrome to classical neuroleptic drugs (e.g., Csernansky, Brown, & Hollister, 1986; Meltzer, Sommers, & Luchins, 1986; Breier et al., 1987; Johnstone et al., 1987). In the previous chapter we described similar findings from our research also: a marginally greater improvement ($p = 0.06$) was obtained on the positive compared to negative syndrome when patients underwent a three- to four-month trial on chlorpromazine or haloperidol (Kay & Singh, 1989). Nonetheless, it is important to consider that the negative symptoms *did* in fact show a highly significant improvement in this study ($p < 0.0001$). Most other investigations also dispel the notion of categorical nonresponse to neuroleptics (see review by Pogue-Geile & Zubin, 1988).

This is not to say, however, that positive and negative symptoms respond in unison, nor that negative symptoms are effectively managed by the classical neuroleptics. Indeed, our research suggests that positive and negative syndromes show a *divergent* pattern of psychopharmacological response and that different neuroleptic medications may be needed to address these two facets of schizophrenia. Our work in this area was guided by three broad objectives: (a) clarification of the biochemical bases of the positive and negative syndromes; (b) validation of their distinctiveness by experimental design, in which drugs serve as a dissecting tool or "therapeutic test"; and (c) development of new pharmacological strategies for treating negative symptoms.

In the present chapter we shall review this series of pharmacotherapeutic studies, from which we have drawn the following tentative conclusions: (a) the positive syndrome alone is exacerbated by anticholinergic antiparkinsonian drugs (Singh, Kay, & Opler, 1987); (b) some negative symptoms are, conversely, improved by anticholinergics (Sandyk & Kay, in press-c); (c) the negative syndrome alone responds favorably to L-dopa (Kay & Opler, 1985) and to pimozide (Feinberg et al., 1988); (d) in contrast, the positive syndrome is more ameliorated than the negative by low-dose bromocriptine (Marangell, Kay, & Lindenmayer, 1989) and clozapine treatment (Lindenmayer et al., 1989); (e) certain newer antipsychotic compounds such as risperidone and possibly sulpiride, which are still in the experimental stages of development, may carry promise for addressing both positive and negative syndromes. Together, these findings support the pharmacological validity of the positive-negative distinction and, moreover, provide evidence that negative symptoms may be successfully targeted by novel psychopharmacological strategies, including certain neuroleptics.

ANTICHOLINERGIC AGENTS

Our first psychopharmacological study concerned the effect of anticholinergic antiparkinsonian drugs on the therapeutic response to neuroleptics (Singh, Kay, & Opler, 1987). These medications are frequently prescribed along with neuroleptics, sometimes in a prophylactic manner, to counter their adverse side effects. In the 1970s, however, our group had reported several double-blind studies in which neuroleptic-treated schizophrenic patients showed a symptomatic worsening when given anticholinergics adjunctively (see review by Singh & Kay, 1985). Particularly involved were the symptoms of thought disorganization, uncooperativeness, bizarre and unusual thoughts, suspicious and paranoid ideation, delusions, disorientation, and sleeplessness. Neppe (1989, p. 162) in his volume on *Innovative Psychopharmacotherapy* concluded that either of two major mechanisms might explain our findings: "Direct anticholinergic effects in the brain [or else] indirect effects, including lowering neuroleptic blood levels and interfering with dopamine blockade." He observed, however, that the evidence for the latter, more peripheral, interpretation was discredited by a number of studies, including our finding of clinical worsening with anticholinergics during a drug-free phase (Singh & Kay, 1979b).

Johnstone, Crow, and colleagues (1983) in Great Britain more recently have replicated our findings of an anticholinergic-neuroleptic antagonism,

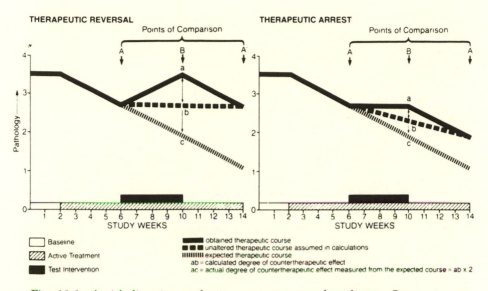

Fig. 11:1. Anticholinergic-neuroleptic antagonism in schizophrenia: Prototypic research design and findings in three studies (combined *n* of 47). (Reprinted with permission from Singh & Kay (1984). Exogenous peptides and schizophrenia. In Shah & Donald (Eds.), *Psychoneuroendocrine Dysfunction*, p. 525. New York: Plenum Publishing Company.)

reporting the therapeutic worsening to be specific to the positive schizophrenic symptoms. This prompted us to reanalyze our data using, retroactively, our current system of positive-negative assessment.

Our research strategy consisted of a double-blind reversal design in which an anticholinergic agent, either benztropine or trihexyphenidyl, was administered for two to four weeks along the course of neuroleptic treatment, either haloperidol or chlorpromazine (Singh, Kay, & Opler, 1987). Data were inspected on a total of 47 schizophrenic inpatients culled from three separate studies (Singh & Kay, 1975a, 1975b, 1979b). To permit assessment of therapeutic arrest and reversal, we contrasted ratings from the anticholinergic phase against the combined preceding and following periods on neuroleptic alone (see methodological discussion of Singh & Kay, 1978), as schematized in Fig. 11:1.

The data analysis (Table 11:1) confirmed our previous reports of overall exacerbation in psychopathology with anticholinergics. In addition, consistent with the findings of Johnstone et al. (1983), we observed significant worsening of the positive syndrome but a corresponding lack of change in negative symptoms. The correlation between positive and negative clusters in their direction and magnitude of change proved nonsignificant, suggesting that these two aspects of psychopathology did not covary in their response to anticholinergics. This reversal of positive symptoms alone by anticholinergic agents was found also when we reanalyzed the data using the system of Angrist et al. (1980) for positive-negative assessment (i.e., the Brief Psychiatric Rating Scale) instead of our own.

We next analyzed response to anticholinergics from a typological vantage point (Singh, Kay, & Opler, 1987). The 47 patients were classified as either positive or negative subtype on the basis of the prospective, pre-treatment placebo baseline assessment. This was done separately using our PANSS composite index as well as the Angrist method (see Table 11:1.)

When these discrete groups entered the anticholinergic phase, the positive subtype was found to deteriorate significantly in general psychopathology as compared with the outlying periods on neuroleptic alone. The negative subtype, conversely, showed no significant clinical change during the anticholinergic phase. The results thus supported the predictive validity of the positive-negative distinction in forecasting differential drug response. However, when applying the procedure of Angrist for classification, neither the positive nor negative subtype showed a significant worsening during the anticholinergic phase, which may reflect on the pharmacological validity of that assessment method (see discussion of rating methodology in Chapter 3).

From a more recent study of a population of 85 chronic schizophrenic patients hospitalized in Rome, Italy, we inferred that certain negative symptoms may be in fact ameliorated by anticholinergic therapy (Sandyk & Kay, in press-c). The sample was grouped as 26 who were receiving anticholinergic medications (trihexyphenidyl or benztropine mesylate) in conjunction with standard neuroleptics, and 59 who were receiving neuroleptics alone. Although the two groups were of comparable age and chronicity of illness, those who were exposed to anticholinergic treatment were distinguished by significantly less severe symptoms of flat affect ($p < 0.002$) and poverty of speech ($p < 0.02$), which are the two features that Crow (1985) proposed would reflect core negative schizophrenia. This finding, though based on a correlational design, is consistent with the theory that increased cholinergic activity may play a major role in the pathophysiology of schizophrenic manifestations (Singh & Kay, 1985), particularly the negative symptoms (Tandon & Greden, 1989; see also Chapter 13), and it has obviously important implications for pharmacotherapy.

L-DOPA

Our next study was inspired by the need for a direct psychopharmacological strategy to target the stubborn, drug-resistant negative profile in

TABLE 11:1

Therapeutic Reversal with Anticholinergic Antiparkinsonian Agents in Schizophrenia

		Positive–Negative Rating Method				
		PANSS			Angrist et al.	
Comparison	n	*Paired t*	p	n	*Paired t*	p
*Syndromes Reversed by AP Agents**						
Positive syndrome	47	2.58	<0.02	47	2.56	<0.02
Negative syndrome	47	1.52	n.s.	47	0.26	n.s.
*Subtypes Vulnerable to AP Reversal***						
Positive subtype	25	2.57	<0.02	28	1.87	n.s.
Negative subtype	22	1.05	n.s.	19	1.48	n.s.
Total group	47	2.41	<0.02			

Note: Based on Singh, Kay, & Opler (1987).

*Clinical worsening on positive and negative syndromes during the AP phase.

**Vulnerability to AP therapeutic reversal (worsening of total psychopathology score) according to positive vs. negative typology, as identified prospectively during the placebo baseline.

schizophrenia. We reasoned that if negative features are not always sensitive to neuroleptics, nor expected to be according to Crow's (1980a, 1980b) hypothesis, they might respond to pharmacological interventions other than dopamine blockade. We were intrigued, therefore, by scattered reports in the Australian and Japanese literature (Buchanan et al., 1975; Inanaga et al., 1975; Ogura, Kishimoto, & Nakao, 1976) on treatment of schizophrenia with L-dopa, which augments brain levels of both dopamine and norepinephrine. These data pointed to therapeutic gains in such deficit-laden areas as communication skills, rapport, and daily functioning. Such findings, together with the amphetamine study of Angrist, Rotrosen, and Gershon (1980) and our own recent work (Sandyk & Kay, in press-d; see Chapter 9), support the notion of a dopaminergic deficiency that underlies the negative syndrome in schizophrenia (as per MacKay, 1980, and van Kammen et al., 1986).

To test the therapeutic effects of L-dopa using our standardized positive-negative scale, we conducted a single-subject experimental study in which Sinemet therapy (L-dopa plus carbidopa) was initiated for a chronic schizophrenic with a longstanding negative syndrome (Kay & Opler, 1985). The study employed a double-blind placebo controlled ABA' design to secure internal validity. After two weeks on placebo alone, the patient underwent 13 weeks on haloperidol plus Sinemet, and then a return to haloperidol and placebo in the last four weeks.

Trend analysis revealed consistent worsening during the 17 weeks of haloperidol-placebo for five parameters that represent deficits as well as for the negative syndrome cluster of seven symptoms (Table 11:2). With the introduction of Sinemet, however, the PANSS negative scale and five individual deficit measures improved significantly ($p < 0.05$) as compared against the combined preceding and following four weeks. No other measures were reliably affected. In particular, there were no significant changes during either phase on the PANSS positive scale nor on any of the seven individual positive symptoms.

Although the single-subject experiment does not permit generalization, the results demonstrated a clear instance of drug response targeting the negative features of schizophrenia. In so doing, the data once again bear out a pharmacotherapeutic differentiation between positive and negative syndromes and, on a theoretical level, lend support to the association of negative phenomena with reduced dopamine functions.

PIMOZIDE

A more recent drug study by our group proceeded from several reports in the European literature (e.g., Pinder et al., 1976; Falloon, Watt, & Shep-

TABLE 11:2
Clinical Changes Under Haloperidol When Combined with Placebo vs. Sinemet*

| Clinical Measures | Clinical Worsening (W) or Improvement (I) | | | |
| | Haloperidol-Placebo | | Haloperidol-Sinemet | |
	Direction	p	Direction	p
Mean negative symptom cluster	W	< 0.005	I	< 0.05
Mean positive symptom cluster	—	> 0.50	—	> 0.50
Poor attention	W	< 0.005	I	< 0.025
Difficulty in abstract thinking	W	= 0.06	I	< 0.05
Passive-apathetic social withdrawal	W	< 0.01	I	< 0.05
Psychomotor rate (retardation)	W	< 0.05	I	< 0.05
Reduction of motor activity	W	= 0.06	I	< 0.05

*Reprinted with permission from Kay & Opler (1985). L-dopa in the treatment of negative schizophrenic symptoms. *International Journal of Psychiatry in Medicine*, 15, 293–298. Amityville, NY: Baywood Publishing Co., Inc.

herd, 1978) that pimozide, a neuroleptic marketed in the United States to treat Gilles de la Tourette's syndrome, may be especially helpful for the deficit symptoms in schizophrenia. This neuroleptic belongs to the diphenylbutylpiperidine group, which also includes penfluridol and flusperilene. The basis for its apparent benefit, though still a matter of speculation, may be its partial dopamine agonist-like effects (Post et al., 1980) or its potent calcium channel antagonism (Gould et al., 1983), which other neuroleptics lack.

To study with a well standardized instrument the action of pimozide on negative symptoms, we selected 10 neuroleptic refractory chronic schizophrenic patients and assessed them biweekly on the PANSS and extrapyramidal symptom scales. The eight-week design, conducted openly, involved establishing a two-week baseline on a standard neuroleptic, generally chlorpromazine or haloperidol, and then switching to pimozide in low but gradually increasing doses over the next six weeks (Feinberg et al., 1988).

Analysis of variance indicated improvement in overall psychopathology by the fourth week of pimozide, yet the therapeutic benefits were highly specific for negative symptoms (Fig. 11:2). Thus, the negative scale of the PANSS, but not the positive scale, showed significant and progressive reduction. Likewise, significant improvement was seen as early as week 2 on the PANSS anergia cluster, representing a deficit feature, but not on the three PANSS clusters that encompass positive items: thought disturbance, paranoid belligerence, and activation. No differences were obtained on measures of extrapyramidal symptoms as well, so that the clinical findings could not be ascribed to improvement in drug-induced motor side effects.

The utility of neuroleptics from the diphenylbutylpiperidine group for negative symptoms, however, remains controversial, since as yet there is no consensus from large scale double-blind investigations. As summarized by Reilly (1989, p. 76) from review of our and other drug studies, "Absolute confirmation of pimozide's selective efficacy in the negative symptomatology and impaired social functioning of chronic schizophrenia may remain tantalizingly out of reach, although much of the available evidence points suggestively in that direction."

LOW-DOSE BROMOCRIPTINE

Although the hypothesis of dopamine overactivity is generally accepted as the basis for positive schizophrenic symptoms and their improvement with neuroleptics (see discussion in Chapter 2), the model does not address the reason for neuroleptic *nonresponse* in many patients. One possible ex-

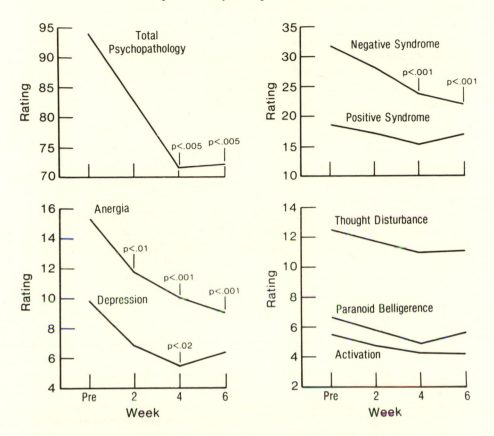

Fig. 11:2. Response to pimozide by neuroleptic refractory schizophrenics (n = 10) in terms of positive and negative symptoms. (Reprinted with permission from Feinberg et al. (1988). Pimozide treatment of the negative schizophrenic syndrome. An open trial. *Journal of Clinical Psychiatry*, 49, 235–238.)

planation comes from the fact that the classical neuroleptics block dopamine receptors after the synapse but not before it. Thus, these medications do not act upon the receptors which may inhibit dopamine synthesis and release and which are perhaps of relevance in correcting the neuroleptic refractory symptoms.

To study this proposition, we undertook a six-week study in which bromocriptine, an ergot alkaloyd with a cyclic peptide side chain, was added in low doses to the ongoing neuroleptic regimen (Marangell, Kay, & Lindenmayer, 1989). This strategy was predicated on observations that low-dose bromocriptine preferentially stimulates dopamine autoreceptors presynaptically, thereby decreasing dopamine synthesis and release (Haubrich &

Pfleugler, 1982). Earlier studies with adjuvant bromocriptine (e.g., Tamminga & Schaeffer, 1979) suggested that this agent may actually worsen psychotic symptoms, but these designs had involved relatively high doses of bromocriptine, in which the medication contrastingly exerts a classical postsynaptic dopamine agonist effect. We predicted that in low doses an opposite, ameliorative action would be obtained, particularly on the positive symptoms if, as per Crow (1980a, 1980b), these are associated with excessive dopamine transmission.

Seven neuroleptic refractory schizophrenic inpatients were recruited from long-term units of a state psychiatric hospital and treated on a closed Research Unit. The patients ranged in age from 27 to 65 years (mean = 45.9) and in length of illness from 8 to 36 years (mean = 11.2). After baseline evaluation on neuroleptic alone, patients were randomly assigned in single-blind fashion to continuation of the neuroleptic-alone regimen or to receiving the neuroleptic in combination with bromocriptine in doses of 2.5 mg per day. At the end of three weeks, all patients were crossed over to the alternate condition (adjuvant low-dose bromocriptine or neuroleptic alone), on which they remained for another three weeks. The differences in PANSS ratings were compared, using one-tailed paired t tests, under the three experimental conditions: baseline, after a three-week course on neuroleptic alone, and after three weeks of adjuvant bromocriptine treatment.

As shown in Table 11:3, the neuroleptic-alone trial showed no significant advantages over the baseline assessment. With bromocriptine, however, there was a 28 percent reduction in total psychopathology, which was accounted for mainly by significant improvements in the positive syndrome (by 27 percent) and, likewise, in the thought disturbance (44 percent) and activation clusters (36 percent). Improvements in negative syndrome and anergia, by comparison, only approached significance ($p < 0.10$). The data thus were consistent with the study hypothesis and suggested that, in low doses, bromocriptine may augment the action of neuroleptics in reducing schizophrenic symptoms, particularly in the positive spectrum of psychopathology.

CLOZAPINE

Lastly, we undertook a 15-week open study with clozapine, an atypical broad-spectrum neuroleptic (Lindenmayer et al., 1990). In contrast to the classical neuroleptics, clozapine is a dopamine nonselective dibenzodiazepine which may have preferential affinity for mesolimbic dopamine receptors (Gross & Langner, 1970) and activity at nondopaminergic, i.e., the alpha-ad-

TABLE 11:3
Changes on the PANSS with Adjuvant Low-Dose Bromocriptine vs. Neuroleptic Alone

PANSS Scale	Baseline Mean (SD)	Neuroleptic Alone Mean (SD)	Bromocriptine + Neuroleptic Mean (SD)	Comprison with Baseline (t) Neurol.	Comprison with Baseline (t) Bromo.	Bromocriptine vs. Neuroleptic (t)
Positive syndrome	13.33(4.23)	12.17(4.02)	9.67(2.07)	.47	2.06**	1.54*
Negative syndrome	13.17(5.04)	13.00(5.62)	9.50(3.99)	.06	1.48*	1.11
Total psychopathology	34.83(11.26)	32.00(10.30)	25.00(5.90)	.60	1.89*	1.48*
Symptom Clusters:						
Thought disturbance	8.67(2.34)	7.83(3.55)	4.83(1.60)	.51	3.29***	1.66*
Activation	5.50(2.25)	5.50(2.07)	3.50(0.84)	.00	2.00**	2.00**
Paranoid/belligerence	5.33(2.25)	4.33(1.63)	3.50(0.84)	1.37	1.28	.70
Anergia	7.00(2.90)	6.00(2.19)	4.83(1.60)	.94	1.48*	.91
Depression	8.33(3.56)	8.33(2.88)	7.17(3.13)	.00	.43	.98

Note: Reprinted with permission from Marangell, Kay, & Lindenmayer (1989). Low dose bromocriptine in the treatment of schizophrenia and tardive dyskinesia. Fourth Annual Meeting of the Society for Research in Psychopathology, Coral Gables, FL.

*p < .10, one-tailed
**p < .05, one-tailed
***p < .01, one-tailed

renergic and serotonergic receptors. Our interest in this compound lies in its reputed benefit for patients who are unresponsive to classical neuroleptics (Gellenberg & Doller, 1979) and the suggestion that this drug may be of equal benefit for positive and negative manifestations (Kane et al., 1988).

Thus, we consecutively recruited 12 DSM-III-R diagnosed schizophrenic inpatients who, by history, had proven refractory to at least three classes of neuroleptics. The sample included eight males and four females of ages 24 to 38 years (mean = 32.5), who had seven to 26 years of illness since their first psychiatric hospitalization (mean = 14.2 years). All patients were stabilized on typical neuroleptics in standard dose ranges at the time of entry into study. After baseline evaluation, patients were tapered off the neuroleptic and placed on clozapine in starting doses of 25–100 mg per day (mean = 68.8 mg) and gradually building up to 100–900 mg per day (mean = 677.5 mg) by the final study week. As elsewhere, we applied the PANSS for measuring positive, negative, and other features of psychopathology, and we also rated patients on the Clinical Global Impressions Scale (CGI) (Guy, 1976) to provide a holistic index of drug response.

The course of clinical changes with clozapine across 15 weeks is illustrated in Figs. 11:3 and 11:4. The significance of changes was tested parametricallly by one-way analysis of variance, treatment-by-sujects design, and nonparmetrically by Cox-Stuart test of trend (see Table 11:4). The results indicated that significant differences from baseline were incurred on all clinical parameters. Specifically, improvements were obtained with clozapine treatment on both the PANSS positive and negative scales, on all five psychopathology clusters, and on the two global psychopathology measures (PANSS and CGI). Whereas the global changes were modest (between 9 percent and 13 percent), the most striking areas of improvement were on the positive syndrome (25 percent) and on the paranoid/belligerence cluster (40 percent). The changes in negative syndrome (11 percent) and anergia (12 percent), though also significant, were considerably smaller. The difference between changes on the positive vs. negative scale, as given by the PANSS composite scores, was statistically significant ($p < 0.005$), although the greater change on the positive syndrome might be attributable to its higher prestudy baseline value.

Of particular interest was the finding that the patients not only sustained their improvements with clozapine over the course of study but continued to improve on some measures even toward the end of the 15-week trial. The Cox-Stuart test of trend across the full period confirmed the consistency of improvements, revealing uniformly significant trends ($p < 0.005$) for all clinical parameters. A similar analysis that focused on only the final ten study weeks indicated that significant trends were obtained from the sixth through fifteenth week on clozapine, suggesting that its action is grad-

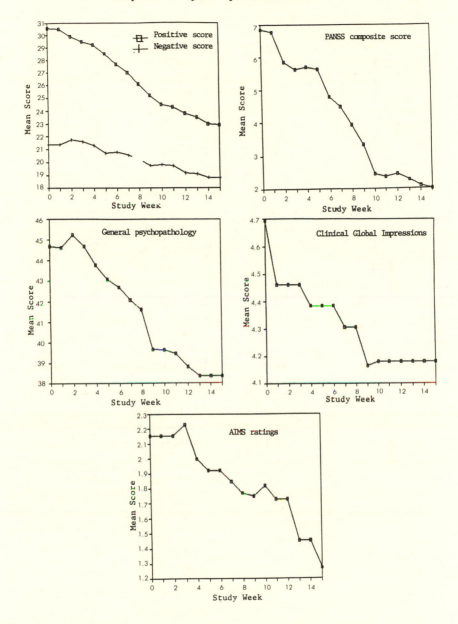

Fig. 11:3. Changes with clozapine on positive, negative, and general psychopathology assessments. (Reprinted with permission from Lindenmayer et al. (1990). Clozapine effects on positive vs. negative symptoms of schizophrenia. Presented at 143rd Annual Meeting of the American Psychiatric Association, NY.)

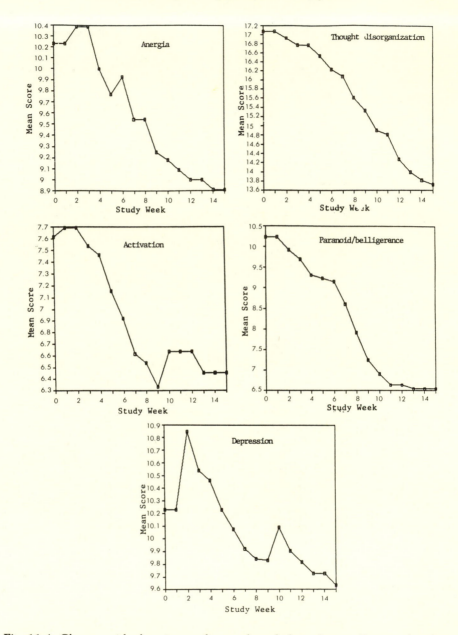

Fig. 11:4. Changes with clozapine on five psychopathology clusters. (Reprinted with permission from Lindenmayer et al. (1989). Clozapine effects on positive vs. negative symptoms of schizophrenia. Presented at 143rd Annual Meeting of the American Psychiatric Association.)

TABLE 11:4
Summary of Clinical Changes on a 15-Week Trial with Clozapine*

Clinical Measure	Pre-study Baseline Mean (50)	Clozapine Week 15 Mean (50)	Percent Improved	ANOVA	Test of Trend Across Study	Test of Trend Weeks 6-15
Clinical Global Impression	5.08(0.67)	4.60(0.52)	9%	$p < .002$	$p < .005$	$p = .31$ (n.s.)
PANSS						
General Psychopathology	48.42(7.88)	42.20(8.20)	13%	$p < .0001$	$p < .005$	$p < .05$
Positive Syndrome	30.58(4.66)	22.90(5.67)	25%	$p < .0001$	$p < .005$	$p < .05$
Negative Syndrome	23.17(7.27)	20.70(6.50)	11%	$p < .0001$	$p < .005$	$p < .05$
Composite Score	7.42(8.04)	2.20(6.02)	—	$p < .0001$	$p < .005$	$p < .05$
Anergia	11.08(3.70)	9.80(2.86)	12%	$p < .0001$	$p < .005$	$p < .05$
Thought disorganization	18.50(3.23)	15.10(4.36)	18%	$p < .0001$	$p < .005$	$p < .05$
Activation	8.25(2.38)	7.10(1.66)	14%	$p < .0001$	$p < .005$	$p < .05$
Paranoid/Belligerence	11.08(2.91)	7.20(2.74)	35%	$p < .0001$	$p < .005$	$p < .05$
Depression	11.08(2.58)	10.60(1.51)	4%	$p < .0005$	$p < .005$	$p = .50$ (n.s.)

*Reprinted with permission from Lindenmayer et al. (1990). Clozapine effects on positive vs. negative symptoms of schizophrenia. Presented at 143rd Annual Meeting of the American Psychiatric Association, NY.

ual, systematic, and progressive over several months. Such continuing improvements were shown on all of the clinical scales except the CGI and the PANSS clusters of activation and depression.

Comparison of each clozapine week against the pre-study baseline, using paired t tests (two-tailed) with alpha set at $p < 0.05$, clarified the speed, sequence, and consistency of changes with clozapine (see Table 11:5). We found that the earliest change was on the positive syndrome, which emerged as significant by only the second clozapine week ($p = 2.35$, $p < 0.05$). Significant overall change on the CGI was seen by week 4 ($t = 2.35$, $p < 0.05$), whereas changes on the negative syndrome proved slower, first achieving significance by week 5 (PANSS negative scale, $t = 3.45$, $p < 0.005$; anergia, $t = 2.57$, $p < 0.05$). Changes on PANSS thought disturbance and general psychopathology were significant by week 7, and activation and paranoid/belligerence improved by week 8.

Accordingly, this study confirmed that clozapine is effective for neuroleptic refractory schizophrenic patients, reducing certain sets of symptoms by up to 40 percent. In contrast to the fairly rapid action of standard neuroleptics and their plateauing after four to six weeks of treatment, we observed increasing therapeutic effects of clozapine through the 15th week of trial. Our findings indicate, in agreement with Kane et al. (1988), that both positive and negative symptoms are ameliorated. Yet our data suggest that the action of clozapine may be most beneficial for positive features, particularly symptoms of paranoid/belligerence.

The foregoing study, however, should not be interpreted as implying that clozapine is less effective than other neuroleptics for targeting the negative syndrome. Paunović and colleagues (1988) in Belgrade, Yugoslavia, reported a very interesting direct comparison of clozapine with pimozide. Using the Serbo-Croatian adaptation of the PANSS, they evaluated the symptomatic changes for 20 well-defined schizophrenic patients from a drug-free baseline through the course of 20 days on either medication. The investigators found a significant improvement in the negative profile under both treatments, consistent with the findings reported in the present chapter (Feinberg et al., 1988; Lindenmayer et al., 1990). These changes, however, were significantly more pronounced and prompt with clozapine, for which the difference from baseline achieved significance already by day 10. A reliable difference between the two drugs also was evident after only ten days of treatment.

CONCLUSIONS AND FUTURE DIRECTIONS

Cumulatively, these psychopharmacological studies give cause for optimism. They indicate that although the negative symptoms may be *relatively* unresponsive to the classical neuroleptic medications, such as haloperidol

TABLE 11:5
Timing of Changes in 15-Week Trial with Clozapine:
Significant Differences from Prestudy Baseline*

Clinical Measures	Clozapine Treatment Week														
	1	2	3	4	5	6	7	8	9	10	11	12	13	14	15
Positive syndrome		X			X	X	X	X	X	X	X	X	X	X	X
Negative syndrome					X	X			X	X	X	X	X	X	X
General psychopathology						X	X	X	X	X	X	X	X	X	X
Clinical Global Impressions				X	X	X	X	X	X	X	X	X	X	X	X
Anergia					X	X	X			X	X	X	X	X	X
Thought disorganization						X	X	X	X	X	X	X	X	X	X
Activation								X		X	X	X	X	X	X
Paranoid/belligerence								X	X	X	X	X	X	X	X
Depression									X	X	X	X	X	X	X

*Reprinted with permission from Lindenmayer et al. (1990). Clozapine effects on positive vs. negative symptoms of schizophrenia. Presented at 143rd Annual Meeting of the American Psychiatric Association, NY.

and chlorpromazine (see Chapter 10), (a) they still improve significantly; (b) they apparently respond preferentially to other neuroleptics, such as pimozide; (c) they may be treated effectively with atypical neuroleptics, such as clozapine, or with non-neuroleptics, such as L-dopa; and (d) positive and negative syndromes do indeed respond differentially to several kinds of psychotropic treatments.

Finally, newer medications are being developed to address the negative and refractory symptoms of schizophrenia. Sulpiride and related neuroleptics from the benzamide group have been developed in France and marketed for their putative anti-autistic (Bobon et al., 1972) and disinhibitory properties (Deniker, 1978). The earlier research on these medications, unfortunately, lacked methodological sophistication; for example, it used poorly operationalized scales and diagnostically mixed groups. More recent research (e.g., Harnyrd et al., 1984; Gerlach et al., 1985) has yielded negative or equivocal results. While amisulpride has shown benefit for anhedonia, anergia, and loss of interest in a nonpsychotic population (Lecrubier et al., 1988), these findings remain to be confirmed in schizophrenic patients.

A perhaps more promising development is the recent application of ritanserin and risperidone to schizophrenia. These compounds have potent serotonergic antagonism and, as such, may have specific advantages for the negative spectrum of symptoms (Niemegeers, 1989). Ritanserin may be used in combination with conventional dopamine blockers, such as haloperidol, to provide a more comprehensive pharmacological treatment for schizophrenia. Risperidone, on the other hand, in itself combines antiserotonergic with antidopaminergic action (Gelders et al., 1989). The first set of studies from Europe using the PANSS has, accordingly, found demonstrable improvements on both negative and positive facets of schizophrenia (De Buck, Hoffman, & De Smet, 1989; De Cuyper, 1989; Jansen & Boom, 1989; Peuskins et al., 1989; Reilly et al., 1989; Turner, Lowe, & Hammond, 1989; also see discussion in Chapter 5) as well as the PANSS depression cluster (Peuskins et al., 1989).

It is hoped that the investigations described in this chapter, beyond supporting the distinctiveness and heuristic value of the positive-negative profiling, may contribute to our neurobiological understanding of the psychopathological processes in schoziphrenia. In the years to come, rational treatments need to be evolved to tackle the drug-refractory symptoms and to address the complexity and heterogeneity of this disorder. Indeed, newer studies are already moving to target the particular symptoms encountered in schizophrenia and away from the stock "one size fits all" approach to medication.

PART V

Newer Models
of Schizophrenia

12

Pyramidical Model of Schizophrenia

THE KRAEPELINIAN TYPOLOGY

The starting point of our research was our fascination with the complexity and heterogeneity of schizophrenia—its symptoms, premorbid history, course, and outcome. We believed that this varied picture, rather than obscuring the nature of schizophrenia, might be the very key that unlocks the mysteries of its origins and treatment. Accordingly, instead of searching for uniformity in schizophrenia where perhaps it does not exist, our strategy was to seek insight into what separates the illness into its various guises. We were hopeful that the diversity in symptoms would provide important clues to the different processes that combine to form this devastating psychiatric disorder. If these components could be identified, then we might have a road map to guide our understanding of the condition and lead the way toward selective treatments for the particular syndromes that are encountered.

Our approach to this problem was primarily a dimensional one, i.e., one aiming to identify the pathological *processes* or *syndromes* that constitute schizophrenia. This stands in contrast to the typological approach that has long dominated the description of schizophrenia and, more generally, psychiatric classification. The assumption behind a typological model is that we may recognize distinct, co-exclusive *types* that differ in fundamental ways, e.g., in their symptoms and course of illness. The schizophrenia subtypes described earlier in this century by Kraepelin (1919), while still underlying the classification in American psychiatry (American Psychiatric Association, 1987), have not sufficed as a basis for reaching decisions on treatment or prognosis. Particularly with the introduction of neuroleptics as the principal therapeutic modality for schizophrenia, it has become plainly evident that the subtyping into paranoid, catatonic, and disorgan-

181

ized schizophrenia has not truly influenced judgments on what kind or combination of medications to prescribe. As such, the Kraepelinian nosology for schizophrenia has not demonstrated pharmacological validity nor great practical value.

IS THE POSITIVE-NEGATIVE MODEL SUFFICIENT?

One of the major advances in schizophrenia research in recent times has been the classification of symptoms as positive, constituting abnormal productions, vs. negative, constituting deficits or loss of functions. Thus far in this volume we have described the validity and importance of this newer conceptualization. But controversy still surrounds the question of whether the positive-negative distinction should be viewed dimensionally, as per Crow (1980a, 1980b), or typologically, as per Andreasen (Andreasen & Olsen, 1982; Andreasen et al., 1982). In addition, there has been little said about how the positive-negative model relates to other subtypes and syndromes of schizophrenia. For example, should it actually supplant the Kraepelinian model or, rather, be regarded as another independent parameter, one that may perhaps interact with the subtypes or else provide some "fine tuning" to nosology? Indeed, despite intensive studies on the validity of positive and negative syndromes, the issue of its *sufficiency* as a descriptive model of schizophrenia has been virtually ignored. We have argued that, in principle, the positive-negative distinction could be valid, i.e., represent separate and meaningful aspects of the disorder, but still incomplete—in other words, not portraying the full complexity of schizophrenia (Singh & Kay, 1987).

These considerations prompted us to go beyond the positive-negative model and to approach schizophrenia from a broader and impartial perspective, one that does not *presuppose* the validity or sufficiency of the positive-negative distinction. This was facilitated by our development of the Positive and Negative Syndrome Scale (PANSS), since this instrument provided a well operationalized assessment of 30 schizophrenic symptoms. Its heuristic benefit was in the examination of a wide spectrum of phenomena, which guards against a self-limiting evaluation. This is important since, as yet, positive-negative research is only in its infancy. To adopt a narrow view at this stage would foreclose opportunities to see the "larger picture." It could conceivably lead us to entertain only our preexisting hypothesis, embodied in a one-sided instrument, and not rival positions, which would thus promote a bias in findings and thwart progress in research.

In particular, we still need to explore the constituent symptoms of the positive and negative syndromes; their relationship to one another; their unitary or pluralistic nature; and their distinctiveness from other facets of schizophrenia, such as depression, which could conceivably masquerade as negative features (cf. Carpenter, Heinrichs, & Alphs, 1985). Above all, a broad scope of assessment permits one to consider whether positive and negative syndromes tell the whole schizophrenia story, or else whether other factors need to be recognized and understood in relation to these syndromes.

Our research design involved a large-scale factor analytic study of the PANSS to determine whether the 30 symptoms separate into identifiable syndromes that might clarify the underlying processes in schizophrenia (Kay, 1990; Kay & Sevy, in press). Although factor analytic studies of psychiatric symptoms are not new to research on schizophrenia (e.g., Lorr, 1962; Guy, 1976), except for one study (Strauss, Carpenter, & Bartko, 1974) a clear-cut negative syndrome has not been delineated. The likely reason, as we argued in Chapter 3, is that the outcome of an investigation is necessarily limited by the validity, reliability, and comprehensiveness of the measures. Since the research focus on negative symptomatology is fairly recent, the earlier scales tended to include few such items. Thus, the difficulty in discerning a negative syndrome may, rather than reflecting on the nature of schizophrenia, simply reflect on the nature of item selection. The 18-item Brief Psychiatric Rating Scale (Overall & Gorham, 1962), for example, encompasses only two generally accepted negative symptoms (blunted affect and emotional withdrawal); for this reason it cannot produce a negative syndrome cluster but only an "anergia" factor (Guy, 1976) that represents a far narrower construct.

Our objectives in the present study (Kay & Sevy, in press) were to examine (a) the factorial validity of the positive-negative distinction, (b) its sufficiency for accommodating the full range of schizophrenia symptoms, (c) the identity of other possible components in schizophrenia, (d) the relationship of these components to the Kraepelinian subtypes, and (e) the significance of this dimensional approach for typology in schizophrenia.

METHODS OF STUDY

Our subjects were 240 schizophrenic inpatients selected from hospital settings in New York City, mainly within a state psychiatric center. All had been initially screened for a chart-based diagnosis of schizophrenia and were then independently interviewed by a research psychiatrist to ascertain fulfillment of DSM-III criteria for this diagnosis (American Psychiatric Association, 1980). Those with major affective illness, schizoaffective disorder, organic brain syndrome, mental retardation, or any additional Axis I diagnosis were specifically excluded from study. This sample, which was gathered over the course of seven years, had been recruited for purposes of research and training and included volunteering patients from both the acute and chronic stages of illness.

From the total of 240 subjects, 179 were male and 61 female; ethnically, 106 were black, 60 white, 72 Hispanic origin, and 2 Asians. The age range was 18 to 68 years (mean = 33.1, SD = 10.21), and the duration since first psychiatric hospitalization was between one month and 42 years (mean = 10.7 years, SD = 8.90). All but two patients were undergoing neuroleptic treatment at the time of study and, as our data show, all were experiencing a significant array of psychotic symptoms.

PANSS ratings of 30 psychiatric symptoms along the seven-point severity scales were performed by consensus of one to three trained psychiatrists immediately after the specified 35–45 minute interview. The interrater reliability (Pearson r) for this sample ranged from 0.81 to 0.89.

The 30 PANSS symptoms were then subjected to principal component factor analysis using equimax rotation to identify the distinct clusters. This statistical procedure was selected as a way to arrive at orthogonal factor patterns that (a) maximally discriminate among patients, (b) are uncorrelated with each other, and (c) are hierarchically ordered in terms of their contribution (Morrison, 1973; Harris, 1975; Marascuilo & Levin, 1983). The computational technique, performed using the CRUNCH statistical program (1986), involved derivation of a correlation matrix; data reduction to a symmetrical tridiagonal matrix; and then application of a QL algorithm as per Bowdler et al. (1968), with rotations, matrix inversions, and scoring calculations as described by Bock (1975). In comparison to other factor analytic techniques, principal component analysis is atheoretical and yields latent hypothetical constructs that are very closely tied to the original variables. Accordingly, after having identified new components, one can subsequently utilize the component scores instead of the original variables without any loss of informaiton (Harris, 1975).

Our findings, as we shall next discuss, addressed four questions: (a) Do positive and negative syndromes constitute distinct and major components of schizophrenia? (b) What other significant components or syndromes in schizophrenia, if any, can be discerned? (c) How do these dimensional syndromes relate to the established Kraepelinian subtypes? (d) Can we recognize in schizophrenia polarized axes of symptoms, i.e., specific clinical dimensions which form opposite poles of the same axis?

COMPONENTS OF SCHIZOPHRENIA

As shown in Table 12:1, the principal component analysis disclosed seven orthogonal components with eigenvalues > 1 that could account for

TABLE 12:1
Results of Principal Component Analysis of 30 Symptoms for 240 Schizophrenic Inpatients (Equimax Rotation)*

Component	Eigenvalue	Percent of Variance	Cumulative Percent
Negative	7.08	23.61	23.61
Positive	3.74	12.48	36.10
Excited	2.55	8.50	44.59
Depressive	2.32	7.73	52.32
Cognitive	1.56	5.21	57.53
Suspicious/persecutory	1.08	3.62	61.15
Stereotyped thinking	1.08	3.59	64.73

*Reprinted from Kay & Sevy (in press). Pyramidical model of schizophrenia. Schizophrenia Bulletin (public domain).

64.7 percent of the total variance (Kay & Sevy, in press). These components, ordered according to the amount of variance that they explain, involved the following dimensions: negative, positive, excited, depressive, cognitive, suspicious-persecutory, and stereotypic thinking. Of these components, the first four had eigenvalues > 2 and explained 52.3 percent of the total variance. They were clearly distinct and, by definition of the orthogonal principal component analysis (Morrison, 1973; Harris, 1975), were statistically unrelated. These four components embraced a substantial set of symptoms, i.e., five or more each; the other three components *all together* included only five symptoms, and these had almost as high loadings with other components (see Table 12:2). Since, as per Harris (1975), these latter components are likely to be describing error variance or factors of minor influence, only the first four components were retained for further analysis.

The findings confirmed the presence of negative and positive syndromes in schizophrenia that are independent of one another. These two syndromes emerged, respectively, as Components 1 and 2 and accounted for the main share of variance (36.1 percent). The component items are identified in Table 12:2, together with their means, standard deviations, and factor loadings. Interestingly, the positive syndrome was restricted mainly to items of delusions and hallucinations, while disorganized thinking was part of a separate but weaker cluster of cognitive items. In this respect, our findings tallied with the study of Bilder et al. (1985), who drew the same conclusions from a different scale and a far smaller sample.

The negative and positive syndromes, however, were in fact not sufficient to explain the phenomenology of schizophrenia. We found, in addition, a cluster associated mainly with excitement and impulsivity, and also a de-

TABLE 12:2
Means, Standard Deviations, and Component Loadings of 30 Schizophrenic Symptoms

Component/ Symptoms	Plotting Code	Mean	(SD)	Equimax Rotated Component Loadings						
				1	2	3	4	5	6	7
NEGATIVE										
Emotional withdrawal	A	3.11	(1.06)	.80	*	*	*	*	*	*
Passive/apathetic social withdrawal	B	2.88	(1.29)	.79	*	*	*	*	*	*
Lack of spontaneity & flow of conversation	C	2.80	(1.45)	.76	*	*	*	*	*	*
Blunted affect	D	3.11	(1.06)	.71	*	*	*	*	*	*
Poor rapport	E	2.77	(1.36)	.71	*	.22	*	*	*	*
Poor attention	F	2.55	(1.35)	.68	*	.24	*	.22	*	*
Active social avoidance	G	2.70	(1.26)	.56	*	*	*	*	.45	*
Motor retardation	H	1.93	(1.08)	.55	*	*	*	*	*	*
Disturbance of volition	I	2.26	(1.30)	.51	*	.24	.31	*	*	*
Mannerisms and posturing	J	1.77	(1.18)	.38	*	*	*	.26	*	*
POSITIVE										
Unusual thought content	K	3.54	(1.50)	*	.84	*	*	*	*	*
Delusions	L	3.59	(1.59)	*	.84	*	.26	*	*	*
Grandiosity	M	2.71	(1.65)	*	.76	*	*	*	*	*
Lack of judgment & insight	N	4.21	(1.30)	.32	.52	*	*	.36	*	*
Hallucinatory behavior	O	2.75	(1.66)	*	.43	*	.39	.25	*	*
EXCITED										
Excitement	P	2.26	(1.19)	*	*	.83	*	*	*	*
Poor impulse control	Q	2.08	(1.15)	*	*	.71	*	*	*	*
Tension	R	2.48	(1.17)	.22	*	.66	.39	*	*	*
Hostility	S	2.15	(1.18)	*	*	.61	*	*	.51	*
Uncooperativeness	T	2.13	(1.27)	.48	*	.49	*	*	.38	*
DEPRESSIVE										
Anxiety	U	2.67	(1.19)	*	*	.28	.71	*	*	*
Guilt Feelings	V	1.87	(1.17)	*	*	*	.66	*	.28	*
Depression	W	2.16	(1.25)	*	*	*	.64	*	.31	*
Somatic concern/delusions	X	2.54	(1.40)	*	.21	*	.60	*	*	*
Preoccupation	Y	2.89	(1.15)	.30	.32	*	.53	*	*	.49
COGNITIVE & OTHERS										
Difficulty in abstract thinking	Z	4.14	(1.35)	.52	*	*	*	.57	*	*
Disorientation	a	1.96	(1.18)	.51	*	*	*	.56	*	*
Conceptual disorganization	b	3.33	(1.49)	.39	.48	*	*	.52	*	*
Suspiciousness/persecution	c	3.07	(1.30)	*	.47	*	.23	*	.61	*
Stereotyped thinking	d	2.95	(1.27)	.30	.41	.27	.31	*	*	.45
Eigenvalue percent				5.68	3.54	2.94	2.92	1.58	1.53	1.25

Note: Reprinted from Kay & Sevy (in press).
Pyramidical model of schizophrenia. *Schizophrenia Bulletin* (public domain).
*Component loadings < .20

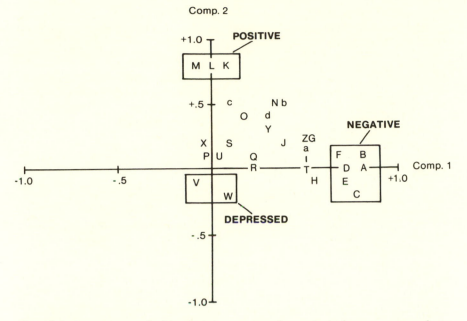

Fig. 12:1. Arrangement of schizophrenic symptoms from principal component analysis. See Table 12:1 for plotting code. (Reprinted from Kay & Sevy [in press]. Pyramidical model of schizophrenia. *Schizophrenia Bulletin* [public domain].)

pressive syndrome that included symptoms of anxiety, guilt feelings, and depression. The emergence of a distinct affective component, despite the diagnostic screening out of affective and schizoaffective patients, suggested that this is a bona fide aspect of schizophrenia and one which, perhaps, does not receive ample attention from clinicians, researchers, and theoreticians.

The interrelationship among syndromes was clarified graphically by plotting their positions in relation to the two principal components, occupying the X and Y axes in Fig. 12:1. We found that the positive, negative, and depressive syndromes formed divergent points of a right triangle that outlined the corners of a single quadrant of the graph. Within this triangular formation, the full range of symptoms was encompassed.

At one corner, a positive syndrome vertex was comprised of the particular symptoms of grandiosity, delusions, and unusual thought content. At the second corner, a negative syndrome vertex included emotional withdrawal, blunted affect, passive/apathetic social withdrawal, poor rapport, lack of spontaneity and flow of conversation, and poor attention. And at the third corner, a depressive syndrome vertex consisted of depression and guilt feelings. The excitement syndrome, which involved symptoms of ex-

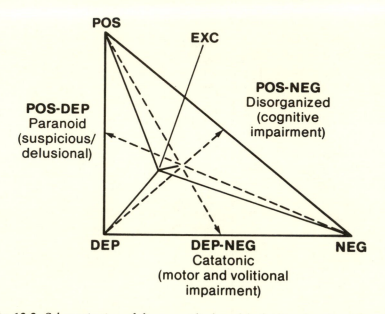

Fig. 12:2. Schematization of the pyramidical model of schizophrenia, with syndromes represented at the angles and center, diagnostic subtypes at the sides, and polarized axes by the transversal arrows. (Reprinted from Kay & Sevy [in press]. Pyramidical model of schizophrenia. *Schizophrenia Bulletin* [public domain].)

citement, tension, and poor impluse control, formed an additional pole that brings this triangular base into a third dimension, yielding the pyramidical shape that is aerially depicted in Fig. 12:2.

It can be seen that this diagram is simply an extraction from the previous graph, one that for the sake of simplicity omits the labeling of the X–Y axis and the individual symptoms coordinates. This configuration of the association among symptoms suggested to us that a "pyramidical model" can accommodate the diversity of symptoms in schizophrenia (Kay, 1990; Kay & Sevy, in press) and, as will be next discussed, is of considerable heuristic value.

DIMENSIONS VS. TYPOLOGY

Although our principal component analysis identified orthogonal symptom complexes, this does not *per force* rule out a typological interpretation of the syndromes. The latter view, however, is less parsimonious: it requires specific assumptions about the discontinuity and mutual exclusivity of these components that are not supported. Earlier typological studies on negative and positive symptoms by Andreasen and Olsen (1982) and our group (Lindenmayer, Kay, & Opler, 1984; Opler et al., 1984) revealed only a small minority of schizophrenic patients who could be classified as showing one set of symptoms without prevalence of the other. An examination of the frequency distribution of the four components in the present study demonstrated, in fact, that negative and positive syndromes were normally distributed, consistent with our previous research (Kay, Fiszbein, & Opler, 1987), whereas the excited and depressive syndromes were skewed to the right. In all cases, however, the distribution curves were unimodal. Thus, these components appeared to represent continuous dimensions, or syndromes, rather than discrete, co-exclusive subtypes.

The orthogonal nature of these syndromes indeed specifies that they are statistically unrelated, so that the presence of one does not imply the presence or absence of the other. Accordingly, positive and negative syndromes are not mutually incompatible; a schizophrenic patient can, and in our experience typically does, show prominent features of more than one syndrome. Where two syndromes prevail, the clinical profile may be revealed by tracing the pathway between the paired poles in Fig. 12:2. In so doing, it is found that the symptoms which are correlated with dual syndromes, as seen by their location between the basal points of triangulation, seem to account for the three Kraepelinian diagnostic subtypes of schizophrenia that are still recognized by American psychiatry (American Psychiatric Association, 1987).

Along the pathway that connects positive and negative syndromes in Fig. 12:1, we see a concentration of cognitive abnormalities that includes conceptual disorganization, stereotyped thinking, difficulty in abstract thinking, and poor judgment; these are important features of the *disorganized* type of schizophrenia. Midway along the positive-depressive poles, alternatively, we observe symptoms characteristic of *paranoid* schizophrenia, namely ideas of suspicion and persecution, somatic delusions, and hostility. Finally, the negative and depressive poles are intersected by features associated with *catatonic* schizophrenia, such as motor retardation, uncooperativeness/negativism, and disturbance of volition.

These findings, which are more broadly schematized in Fig. 12:2, suggest that the Kraepelinian typology derives from *hybrid* rather than pure constructs. It reflects not single pathological processes but, instead, symptoms related to paired components. Thus, we may recognize uncorrelated but co-occurring syndromes which, in their combination, produce the familiar subtypes of schizophrenia. Such a model clearly distinguishes between syndromes and typology. It argues first against regarding positive and negative symptoms as schizophrenia *subtypes*, as per Andreasen and Olsen (1982), since these factors are not inversely related or co-exclusive. Second, it argues against viewing paranoid, disorganized, and catatonic subtypes as genuine syndromes, since these did not emerge as true components. Instead, as noted above, the paranoid type seems to involve an interaction between positive and depressive syndromes; the disorganized type a positive-negative interaction; and the catatonic type a negative-depressive interaction.

A PROGNOSTIC AXIS IN SCHIZOPHRENIA

Within this pyramidical model, an examination of the transverse from the base vertices to the opposing sides, depicted by the broken arrows in Fig. 12:2, suggested the presence of co-exclusive symptoms that form bipolar axes in schizophrenia. For example, the diagonal across from the positive syndrome vertex extends distally to signs of motor and volitional impairment. In other words, the positive syndrome stands apart in its unrelatedness to these facets of psychopathology, which instead are linked to both negative and depressive syndromes. Likewise, the negative syndrome stands apart from paranoid ideation, and the depressive syndrome apart from cognitive dysfunction.

This last relationship is especially intriguing because depression and cognitive deficit carry opposite prognostic value in the active stage of schizophrenia. Specifically, depression conveys a favorable outlook (Vaillant, 1964; Kay & Lindenmayer, 1987; Lindenmayer & Kay, 1989), while cognitive dysfunction is generally believed to portend a poor outcome (Chapman et al., 1975; Kay & Singh, 1979). Indeed, as described in Chapter 10, our recent 2.7 year follow-up of 46 schizophrenic patients found that the best single predictors of good vs. poor functional reconstitution were, respectively, symptoms of depression vs. thought disturbance (Kay & Murrill, 1990).

It seems, therefore, that the empirically based pyramidical model for conceptualizing schizophrenic symptoms discloses a bipolar prognostic axis characterized by affective and cognitive features that signify opposite predictions about the course of illness.

CONCLUSIONS FROM THE PYRAMIDICAL MODEL

The results of this factor analytic study suggest the following conclusions: (a) a two-factor model of schizophrenia is inadequate; we can identify four defining symptoms complexes—negative, positive, excited, and depressive; (b) these features are statistically independent and not mutually exclusive; (c) these syndromes form a pyramidical set of axes that encompasses the diversity in symptoms and may reflect separate pathological processes in schizophrenia; (d) positive and negative syndromes show factorial validity, even though alone they are not sufficient for a model of schizophrenia; (e) the positive syndrome, as it is presently conceived (Andreasen, 1985; Crow, 1985), proves to be nonunitary, with thought disorganization part of a cognitive factor and not tied to the interrelated cluster of delusions and hallucinations; (f) the co-occurrence of positive, negative, and depressive components may account for the paranoid, disorganized, and catatonic subtypes that are traditionally recognized; (g) the transversal relationships in this model suggest polarized phenomenological axes that may have relevance for prognosis and other aspects of the schizophrenic disorder; (h) from the psychometric standpoint, these data support the use of the PANSS for measuirng negative symptoms independently of positive and depressive symptoms, thus addressing basic concerns about the construct validity of negative syndrome assessment (e.g., Carpenter, Heinrichs, & Alphs, 1985; Sommers, 1985; Zubin, 1985).

Of course, it is necessary to establish that the present findings are upheld in other samples and particularly under drug-free conditions, i.e., without possible contamination from extrapyramidal symptoms. It should be recalled, however, that in our drug-free double-blind study of 62 schizophrenic inpatients (Kay & Singh, 1989; see Chapter 10), we found as well that postivie and negative syndromes were statistically unrelated. In addition, both syndromes proved to be stable between the drug-free placebo baseline and three to four months of subsequent neuroleptic treatment with chlorpromazine or haloperidol.

In terms of cross-validation on a different sample, this has recently been completed by Lepine, Piron, and Chapotot (1989) in Paris. Independently and blind to our findings, they had also conducted a principal component analysis on PANSS data from 101 French patients with a DSM-III-R diagnosis of schizophrenia (American Psychiatric Association, 1987). Their study revealed eight factors before rotation that had eigenvalues > 1. After orthogonal varimax rotation they arrived at four clearly defined factors that, despite any crosscultural differences in sampling, bore a striking resemblance to our findings: negative symptoms, hostility/excitement, anxiety/depression, and paranoid symptoms. It should be noted that what Lepine and colleagues described as "paranoid" symptoms comprised essentially the same items that we have referred to as "positive": delusions, grandiosity, and hallucinations. Indeed, their four factors corresponded precisely to those discerned in our American study, except that the positive/paranoid syndrome emerged as Component 2 in our sample but as Component 4 in theirs. The amount of variance explained by these four factors also was strikingly similar in the two studies: 52.3 percent in our sample as compared to 52.8 percent in the French sample.

Interestingly, Lepine has thus far examined a much larger French population on the PANSS, involving a total of 700 patients of different psychotic diagnoses (personal communication, Oct. 1989). His broadened database indicates that the same four factors seemed to emerge, suggesting that there are perhaps universal crossdiagnostic components.

Future extensions of this line of research are to be directed at identifying the biological and historical covariates of the syndromes in this model of schizophrenia. Especially important is the question of whether these distinct components can be accounted for by differences on genetic, premorbid, catamnestic, psychopharmacological, and neurobiological variables. For example, we may wish to compare the syndrome profiles of familial vs. nonfamilial schizophrenic patients to learn more about genetic influences. This can be undertaken by inspecting the syndrome scores, as given by the PANSS components, in relation to such distinctions. As we have noted, statistically these components bear a direct linear relationship to the original variables and serve to summarize their contribution without any loss of information (Harris, 1975). Using Table 12:2 as a guide, a patient's component scores can be calculated as follows: (a) convert the raw score of PANSS items into standard (z) scores by subtracting the normative mean from the rated score and then dividing by the standard deviation; (b) multiply each standard score by its respective item component loading; and (c) average across the set of items that comprise each component.

Based on the factor analytic study as well as the other evidence described in this volume, there is ample reason to think that the negative, positive, excited, and depressive syndromes might involve different pathogenetic mechanisms. In the next chapter we shall expound a new theoretical proposal for explaining the origins and nature of the negative and positive syndromes, their pathophysiology, and the basis for their co-occurrence in schizophrenia. This model, which incorporates observations from our studies and numerous other sources, departs from the positions of Crow (1980a, 1980b), Andreasen (1985), MacKay (1980), and others in proposing specific etiological agents and integrating positive and negative symptoms into a single explanatory mechanism.

Aside from the theoretical ramifications, the present data confirm the multiplicity of symptom components in schizophrenia. Clearly, not all facets of the disorder are addressed by the classical neuroleptics, as evidenced by their partial efficacy as well as their selective efficacy. What seem to be needed are medications that are tailored to the particular symptom profile of the individual patient. Through the PANSS we now have an instrument for quantifying the intermix of schizophrenic symptoms in each given case. Our ultimate goal is to apply the pyramidical model toward refining the treatment of this vexing disorder. We hope that our findings help to clarify its heterogeneity and, in this way, also help to illuminate the path toward a new generation of syndrome-specific treatments.

13

Interpretation of the Positive-Negative Distinction

WITH REUVEN SANDYK, M.D., M.SC.*

Up to this point, our exposition has emphasized the nature of positive and negative syndromes, their validity as distinct processes in schizophrenia, and their significance premorbidly, symptomatically, prognostically, and psychopharmacologically. In the present chapter we plan an excursion beyond our data proper into the realm of interpretation. We shall attempt a conceptual synthesis of studies in the field, including our own, and thereupon propose to explain the pathophysiological basis of positive and negative syndromes. From this we will conclude with an integrated hypothesis of the pathophysiology of schizophrenia.

It is indeed striking that, despite the evidence that positive and negative symptom classes reflect different dimensions of the disease, there is at present no integrated model for understanding the pathophysiology of these symptoms and their co-occurrence in schizophrenia. In this chapter we shall advance the position that negative phenomena of schizophrenia may be a variant of parkinsonism. It will be seen that this view is supported by the overlap with Parkinson's disease in terms of clinical features, neurochemistry, and pharmacology, as well as neuroradiological and neuropatho-

*Research Fellow in Biological Psychiatry & Pharmacology, Department of Psychiatry, Albert Einstein College of Medicine/Montefiore Medical Center, Bronx, New York

Visiting Professor of Neurology, Department of Nutritional Sciences, Rutgers University, Cook College, New Brunswick, NJ

logical aspects. As such, negative symptoms may be a manifestation of disease of the basal ganglia and constitute the core pathology of schizophrenia. Positive symptoms, conversely, may reflect an "accessary" process related to a compensatory increase in dopaminergic and possibly noradrenergic activity following an injury to the striatal and mesolimbic/mesocortical dopaminergic neurons and brainstem noradrenergic systems, respectively. Finally, the significance of this hypothesis with respect to the pathophysiology and management of schizophrenia will be discussed.

POSITIVE-NEGATIVE MODELS

Hughlings Jackson (1887), in describing neurological conditions, had originally proposed that negative symptoms result directly from damage to brain areas that are responsible for production of human behavior. He regarded positive symptoms as a release phenomenon exercised by the damaged brain. Although Bleuler (1908) never used the term "negative symptoms," he perceived them as the fundamental deficiency of schizophrenia, while positive symptoms such as delusions and hallucinations played a variable "accessory" role in the illness.

Crow (1980a) presented the hypothesis that these symptom classes reflect two etiologically and prognostically distinct schizophrenic processes, in which negative symptoms are associated with gross structural abnormality (i.e., cerebral atrophy) and positive symptoms with biochemical dysregulation involving dopaminergic overactivity. In this much cited model, the two syndromes are independent and may occur separately or simultaneously. It will be recalled (Chapter 2) that Andreasen (1982) popularized Crow's model as a typological one, referring to positive and negative "subtypes," although her own data indicated that a majority of schizophrenic patients have mixed syndromes.

Subsequent research by our group has found that these phenomena represent orthogonal components (Kay & Sevy, in press), coexist in the majority of schizophrenic patients (Kay, Fiszbein, & Opler, 1987), and are uncorrelated in the drug-free state (Kay & Singh, 1989). For purpose of the present discussion, therefore, the term "negative schizophrenia" is applied as a dimensional rather than typological construct, i.e., as a condition characterized by a predominance of negative symptoms.

In a direct exchange with Crow (1980b), MacKay (1980) presented a divergent hypothesis that has never attained comparable recognition. He proposed that negative symptoms may reflect chronic dopaminergic underactivity, while positive symptoms emerge when there is a burst of dopaminergic overactivity. According to MacKay (1980), the negative symptoms in schizophrenia are chronically present and form the background on which positive symptoms are periodically acutely superimposed. Neither Crow nor MacKay, however, could explain why these two types of symptoms occur together in schizophrenia.

In terms of symptom presentation, flat affect, reduced quantity of speech, emotional withdrawal, motor reduction, and cognitive deficit have been considered the key elements of the negative syndrome by most investigators. We have seen that patients with this clinical profile are more likely to have been born in winter (Opler et al., 1984), to have had poor premorbid cognitive and social adjustment (Opler et al., 1984; Pogue-Geile & Harrow, 1984, 1985), to respond inadequately to neuroleptics (Breier et al., 1987; Meltzer, Sommers, & Luchins, 1986; Johnstone et al., 1987), to have family members with history of schizophrenia (Kay, Opler, & Fiszbein, 1986), and to show morphological brain abnormalities (Andreasen et al., 1982; Weinberger et al., 1980). In contrast, positive symptoms are characterized phenomenologically by delusions and hallucinations and also by a more favorable response to neuroleptics and absence of gross structural brain abnormalities on CT scan (Andreasen, 1985).

SIMILARITY OF NEGATIVE SYNDROME AND PARKINSONISM

The characteristic symptoms of negative schizophrenia, such as blunted affect, poverty of speech, emotional withdrawal, motor reduction, and cognitive deficits (Crow, 1980a, 1985; Andreasen, 1985), are also hallmarks of Parkinson's disease (Lidsky, Weinhold, & Levine, 1979; Pirozzolo, Hansch, & Mortimer, 1982; Alpert & Rush, 1983; Rogers, Lees, Trimble, & Stern, 1986; Growdon & Corkin, 1986). In particular, akinesia is one of the features of parkinsonism most likely to be confounded with negative schizophrenia (Hoehn, Crowley, & Rutledge, 1976; Sommers, 1985; Sandyk & Kay, in press-a, in press-d). Hoehn et al. (1976) found in 37 untreated Parkinsonian patients a high correlation between MMPI-8 scores (which are indicative of schizophrenic-like looseness of thinking) and akinesia. This correlation was the highest between any psychological and any neurological or biochemical variables in these patients. In addition, we found a significant association between features of negative syndrome in schizophrenia and positive glabellar tap reflex, which reflects decreased striatal dopaminergic activity (Sandyk & Kay, in press-d; see Chapter 9).

Narrowly defined, akinesia represents a motor anomaly characterized by slowness of movement, poor arm swing, and rigid posture (Chien, DiMascio, & Cole, 1974). More broadly viewed, akinesia overlaps with negative symptoms along dimensions other than pure motor behavior (Rifkin, 1981; Rifkin, Quitkin, & Klein, 1975; Van Putten & May, 1978; Van Putten, May, &

Wilkins, 1980); it includes lack of emotional reactivity, lack of goal-directedness, retarded spontaneous speech, sluggishness, decreased sociability, and decreased physical movements. In addition, the classic "mask-like facies" of parkinsonism cannot be distinguished from the absence of facial expression in blunted affect that is attributed to the negative syndrome (see Sommers, 1985). Thus, negative schizophrenia and parkinsonism apparently share common clinical features that cannot be easily distinguished from each other.

Carpenter et al. (1985) cautioned that, in assessing negative phenomena, one must be careful to avoid confound from parkinsonian symptoms. Indeed, studies by our group (Kay, Opler, & Fiszbein, 1986) have indicated a significant direct correlation between negative syndrome on the Positive and Negative Syndrome Scale (PANSS) and scores on the 'Extrapyramidal Symptoms Scale,' even though the PANSS negative scale excludes motor items (Kay, Fiszbein, & Opler, 1987).

We propose that this overlap between symptoms of negative schizophrenia and parkinsonism is not merely coincidence, confound, or rater misjudgment. We suggest the possibility that negative schizophrenia may, in fact, constitute a variant form of parkinsonism and, therefore, may reflect a primary disorder of the basal ganglia. As we shall discuss, this hypothesis is supported by a network of neurochemical, pharmacological, neuroradiological, and neuropathological data. We furthermore contend that positive symptoms, which are generally believed to issue from increased dopaminergic functions, are the result of compensatory mechanisms to overcome the primary dopaminergic deficiency. In addition, we postulate that positive symptoms may reflect compensatory mechanisms of brainstem noradrenergic mechanisms. Our hypothesis suggests that the two prominent symptom clusters in schizophrenia are interrelated and attributable to a single neurostructural impairment, which is also responsible for the parkinsonian symptoms that frequently emerge with neuroleptic treatment.

Table 13:1 summarizes the range of similarities between negative schizophrenia and parkinsonism. In the following sections we review the evidence that they constitute a single pathophysiological entity. We will attempt to show that this hypothesis provides novel implications toward future research and treatment strategies for negative schizophrenia.

THE CO-OCCURRENCE OF SCHIZOPHRENIA AND PARKINSONISM

The presence of psychotic features in conjunction with parkinsonism has been cited extensively in the past (Jackson, Free, & Pike, 1923; Jelliffe, 1927; Fairweather, 1947; Hollister & Glazener, 1961). More than 60 years

TABLE 13:1
Comparison of Negative Schizophrenia and Parkinsonism

Areas of Study	*Features in Common*
Symptoms	Decreased motor activity
	Blunted affect
	Impoverished speech
	Social withdrawal
	Anhedonia
	Emotional withdrawal
	Cognitive dysfunction
	Extrapyramidal symptoms
	Frontal lobe symptoms
Epidemiology	Predominant in male gender
Neurochemistry	
(1) Neurotransmitters	Decreased dopamine functions
	Increased cholinergic functions
	Decreased serotonergic functions
	Decreased norepinephrine functions
(2) Neuroendocrinology	Glucose intolerance
	Melatonin secretion
	DST-nonsuppression
(3) Neuropeptides	Decreased CCK
Pharmacology	
	Response to L-dopa
	Response to amphetamines
	Response to anticholinergics
	Response to atypical neuroleptics
	Lesser response to neuroleptics
Neuroradiology	
(1) CT scan	Cortical atrophy
	Enlarged lateral ventricles
	Pineal gland calcification
(2) Blood flow and PET studies	Hypofrontality
Pathology	Periventricular, diencephalic gliosis
	Basal ganglia degeneration
	Lewy body formation
	Neurobrillary tangles
Differences	*Distinguishing Features of Parkinsonism*
	Later age of onset
	Predominance of motor symptoms
	Relative lack of positive symptoms
	Relatively intact premorbid adjustment

ago McCowan and Cook (1928) described the mental status in some cases of parkinsonism as "extremely difficult to distinguish from ordinary cases of paraphrenia." Psychotic symptoms are particularly notable in postencephalitic parkinsonism; during the acute illness, some of these patients develop catatonic psychotic states, hallucinations, akinetic mutism, obsessional behavior, and Korsakoff's psychosis (Benedek, 1925).

In 1971, Misra and Hay published the case reports of three patients who developed symptoms of acute schizophrenia in the context of an encephalitic process. One patient developed post-encephalitic parkinsonism and a second remained in a chronic schizophrenic state. Crow et al. (1976) observed four cases in which an illness with schizophrenic features developed in conjunction with long-standing parkinsonism. Based on these observations, they concluded that the "dopaminergic overactivity hypothesis of schizophrenia faces the difficulty that parkinsonism and schizophrenia-like illness can coexist as post-encephalitic sequelae" (p. 232).

Friedman et al. (1987) reported a patient with schizophrenia who later during the course of the illness developed what appeared to be a form of idiopathic parkinsonism. More recently, Friedman and Lannon (1989) described five patients with parkinsonism who, during the course of the disease, suffered a severe psychotic illness that responded to clozapine. Attenuation of psychotic symptoms with clozapine is, in fact, associated with improvement in parkinsonism (Friedman & Lannon, 1989), underscoring the possibility that both conditions are interrelated. Indeed, Mettler suggested a basal ganglionic dysfunction in schizophrenia on grounds of: (a) a high incidence of parkinsonian symptoms among schizophrenic patients (Mettler, 1955), and (b) a high incidence of "schizoid states" in Parkinson's disease patients (Mettler & Crandell, 1959). Bowman and Lewis (1980) furthermore observed a high prevalence of schizophrenic features in diseases of the basal ganglia.

Several studies have suggested more specifically that the negative syndrome of schizophrenia is associated with an increased risk of parkinsonism. Epidemiologically, both negative schizophrenia (Kay, Opler, & Fiszbein, 1986; Todd, 1989) and Parkinson's disease (De Jong, 1966) are associated with predominant male gender, which may represent a genetic or consitutional marker of vulnerability. Neuroradiologically, schizophrenic patients with increased lateral ventricular size, which Andreasen et al. (1982) described as a marker of the negative syndrome, have been reported to be at high risk for developing neuroleptic-induced parkinsonism (Luchins, Jackman, & Meltzer, 1983). More recently, Hoffman et al. (1987) found that the severity of drug-induced parkinsonism covaries significantly with a larger ventricular brain ratio (VBR). In addition, negative symptoms of schizophrenia and a pattern of cognitive dysfunction common in idiopathic parkinsonism were also significantly associated with drug-induced parkinsonism (Hoffman et al., 1987). These findings suggest that cerebral atrophy and abnormalities in dopaminergic functions may underlie the increased risk for drug-induced parkinsonism as well as the behavioral and cognitive abnormalities of negative schizophrenia.

FRONTAL LOBE DEFICITS

There is considerable evidence that negative schizophrenia is associated with frontal lobe dysfunction (Seidman, 1983; Goldberg, 1985; Goldberg et al., 1987; Merriam et al., in press). Personality alterations similar to negative schizophrenia frequently accompany frontal lobe disease (Teuber, 1964; Luria, 1966; Blumer & Benson, 1975). Among these are blunted affect, apathy, impaired social judgment, and psychomotor abnormalities (Blumer & Benson, 1975; Flint & Eastwood, 1988). In schizophrenia, blunted affect has been shown to correlate with impairment on motor tasks that depend on frontal lobe integrity (Cox & Ludwig, 1979). Neuropsychological studies have revealed pronounced cognitive deficits in negative schizophrenia which are consistent with frontal lobe damage (Kolb & Whishaw, 1983; Goldberg et al., 1987). Specifically, the patients score poorly on the Wisconsin Card Sorting Test, which suggests a prefrontal-type cognitive deficit (Goldberg et al., 1987), and they show neurological soft signs associated specifically with the frontal region (Merriam et al., in press).

Parkinson's disease also is associated with various personality changes and cognitive deficits that are observed after frontal lobe lesions (Javoy-Agid & Agid, 1980; Agid et al., 1986). These abnormalities may be related in part to lesions in the basal ganglia (Rafal et al., 1984) and the mesocortical dopaminergic system (Javoy-Agid & Agid, 1980), or to damage of diencephalic neurons which project to the prefrontal cortex (Agid et al., 1986). Similarly to negative schizophrenia, metabolic studies have indicated hypofrontality in patients with Parkinson syndromes (Bes, Guell, & Fabre, 1983; D'Antona et al., 1985). In addition, parkinsonian patients showed deficits on the Wisconsin Card Sorting Test (Taylor, Saint-Cyr, & Lang, 1986), which is characteristic of prefrontal cortical damage (Goldberg et al., 1987).

NEUROCHEMICAL STUDIES

(1) The Dopaminergic System and Negative Schizophrenia

There is substantial evidence that negative schizophrenia, like parkinsonism, is related to decreased dopaminergic functions and, thus, is responsive to dopamine agonists:

(a) Prolonged administration of alpha-methyl-p-tyrosine in primates, a drug that inhibits tyrosine hydroxylase and thus limits catecholamine synthesis, has been shown to produce a syndrome characterized by decreased social interactions and initiative, reduced social expression, and retarded motor activity. Some of these symptoms appeared to be partially reversed with L-dopa treatment (Redmond et al., 1971).

(b) Administration of L-dopa (Gerlach & Luhdorf, 1985; Alpert & Rush, 1983; Friedhoff, 1983) and amphetamines (Angrist, Rotrosen, & Gershon, 1980) has been reported to improve blunted affect, emotional withdrawal, and apathy in patients with prominent negative symptoms.

(c) Encephalitis lethargica, a presumed viral illness with a propensity to affect the dopaminergic neurons, is associated with emotional deterioration and "psychic torpor" similar to that identified with negative symptoms (Economo, 1931).

(d) Neuroleptic drugs, which block dopaminergic receptors, frequently produce affective flattening, anhedonia, loss of initiative, and apathy (Andreasen, 1985). These effects are attributed to the specific properties of neuroleptic drugs and not to their nonspecific sedative effects (Wise, 1982).

(e) Homovanillic acid (HVA) accumulation in the cerebrospinal fluid (CSF), serving as an indicator of dopamine turnover, has been reported to be decreased particularly in schizophrenics characterized by retarded depression, emotional blunting, and poor premorbid social adjustment (van Praag & Korf, 1971; Bowers, 1974). Van Praag and Korf (1971) reported that patients with low HVA accumulation following administration of probenecid were more likely to develop extrapyramidal side effects regardless of the dose of neuroleptic used. More recently, van Kammen et al. (1986) found that schizophrenic patients with CSF dopamine utilization below the mean had more severe negative symptoms.

(f) Apomorphine-induced growth hormone response in schizophrenic patients significantly correlates with negative symptom scores on the Schedule for Affective Disorders and Schizophrenia-Change Version (SADS-C), suggesting that these patients may have decreased dopaminergic activity (Carpenter, Heinrichs, & Alphs, 1985).

(g) Facial seborrhea, which is associated with decreased hypothalamic dopaminergic activity, has been found to covary significantly with parkinsonian motor disability and the two major features of negative schizophrenia described by Crow (1985), namely blunted affect and poverty of speech (Sandyk & Kay, in press-e).

(h) Patients with enlarged lateral ventricles on CT scan have decreased CSF HVA levels (van Kammen et al., 1986; Lindstrom, 1985) and are more likely to develop parkinsonism (van Praag & Korf, 1971; Chase, 1974).

(2) The Cholinergic System and Negative Schizophrenia

Several lines of evidence suggest that negative schizophrenia, like parkinsonism, is associated with cholinergic hyperactivity (see for review, Tandon & Greden, 1989). Pharmacological evidence includes:

(a) Administration of cholinomimetics to normal controls produces a syndrome characterized by psychomotor retardation, anergy, malaise, lethargy, and slowed thoughts (Bowers, Goodman, & Sim, 1964; Davis et al., 1976), a behavioral profile resembling that of negative schizophrenia.

(b) Anticholinergics have been reported to produce substantial improvement in negative symptoms, particularly in the areas of affective blunting, anhedonia-asociality, and avolition-apathy (Tandon, Greden, & Silk, 1988; Tandon & Greden, 1987; Fayen et al., 1988). Comparable improvements are not found for the positive symptoms of schizophrenia, which instead are exacerbated by anticholinergic drugs (Johnstone et al., 1983; Singh, Kay, & Opler, 1987).

(c) Atypical neuroleptics such as clozapine (Honigfeld, Patin, & Singer, 1984) and zotepine (Fleischhacker et al., 1987), which are reported to be more effective in negative schizophrenia, possess high anticholinergic activity; this might account for their efficacy with negative symptoms (Tandon & Greden, 1989).

(d) Cholinergic drugs have consistently been found to decrease drive-reduction behavior (Domino & Olds, 1968), which may be related to the prominent negative symptoms of anergy, apathy, and avolition.

(3) The Noradrenergic System and Negative Schizophrenia

Deficit symptoms such as those observed in negative schizophrenia may be produced by reduction in the noradrenergic reward system (see Carpenter, Heinrichs, & Alphs, 1985). In rats, 6-hydroxydopamine lesions of the noradrenergic reward system result in symptoms reminiscent of the negative phenomena of schizophrenia (Stein & Wise, 1971). It has been suggested (Carpenter, Heinrichs, & Alphs, 1985), therefore, that loss of the structural integrity of the noradrenergic reward system may be causally related to symptoms of negative schizophrenia. Van Kammen et al. (1983) found low CSF dopamine-beta hydroxylase (DBH) activity in a subgroup of schizophrenic patients with cerebral atrophy. Wise and Stein (1973) noted a decrease in central DBH activity in whole brainstem of schizophrenics who had presented predominant deficit symptoms. Markianos and Tripodianakis (1985) reported low plasma DBH in demented schizophrenics. Rosen et al. (1985) found that lower levels of platelet ^{3}H-clonidine binding sites were associated with more negative symptoms and lesser response to neuroleptics in drug-free schizophrenics. Decreased cerebral noradrenergic function has also been demonstrated in patients with parkinsonism (van Dongen, 1981; Hurst et al., 1985; Jellinger, 1986b; Cash et al., 1987; Sandyk & Iacono, in press). Specifically, degeneration of noradrenergic neurons in the locus coeruleus has been associated with the akinesia and decreased cognitive functions in these patients (Narabayashi et al., 1984; Cash et al., 1987).

(4) The Serotonergic System and Negative Schizophrenia

Several investigators found decreased CSF serotonin (5-HT) metabolites in schizophrenic patients (Ashcroft et al., 1966; Potkin et al., 1983). The latter group noted that the decrease in CSF 5-hydroxyindoleacetic-acid (5-HIAA) was present only in patients with enlarged ventricles. These findings suggest that decreased 5-HT metabolism may be more closely related to negative schizophrenia. It is noteworthy that both clozapine and risperidone, which have 5-HT antagonistic properties, significantly reduce negative symptoms without worsening parkinsonism (Kane et al., 1988; Peuskins et al., 1989). Decreased brain and CSF 5-HT levels have been found also in patients with Parkinson's disease, specifically in depressed parkinsonian patients (Jellinger, 1986a; Sandyk & Fisher, 1988).

Neuropeptides

Several peptidergic abnormalities have been implicated in schizophrenia (Meltzer, 1987). Decreased brain cholecystokinin (CCK) levels have been found both in patients with negative schizophrenia (Ferrier et al., 1983) and in those with Parkinson's disease (Studler et al., 1982).

NEUROENDOCRINE STUDIES

(1) Glucose Metabolism

In 1899 (p. 113) Sir Henry Maudsley in *The Pathology of the Mind* wrote that "Diabetes is a disease which often shows itself in families in which insanity prevails." High prevalence of impaired glucose tolerance has been indeed reported in patients with a variety of neuropsychiatric disorders as well as schizophrenia (Brambilla, Guastalla, & Guerrini, 1976; Wilkinson, 1981). Tonnard-Neuman (1968) found that 25 percent of his group of several hundred female schizophrenic patients developed hyperglycemia when treated with neuroleptics. In a quarter of the affected patients, hyperglycemia remitted following dose reduction or discontinuation of therapy. Other studies (Schwartz & Munoz, 1968) found that phenothiazines had little effect on patients' diabetic state.

A high prevalence of abnormal glucose tolerance has been observed also in patients with Parkinson's disease. Elner and Kandel (1965) reported an 83 percent incidence of abnormal glucose metabolism in 80 patients with Parkinson's disease, and Boyd et al. (1971) found 50 percent of parkinsonian patients to have abnormal intravenous glucose tolerance tests. Lipman et al. (1974) found a 52.4 percent incidence of abnormal glucose tolerance in parkinsonian patients and speculated that "hypothalamic involvement might be logically suspected as explaining the abnormal glucose metabolism in these cases" (p. 577). Indeed, a number of investigators have noted changes in the hypothalamus in Parkinson's disease (Lewy, 1923; den Hartog & Bethlem, 1960; Langston & Forno, 1978). Similarly, pathological lesions in the hypothalamus have been detected also in schizophrenic patients (Morgan & Gregory, 1935; Stevens, 1982; Nieto & Escobar, 1972), an observation which may account for the high incidence of diabetes mellitus in these patients.

A particularly high prevalence of diabetes mellitus has been reported recently in schizophrenic patients with drug-induced parkinsonism (Sandyk & Kay, in press-b; Sandyk, Kay, & Iacono, in press). In a group of 44 consecutive patients with abnormal involuntary movements who were referred to a movement disorders clinic, we identified 16 (36.4 percent) who had drug-induced parkinsonism together with diabetes mellitus. These patients were distinguished as having an almost pure parkinsonian syndrome, lower ratings of tardive dyskinesia (TD), and a far higher rate of dementia. They had also significantly more severe global parkinsonism as compared to nondiabetic patients. Since parkinsonism is a covariate of negative schizophrenia (Luchins, Jackman, & Meltzer, 1983; Hoffman, Labs, & Casey, 1987; Sandyk & Kay, in press-a, in press-d), the risk of diabetes mellitus may be a facet of an underlying Parkinson's disease.

(2) Pineal Melatonin Functions

Pathological changes in the form of gliosis have been detected in the pineal gland of schizophrenic patients (Nieto & Nieto, 1988). In addition, several studies have found decreased melatonin secretion in schizophrenic patients (Ferrier et al., 1982; Fanget et al., 1989). We have elsewhere suggested that diminished melatonin secretion may be associated with the pathophysiology of a subgroup of schizophrenic patients characterized by cerebral atrophy and ventricular enlargement, negative symptoms, impaired cognitive and psychosexual development, onset at pubescence, poor response to neuroleptic medication, and an increased risk of extrapyramidal symptoms (Sandyk & Kay, in press-g). We found also a high prevalence of pineal gland calcification among schizophrenic patients with drug-induced parkinsonism (Sandyk & Kay, in press-f).

The role of the pineal gland in parkinsonism is poorly understood, but there is indirect evidence that decreased melatonin secretion is associated also with the pathophysiology of Parkinson's disease (Sandyk, in press). Indeed, we found that pineal gland calcification was associated with drug-induced parkinsonism in neuroleptic-treated schizophrenic patients (Sandyk & Kay, in press-f), an observation which underscores the association of abnormal pineal functions in both negative schizophrenia and parkinsonism.

(3) Dexamethasone Suppression

Numerous studies have reported that a high proportion of schizophrenic patients are dexamethasone nonsuppressors (e.g., Saffer, Metcalfe, & Coopen, 1985; Tandon et al., 1989). Dexamethasone non-suppression is generally attributed to hypothalamic-pituitary adrenal (HPA) axis hyperactivity (Rose & Sachar, 1981) and is reportedly associated with negative schizophrenia (Saffer, Metcalfe, & Coopen, 1985; Tandon et al., 1989). Dexamethasone non-suppression has been observed also in patients with Parkinson's disease (Pfeiffer et al., 1986; Kawamura et al., 1987); one study found non-suppression related to parkinsonian akinesia and freezing (Kawamura et al., 1987), thus underscoring the similarity of parkinsonism with negative schizophrenia.

PHARMACOLOGICAL STUDIES

Based on evidence that negative schizophrenia is associated with reduced dopaminergic and increased cholinergic activity, several investigators have initiated therapeutic trials with dopaminergic and anticholinergic drugs in negative schizophrenia. Dopaminergic agonists such as amphetamine and L-dopa, which alleviate symptoms of parkinsonism, have been reported to improve some negative features of schizophrenia (Angrist, Rotrosen, & Gershon, 1980; Alpert & Rush, 1983; Friedhoff, 1983; Desai et al., 1984; Kay & Opler, 1985). Angrist et al. (1980) observed that neuroleptic-free patients with predominant negative symptomatology who were treated with a single dose of d-amphetamine (0.5mg/Kg) showed significant reduction of negative symptoms three hours after its administration. This effect was not obtained in schizophrenic patients with predominant positive symptoms. Similarly, prolonged treatment with L-dopa has been reported to be effective in improving blunted affect, emotional withdrawal, and apathy in patients with prominent negative symptoms (Alpert & Rush, 1983; Friedhoff, 1983) and in ameliorating the negative but not the positive syndrome scale of the PANSS (Kay & Opler, 1985). Desai et al. (1984) reported two patients in whom oral d-amphetamine produced long-term improvement of negative symptoms (alogia, affective flattening, anhedonia).

An open pilot study on the effects of the anticholinergic antiparkinsonian drug, trihexyphenidyl, on negative symptoms demonstrated substantial improvement in the areas of affective flattening, anhedonia-asociality, and avolition-apathy in four out of five patients (Tandon, Greden, & Silk, 1988; Tandon & Greden, 1987). Another study reported a similar improvement of negative symptoms with trihexyphenidyl in comparison with amantadine when these agents were employed to treat neuroleptic-induced extrapyramidal side-effects (Fayen et al., 1988). Conversely, independent studies by Johnstone et al. (1983) and Singh, Kay, & Opler (1987) found that anticholinergics compounds significantly exacerbate the positive spectrum of psychopathology in schizophrenia. This may be related in part to the anticholinergic effects of neuroleptics, as cholinergic underactivity has been hypothesized to be associated with positive symptoms (Tandon & Greden, 1989).

These preliminary observations support the dopaminergic deficiency-cholinergic excess model of negative schizophrenia (Tandon & Greden, 1989). A similar model has been suggested for parkinsonism, for which both dopaminergic and anticholinergic agents are presently the most efficacious drugs in its management.

Recently, Friedman et al. (1987) and Friedman and Lannon (1989) described six patients with coexisting schizophrenia and Parkinson's disease for whom parkinsonism was successfully treated with levodopa and the schizophrenic disorder with clozapine. It is noteworthy that clozapine, which unlike most classical neuroleptics does not promote the emergence of parkinsonism, has been described as an efficacious antipsychotic drug for negative schizophrenia (Honigfeld, Patin, & Singer, 1984). Likewise, risperidone, which similarly does not induce such effects, significantly diminishes the negative syndrome (Peuskins et al., 1989). These psychopharmacological findings underscore the parallel between negative schizophrenia and parkinsonism.

RADIOLOGICAL STUDIES

Computed tomographic (CT) scan studies of the brains of schizophrenic patients with negative schizophrenia have demonstrated ventricular enlargement, third ventricular dilatation, cortical and cerebellar atrophy, and atypical asymmetry between the cerebral hemispheres (Weinberger & Wyatt, 1980; Andreasen et al., 1982; Maser & Keith, 1983; Nasrallah et al., 1983; Dewan et al., 1983; Houston et al., 1986). The most consistent abnormality included enlargement of the lateral ventricles associated with an increased ventricular brain ratio (VBR) (Andreasen et al., 1982; Weinberger, Torrey, & Neophytides, 1979; Weinberger & Wyatt, 1980). These abnormalities are in accord with the concept that negative schizophrenia is associated with organic brain damage (Crow, 1980) and with the neuropathological findings reported by Stevens (1982), which demonstrated neuronal damage in diencephalic, periventricular, and mesencephalic periaqueductal regions. Enlarged lateral ventricles have been reported also in patients with drug-induced parkinsonism (Luchins, Jackman, & Meltzer, 1983; Hoffman, Labs, & Casey, 1987; Sandyk & Kay, in press-a), and it has been suggested that ventricular dilatation may be a risk factor associated with increased susceptibility for the development of drug-induced parkinsonism. Hoffman et al. (1987) found a significant association between increased VBR, parkinsonism, and negative schizophrenia. Our own analysis (Sandyk & Kay, in press-a) revealed a significant association between VBR and the severity of bradykinesia in patients with drug-induced parkinsonism.

Neuroradiological changes similar to those observed in negative schizophrenia have been found also in patients with Parkinson's disease (Selby, 1968; Steiner, Gomori, & Melamed, 1985; Sroka et al., 1981; Gath, Jorgensen, & Sjaastad, 1975). Indeed, it has been considered that cerebral atrophy is an essential feature of Parkinson's disease (Selby, 1968). Selby (1968) found a 57 percent incidence of cortical (sulcal) atrophy and 30 percent ventricular enlargement in 250 parkinsonian patients, and he noted a "greater incidence of ventricular dilatation in the parkinsonian patients with an impaired mental state."

Gath et al. (1975) found cortical atrophy in 47 percent and ventricular dilatation in 78 percent of their parkinsonian patients, the latter feature being the dominant abnormality in their series, in contrast to that of Selby. Neither study showed any significant correlation between duration of the Parkinson's disease and either cortical and ventricular dilatation. Becker et al. (1976) found that 53.4 percent of 172 parkinsonian patients had ventricular dilatation, which was observed to occur earlier than cortical atrophy. Sroka et al. (1981) found abnormal CT scan in 65 percent of 93 parkinsonian patients. These included 40 percent generalized atrophy (ventricular and sulcal enlargement); 40 percent primary cortical atrophy; and 12 percent primary ventricular enlargement. Ventricular enlargement was more strongly correlated with organic mental disorder than cortical atrophy. Portin et al. (1984) found a significant correlation between parkinsonian mental disturbances and cerebral atrophy in 28 patients. Correlations between motor symptoms and cerebral atrophy were less pronounced. Since Parkinson's disease is associated also with pathological changes in extrastriatal structures (Greenfield & Bosanquet, 1953; Jellinger, 1986a, 1986b), these alterations probably lead to structural changes in the brain, as mediated in part through the various connections of the nigrostriatal system.

PATHOLOGICAL STUDIES

(1) Diencephalic Pathology

Since the turn of the century, there have been many attempts to find structural abnormalities in the brain of schizophrenic patients. In a landmark neuropathological study on 25 schizophrenic patients, Stevens (1982) reported a patchy, fibrillary gliosis that, in various degrees and distributions, affected principally the periventricular regions of the diencephalon and substantia innominata. There was neuronal loss or infarction in the globus pallidum in five patients. Nieto and Escobar (1972) also noted a widespread gliosis with a predilection for the periventricular and perivascular regions in the diencephalon and midbrain of schizophrenic patients studied at postmortem examination. These findings were confirmed by Fishman (1975), who similarly observed gliosis, especially in the midpons and medial reticular nuclei. Lesch and Bogerts (1984) found reduced thickness of the periventricular gray matter of 15 schizophrenic patients, four of whom had predominant negative symptoms. The finding of subependymal gliosis in the diencephalon and hypothalamus or of pallidal neurons dropout in these brains from schizophrenic patients is consistent with the evidence of moderate enlargement of the third and lateral ventricles, which may be characteristic of negative schizophrenia (Weinberger, Torrey, & Neophytides, 1979; Dewan et al., 1983; Houston et al., 1986).

(2) Basal Ganglia Pathology in Schizophrenia

Buscaino (1920) was the first to point out possible involvement of the basal ganglia in the genesis of schizophrenic symptoms; he stated that, particularly in typical catatonic patients, serious alterations, especially of the globus pallidus, could be found. Similar observations were reported in an extensive study by Hopf (1952). Recently, Stevens (1982) described neuronal loss within the pallida in four cases and pallidal gliosis in six of 28 qualitatively investigated schizophrenics. Bogerts et al. (1985) performed a morphometric study of the basal ganglia in 13 schizophrenic patients and found decreased volume of the internal pallidum. The latter was interpreted as degenerative shrinkage of unknown etiology.

The pathological lesions in chronic schizophrenia overlap with those found in post-encephalitic parkinsonism, with the exception that Lewy bodies are absent in patients with post-encephalitic parkinsonism (van Dongen, 1981; Howard & Lees, 1987). Lewy bodies are the hallmark of Parkinson's disease (Forno, 1986). The frequency and occurrence of Lewy bodies in the brain of "patients with psychosis or mental deficiency" is similar to that in a large sample of individuals "without predominance of psychiatric symptoms" (Woodard, 1962). Lewy bodies were found, however, to be much more frequent (28 percent) in cases of "mental disturbance without established morphological basis"; the clinical features found in these patients with Lewy bodies are paranoia, violence, confusion, affective disorder, and intellectual deterioration (Woodard, 1962). In the same study, interestingly, Woodard (1962) found a relatively high prevalence of Alzheimer's pathology, suggesting an interrelationship between schizophrenia and Alzheimer's disease. Coexisting Parkinson's and Alzheimer's pathology has been also observed in patients with idiopathic Parkinson's disease (Growdon & Corkin, 1986; Gibbs & Lees, 1989) and those with postencephalitic parkinsonism (van Dongen, 1981).

Gliosis, the most ubiquitous abnormality found in the brains of schizophrenic patients (Nieto & Escobar, 1972; Stevens, 1982), reflects a response to brain injury. The location of gliosis in these patients indicates injury in proximity to or involving principally the subependymal and subpial regions of the midbrain, diencephalon, and basal forebrain (Stevens, 1982). Although cerebral gliosis is merely indicative of past injury, several reports have suggested that the observed gliosis in schizophrenia may be secondary to infectious or immunologic disorder (Albrecht, Torrey, & Boone, 1980; Tyrrell et al., 1979). Fishman's (1975) findings of glial knots and perivascular infiltration in the brainstem of schizophrenic patients is consistent with past or present encephalitis.

It is noteworthy that the pathological lesions of postencephalitic parkinsonism are most severe in the brainstem and basal ganglia (Howard & Lees, 1987). These lesions include nonpurulent, nonhaemorrhagic perivascular infiltration and nerve cell necrosis limited to the gray matter, with preferential localization to the midbrain. Although the changes are most severe in the brainstem and basal ganglia, there is also involvement of the cerebral cortex and spinal cord. The neurofibrillary tangle in the substantia nigra is regarded as the hallmark of post-encephalitic parkinsonism (Forno, 1986). Typically the tangles are found in connection with severe diffuse nerve cell loss. Since postencephalitic parkinsonism may be associated with schizophrenic symptoms (Howard & Lees, 1987), Crow (1983) cited the presence of such symptoms in these patients as supportive evidence for the theory that schizophrenia could be due to a virus which is transmitted predominantly from schizophrenic patients to genetically predisposed individuals. Indeed, Alizan et al. (1980) found an increased frequency of HLA B14 (44 percent) in postencephalitic parkinsonism as compared with matched controls, which suggested to him a genetic susceptibility for this disorder.

In addition, increased levels of serum antibodies against herpes simplex virus (HSV) have been found in patients with Parkinson's disease, but their relationship to the pathogenesis of the disease remains unknown (see Marttila et al., 1984). Furthermore, Pouplard and Emile (1984) demonstrated in the sera of 62.7 percent of parkinsonian patients circulating antibodies reacting against sympathetic ganglion neurons, which suggests that autoimmune mechanisms may be involved in the pathogenesis of Parkinson's disease (Abramsky & Litvin, 1978). Thus, it is possible that the delayed appearance of parkinsonism following a seemingly full recovery from acute encephalitic illness may be due to a continuing virally mediated striato-nigral damage. A similar mechanism may conceivably operate in the pathogenesis of schizophrenia.

COMPENSATORY MECHANISMS AND POSITIVE SCHIZOPHRENIA

(1) Dopaminergic Mechanisms

While negative schizophrenia may thus relate to decreased dopaminergic functions, as per MacKay (1980), positive schizophrenia has alternatively been thought to reflect a neurochemical abnormality associated with increased dopaminergic functions (Crow, 1980a; MacKay, 1980; Andreasen, 1985). Yet it remains unclear how increased dopaminergic functions are linked to the positive symptoms and why these paradoxically occur together in patients with negative symptoms.

Studies derived from parkinsonian patients have suggested that the clinical symptoms of parkinsonism emerge following 80 percent loss of striatal dopamine neurons (Hornykiewicz & Kish, 1986). A phase of subclinical parkinsonism usually precedes the onset of the motor symptoms (Hornykiewicz & Kish, 1986). It has been shown that the preclinical phase of parkinsonism is associated with compensatory mechanisms of striatal dopamine neurons aimed at overcoming the progressive dopaminergic deficiency (Zigmond et al., 1984; Agid et al., 1986). Similarly, the increased dopaminergic activity which is associated with the positive symptoms of schizophrenia may reflect a compensatory increase in dopamine turnover in the mesolimbic pathways as a result of damage to dopaminergic neurons. The favorable response of positive symptoms to neuroleptics is consistent with this position. As such, this hypothesis may offer an integrated model of schizophrenia that explains, with a single underlying pathophysiological mechanism, the emergence of both positive and negative symptoms as well as their coexistence in the same patient.

(2) Norepinephrine Mechanisms

Positive symptoms may also be associated with compensatory mechanisms at the level of the noradrenergic locus coeruleus (LC). There is evidence that productive psychotic behavior is related to increased brain norepinephrine (NE) turnover. Amphetamine-induced psychosis (Mason, 1979) and L-dopa-induced psychosis in parkinsonian patients (Birkmayer et al., 1974) are associated with increased NE levels in several brain regions, and it has been suggested that the antipsychotic effects of neuroleptics may be related in part to their blockage of beta and alpha$_2$-adrenoreceptors (van Dongen, 1981). Elevated NE levels in the LC terminals have also been found in patients with paranoid schizophrenia (van Dongen, 1981). Increased NE turnover in schizophrenia may reflect a compensatory increase in LC activity subsequent to damage of the LC or its projections to other regions of the CNS. LC fibers regenerate after damage, in contrast to most other CNS regions. After damage, the intact part of the fiber shows sprouting and regrowth, and the regrown LC fibers contain and accumulate NE (van Dongen, 1981). The regrowth of LC fibers is age- and region-dependent. The various LC terminal regions have different critical periods of regrowth, with aging being a limiting factor. It has been shown that the original connections are often accurately restored, but occasionally hyperinnervation is found (Bjorklund & Lindvall, 1979). Similar compensatory mechanisms have been shown for the alpha$_2$-adrenoreceptors (U'Prichard et al., 1971).

Since the activity of NE LC neurons is linked to cognitive functions and level of arousal (van Dongen, 1981), reinnervation and hyperinnervation of the NE LC neurons may account also for the alterations in the level of arousal, attention, and information processing capacity observed in schizophrenic patients (Cornblatt et al., 1985; George & Neufeld, 1985). It is the hyperarousal in schizophrenia that is believed to underlie the florid symptoms such as hallucinations, delusions, and disorganized thinking (Kay, 1981; Kay & Singh, 1979), and its regulation may explain the therapeutic action of neuroleptics (Venables, 1966; Gruzelier & Hammond, 1978).

INTEGRATED MODEL OF SCHIZOPHRENIA

It appears, based on the above discussion, that negative schizophrenia is associated with decreased dopaminergic activity (MacKay, 1980) and increased cholinergic activity (Tandon & Greden, 1989). This neurochemical profile is also characteristic of the parkinsonian state, suggesting that we may be dealing with the same fundamental disease process. Indeed, we have seen that the clinical features of negative schizophrenia are found as well in parkinsonism. Also, the favorable response of negative symptoms to dopaminergic drugs and anticholinergic agents supports the hypothesis that negative schizophrenia may be a variant of parkinsonism.

Positive schizophrenia, on the other hand, may reflect a compensatory increase in dopaminergic activity as a result of damage to dopaminergic pathways. This view is consistent with the seminal model of Bleuler (1908), who regarded negative features as cardinal in schizophrenia and positive features as accessory symptoms. Similarly, the emergence of spontaneous or levodopa-induced psychotic symptoms in patients with parkinsonism may reflect increased dopaminergic activity either as a compensatory mechanism or drug-induced. Thus, the coexistence of negative and positive symptoms in the same patient may reflect different processes in the dopaminergic system.

Table 13:2 summarizes the key elements hypothesized in the pathophysiology of schizophrenia vs. Parkinson's disease. Our model postulates similarities in the origins, anatomical regions affected, and neurochemical disturbances. It is, of course, important to recognize that there are a few dif-

TABLE 13:2
Pathophysiological Model of Schizophrenia and Parkinsonism

Origins:	Genetic and/or constitutional vulnerability to viral infectious disease
Anatomical regions affected:	Basal ganglia, periventricular, and limbic systems
Neurochemical disturbances:	Low dopamine, low serotonin, increased dopaminergic and noradrenergic activity
Onset in adolescence (schizophrenia):	(1) Core negative symptoms (affective, social, cognitive, and motor deficits) (2) Compensatory mechanisms (increased dopamine functions and brain norepinephrine turnover) (3) Associated positive symptoms (hyperarousal, hallucinations, delusions, etc.)
Onset in late adulthood (Parkinson's disease):	(1) Core negative symptoms (with particular prominence of motor deficits) (2) Diminished capacity for compensatory adaptation (3) Paucity of associated positive symptoms

ferentiating features which are salient enough to mask the fundamental similarities outlined herein.

It will be recalled from Table 13:1 that a crucial difference between schizophrenia and Parkinson's disease is in the timing of the onset. Schizophrenia tends to be manifested symptomatically in mid- to late adolescence or early adulthood, whereas Parkinson's disease usually affects individuals in late adulthood. This very difference in the age of onset could explain the differences in the clinical presentation, namely the predominance of motor deficits and the relative lack of positive symptoms in patients with Parkinson's disease.

In cases of late onset of illness, we would expect lesser pathological impact on cognitive and social functions, which by now have been fully developed in the individual and are well established. In schizophrenia, by contrast, the maturational course is itself interfered with by the disease process, leading to premorbid social and cognitive dysfunctions that seem to antedate the negative schizophrenic syndrome (Pogue-Geile & Harrow, 1984, 1985; Kay, Opler, & Fiszbein, 1986) and, subsequently, to resist neuroleptic intervention (Kay & Singh, 1979).

Secondly, we may expect diminished capacity for compensatory adaptation in the aged organism. Accordingly, one would predict in Parkinson's disease a comparatively lesser increase in dopaminergic functions and norepinephrine turnover, and hence a paucity of associated positive symptoms that emerge.

Finally, in understanding the distinction between negative schizophrenia and Parkinson's disease, we stress that our proposal is not that they are the same condition, but rather that they are variants of the same disorder, sharing a common pathophysiological mechanism. Further studies on the comparison of the two illnesses in terms of genetic liability, premorbid history, and catamnestic course are clearly required.

The hypothesis that negative schizophrenia is a variant of Parkinson's disease carries several implications: (a) Pharmacologically, negative schizophrenia might be managed like parkinsonism, i.e., with dopaminergic and anticholinergic drugs rather than neuroleptics, which in fact may facilitate the progression of the disease. (b) L-deprenyl, an MAO-B inhibitor which has been shown to halt the progression of Parkinson's disease (Birkmayer et al., 1985; Tetrud & Langston, 1989), may be useful in negative schizophrenia. (c) Patients with both negative and positive features might be managed like psychotic parkinsonian patients, namely with levodopa combined with clozapine (Friedman & Lannon, 1989). (d) Adrenal medullary tissue transplantation, which has shown promising results in parkinsonism, may be a future promising therapy for drug-resistant negative schizophrenia.

14

Conclusions and Implications

In this volume we presented the rationale, strategies, and findings of our research on positive and negative syndromes of schizophrenia. Although there were multiple aims to our work, chief among them was the effort to better understand the heterogeneity of schizophrenia, and thereby to gain fresh insights into its etiology and treatment. Our strategy involved, first, the development and standardization of a strictly operationalized and standardized symptom rating scale, the PANSS. Thereafter we applied it in a series of multidimensional investigations that included typological, cross-sectional, prospective, longitudinal, phasic, drug-free, psychopharmacological, and factorial studies. Although the various results have been described separately throughout the book, we are now in a position to convey the overall picture. We shall therefore proceed to briefly sum up the primary conclusions and implications, literally from "a" to "z."

(a) Positive and negative syndromes can be reliably and validly measured. To attain these properties, however, the instrument of assessment needs to be devised according to the same principles and standards that are mandated generally for psychological test development (American Psychological Association, 1985).

(b) A useful method for evaluating positive and negative syndromes must be comprehensive both in its representation of the constituents of these syndromes (content validity) and in its inclusion of other facets of psychopathology that provide a basis for comparison (construct validity).

(c) Unless the same assessment method is uniformly applied in different studies, the results will not be comparable. This implies, first, that researchers should ideally adopt a single method or set of methods to study a given phenomenon. Second, for multicenter and international use, it is important that a standard training procedure for the particular method be made available and that the assessment method be translated and restandardized in other languages.

(d) Refinement in psychiatric diagnosis may in the future be achieved by

214

a two-tier system which, beyond the traditional nosology, seeks to identify dimensional profiles (van Praag et al., 1987). The development of the SCID-PANSS for psychotic disorders (Chapter 8) is a first step in this direction.

(e) There is ample evidence for the validity of the positive-negative distinction in schizophrenia. This appears to reflect on differences in pathogenesis, since the two syndromes correlate differentially with fundamental parameters, such as premorbid adjustment, cognitive development, information processing, neuropsychiatric profile, dopaminergic functions, family history of psychiatric disorder, drug response, and the subsequent course of illness.

(f) The positive-negative distinction seems to better fit a dimensional rather than typological model, since the typological assumptions of the discontinuity and co-exclusivity of these features are not supported. Positive and negative syndromes prove to be theoretically unrelated, and in fact a majority of schizophrenic patients show prominent symptoms of both kinds.

(g) An accurate reading of positive and negative phenomena requires that one control for general severity of psychopathology and neuroleptic status, either of which can mediate an intercorrelation between the syndromes.

(h) Despite prevailing opinion, and contrary to Crow's (1980a) hypothesis, the negative syndrome is consistently found to be unrelated to the progression of illness. Both negative and positive symptoms are equally pronounced in all phases of the active psychosis.

(i) The syndromes are quite stable over time after the first two years of illness, i.e., in the subacute and chronic stages. Although the absolute severity of the syndromes may change, especially with neuroleptic treatment, their relative prominence in one's psychiatric profile appears to be fairly constant.

(j) The meaning of the positive-negative distinction may be considered phase-specific, this in keeping with the evolving nature of the disease process. The characteristic impression of negative schizophrenia as a regressed condition with a guarded prognosis seems applicable only in the chronic condition.

(k) In chronic schizophrenia, the negative syndrome is uniquely associated with familial psychosis and an ominous cognitive disorder that is characterized by apparent developmental failure, prefrontal signs, and specific information processing deficits. From the standpoint of the contribution of nature vs. nurture, a *combination* of genetic and developmental liabilities is therefore implicated.

(l) In acute schizophrenia, however, a negative syndrome denotes a more benign family history and course of illness. A positive syndrome, alternatively, portends a worse long-range outcome in the subacute and chronic stages.

(m) Prognostically, positive symptoms predict poorer social adjustment, whereas negative symptoms predict poorer occupational functioning. Outcome prediction can be further enhanced, however, by combining the phenomenological predictors with other established prognosticators for schizophrenia, such as premorbid functioning and process vs. reactive onset of illness, which appear to be independent of the positive-negative distinction.

(n) In response to classical neuroleptics, both syndromes are significantly ameliorated, but the reduction in negative symptoms is marginally less. These findings suggest that neither group of symptoms is entirely irreversible and challenge Crow's (1980a, 1980b) premise that the negative syndrome reflects a structural brain deficit.

(o) The association of positive symptoms with hyperdopaminergia, as per Crow (1980a), seems to be sustained. These productive manifestations may have their roots in arousal dysregulation, which can ordinarily be brought under control by dopamine blocking agents.

(p) Newer treatment approaches that are directed at the negative syndrome carry promise. These include unconventional and atypical neuroleptics, non-neuroleptic compounds, and drugs that combine dopamine blocking action with serotonergic antagonism.

(q) Certain medications, such as L-dopa and pimozide, seem to target the negative syndrome; others, such as low-dose bromocriptine, enhance the response of positive symptoms, whereas anticholinergics seem to worsen the positive dimension. Some medications that are still in the experimental stages of development, such as risperidone, show promise for addressing both syndromes as well as depression.

(r) The stability, validity, and significance of positive and negative syndromes are confirmed in drug-free study of schizophrenia. Very high longitudinal reliability is seen off medication, and significant correlations from off- to on-drugs are found even three to four months after intervention with neuroleptics.

(s) Notwithstanding the validity and importance of positive and negative syndromes, a two-factor model is insufficient to accommodate the diverse phenomenology of schizophrenia. With principal component analysis as a base, we may recognize four major factors—negative, positive, excited, and depressive—which are statistically independent and not co-exclusive.

(t) The mathematical properties that describe the relatedness among these factors form the basis of a "pyramidical model" of syndromes in schizophrenia. The model suggests that the traditional subtyping as paranoid, disorganized (hebephrenic), and catatonic schizophrenia can be explained by the interaction of co-occurring syndromes, which constitute the more fundamental elements of psychopathology. The importance of these four factors and their interactions for understanding the pathogenesis of schizophrenia is to be explored in future research.

(u) The pyramidical model also reveals a bipolar prognostic axis in schizophrenia, consisting of depression (good prognosis) at one end vs. thought disorganization (poor prognosis) at the other. A specific association of thought disorganization with unfavorable outcome could account for our findings that a positive syndrome anticipates poorer long-term outcome.

(v) Although the positive-negative distinction shows factorial validity, thought disorganization emerged as a symptom that is not an intrinsic constituent of the positive component. Depression, as measured on the PANSS, was clearly differentiated from the negative component.

(w) In understanding the pathophysiological significance of the negative syndrome, we have hypothesized that it may constitute a variant of Parkinson's disease. This view is based on a striking overlap between negative schizophrenia and Parkinson's disease with respect to clinical features, epidemiology, neurochemistry, pharmacology, neuroradiology, and neuropathology.

(x) According to our hypothesis, negative symptoms constitute the core disease of schizophrenia and are related to a striatal dopamine-acetylcholine imbalance rooted in disorder of the basal ganglia. Positive symptoms, conversely, reflect an "accessory" process deriving from a compensatory increase in dopaminergic activity that follows the injury to the striatal and mesolimbic/mesocortical dopaminergic neurons.

(y) In contrast to Parkinson's disease, schizophrenia develops much earlier in one's life span. Therefore, it interferes with cognitive and social development, causing perhaps irreversible deficits, and is more likely to be associated with compensatory adaptation in the young organism that is manifested as positive symptoms.

(z) Thus, the negative symptoms of schizophrenia might be managed like Parkinson's disease, including the use of dopamine agonists and the MAO-B inhibitor, L-deprenyl. Aside from psychopharmacological strategies, future research will need to also investigate the avenue of surgical intervention for schizophrenic patients with profound and intransigent negative symptoms. Specifically, adrenal medullary tissue transplantation, which is employed in Parkinson's disease, might be considered.

In this text we have introduced new methods, findings, models, hypotheses, and prospects for further study. Whether this work makes a valuable contribution will be determined by the course of future investigation. We hope, at the very least, to have inspired some different paths of thinking about schizophrenia and, perhaps, to have encouraged the opening of doors that otherwise would remain sealed. Therefore, although we now close our final chapter on schizophrenia, we emphasize that "the final chapter" has yet to be written. With this elusive goal ever goading and taunting us, we set the pen down and eagerly return to the source of inspiration, our patients.

Appendices

Appendix A

PANSS INTERVIEW GUIDE

Prototypic Questions for the PANSS Patient Interview in Pursing Major Areas of Psychopathology

1) *Judgment and insight*

   What brought you to the hospital (clinic, etc.)?

   Are you in need of treatment? Medicine? Hospitalization?

   Is your hospitalization a mistake? A punishment? Part of a scheme or plot?

   Do you have a psychiatric disorder? Have you had one in the past?

   What are the symptoms of your illness?

   (If receiving chemotherapy:) Why are you taking medicine?

   Are you ready to be discharged from the hospital (clinic, etc.)?

   What are your immediate plans? Your plans for the future?

2) *Hallucinations*

   Do you ever have strange experiences? Hear strange noises?

   Do you sometimes hear things that others don't hear?

   Do you sometimes receive personal communications from the radio or television? From God?

   Can you sometimes hear your thoughts aloud inside your head? Do they sound like voices?

   Do you sometimes hear voices inside your head? When? How often? How clear are they? How loud are they?

   Whose voices do you hear inside your head? How many are there? Do they speak to you, comment about you, or speak to each other?

   What do the voices say? Are they good or bad voices? Are you afraid of them?

   Do the voices tell you what to do? Give you direct orders?

   Do you obey the voices' commands? Must you?

Do ordinary things ever appear strange or distorted?

Do you ever have "visions" or see things that others don't? How often? How clear are these visions?

Do the visions occur together with the voices or separately?

Do you ever smell things that others don't?

Do you get strange sensations from within your body or feel something strange inside you?

What do you make of these voices (visions, etc.)? How did they come about? Are they a problem for you?

3) *Delusions (general)*

When you are by yourself, what do you think about?

What are your convictions or beliefs about life?

Do you have a particular philosophy that you follow?

4) *Ideas of suspicion and persecution*

How do you get along with others?

Do you like people? Dislike people? Are you annoyed with people? Afraid of people? Why?

Do you prefer to be alone? Why?

Do people like you? Dislike you? Why?

Do you trust most people that you know? Are there some whom you distrust? Who? Why?

Do people sometimes talk about you behind your back? What do they say? Why?

Do some people harbor ill will toward you? Spy on you? Plot against you? Attempt to harm you? Attempt to kill you?

What is the evidence of this? Who is behind all this? Why does this happen?

5) *Grandiosity*

How do you compare to the average person? Better or worse?

Are you special in some ways?

Do you have talents or abilities that most people don't have?

Do you have ESP? Can you read another person's mind?

Do you have special or unusual powers?

Do you consider yourself wealthy? Famous? Have you ever appeared on television, radio, movies, or stage? Made records?

Do you rate higher than others in terms of your moral standards? Does this make you special in some respect?

Do you have a special mission in life? How did this come about?

Are you a religious person? What is your relationship with God? Are you closer to God than others are? Are you one of God's angels (children, emissaries, etc.)?

6) *Guilt feelings*

Do you feel less worthwhile than the average person?

Do you consider yourself a bad person in some ways?

Do you feel guilty about something you may have done in the past?

Have you done something to deserve punishment? What kind of punishment do you deserve?

Is your present situation (hospitalization, illness, etc.) some kind of punishment? How do you know this?

Have you had thoughts of harming yourself as one kind of punishment? Have you ever acted on those thoughts?

7) *Somatic concern*

How have you been feeling?

Is there any problem with your physical health? With the way your body has been functioning?

Do you have some medical illness or disease? If so, how serious is it?

How is your head? How is your heart?

Any trouble with your lungs? Arms? Legs? With any other part of your body?

Does your head or body ever feel strange?

Has your head or body changed in shape or size?

What is causing these problems?

8) *Depression*

What is your typical mood like?

Are you mostly happy? Sad? Why?

How unhappy have you been feeling?

When do you feel the saddest? How long do these feelings last?

Do you sometimes cry? How often?

Has your mood affected your appetite? Your sleep? Your ability to work?

Have you had any thoughts of harming yourself or ending your life? Have you attempted suicide?

9) *Anxiety*

Is anything worrying you?

Have you been feeling nervous? Tense?

Would you please hold your hands out straight (to inspect for tremor)?

Now may I see your palms (to inspect for perspiration)?

Are you afraid of something? Of someone?

How anxious have you been feeling?

Do you ever get into a state of panic?

Have your worries or nervousness affected your appetite? Your sleep? Your ability to work?

10) *Orientation*

What day of the week is it? What is today's date (day, month, year)? What season are we in?

Where are we now located (city, state, district/borough, and street address)?

What is the name of this hospital (clinic, etc.)? What ward (service, division, etc.) are we on?

What is the name of the doctor who is treating you?

What are the names of the other hospital (clinic, etc.) staff members? What are their jobs?

What are the names of some of your friends in the hospital (clinic, etc.)? What are the names of your friends at home?

Do you know the name of our Mayor (Town Supervisor, etc.)? Our Governor? Our President?

11) *Abstract thinking**
   Similarities

1. How are a ball and orange alike?
2. Apple and banana?
3. Pencil and pen?
4. Nickel and dime?
5. Table and chair?
6. Tiger and elephant?
7. Hat and shirt?
8. Bus and train?
9. Arm and leg?
10. Rose and tulip?
11. Uncle and cousin?

---

*Only a sampling of similarities and proverbs at different levels of difficulty (e.g., one item selected from each quarter of the full test sets) needs be administered with the interview. When one is using the PANSS longitudinally, items should be systematically rotated with successive interviews so as to provide different selections from the various levels of difficulty, thus minimizing repetition.

12. The sun and the moon?
13. Painting and poem?
14. Hilltop and valley?
15. Air and water?
16. Peace and prosperity?

B. *Proverbs*

What does the saying mean:

1. "Plain as the nose on your face"
2. "Carrying a chip on your shoulder"
3. "Two heads are better than one"
4. "Too many cooks spoil the soup"
5. "Don't judge a book by its cover"
6. "One man's food is another man's poison"
7. "All that glitters is not gold"
8. "Don't cross the bridge until you come to it"
9. "What's good for the goose is good for the gander"
10. "The grass always looks greener on the other side"
11. "Don't keep all your eggs in one basket"
12. "One swallow does not make a summer"
13. "A stitch in time saves nine"
14. "A rolling stone gathers no moss"
15. "The acorn never falls far from the tree"
16. "People who live in glass houses should not throw stones at others"

Appendix B

INDEX TO FOREIGN LANGUAGE TRANSLATORS OF THE PANSS

Language	Translators	Address
Spanish	Luis Silva Fuentes, M.D. Abraham Fiszbein, M.D.	Departamento di Psiquiatría Facultad de Medicina Universidad de la Frontera Temuco Chile
French	(1) J. P. Lepine, M.D.	Assistance Publique Hôpitaux de Paris Hôpital Bichat 46, rue H. Huchard 75018 Paris France
	(2) Janssen Research Foundation	Turnhoutseweg, 30 B-2340 Beerse Belgium
	(3) Xavier DeVriendt, M.D., F.R.C.P. Y. Lapierre, M.D. Astra Pharma Inc.	Centre Hospitalier Robert Giffard 2601, de la Canardière Beauport, Québec G1J 2G3 Canada
	(4) Mireille Cyr, Ph.D. Jean Toupin, Ph.D.	Institut Philippe Pinel de Montréal 10905 est, boulevard de Henri-Bourassa Montréal, Québec H1C 1H1 Canada
German	(1) Gerhard Heim, Dipl.-Psych.	Freie Universität Berlin Universitätsklinikum Rudolf Virchow Stadort Charlottenburg Psychiatrische Klinik, Eschenallee 3

		D-1000 Berlin 19 West Germany
	(2) Janssen Research Foundation	Turnhoutseweg, 30 B-2340 Beerse Belgium
Italian	Flavio Pozzi, M.D.	Department of Neuroscience Janssen Italy V.lle Castello Della Magliana 38 00148 Rome Italy
Portuguese	(1) Mário Simões, M.D.	Psychiatric University Clinic c/Caxes,2,2°,E E-28026, Madrid Spain
	(2) Dra. Ana Luiza Vessoni	Escola Paulista de Medicina Departamento de Psiquiatria R. Botucatu, 740-3° andar CEP:04023, São Paulo Brazil
Dutch	(1) Don H. Linszen, M.D. Tom Kuipers, M.D.	Adolescent Clinic Psychiatric Centre University of Amsterdam Academisch Medisch Centrum Meibergdreef 9 1105 A2 Amsterdam Zuidoost The Netherlands
	(2) Janssen Research Foundation	Turnhoutseweg, 30 B-2340 Beerse Belgium
Swedish	Lars von Knorring, M.D.	Psychiatric Research Center University of Uppsala S 750 17 Uppsala Sweden
Hungarian	Istvan Bitter, M.D.	Semmelweis Orvastudományi Egyetem Psychiátriai Klinika H-1083 Budapest Balassa u.6 Hungary
Serbo-Croatian	Vladimir R. Paunović, M.D., D.Sci.	Department of Psychiatry University Clinical Center School of Medicine University of Belgrade Pasterova 2

		11000 Beograd Yugoslavia
Japanese	Hiroshi Yamada, M.D.	Department of Psychiatry Tokyo Metropolitan Matsuzawa Hospital 2-1-1, Kamikitazawa Setagayaku Tokyo 156 Japan
Chinese	Michael R. Phillips, M.D., M.A., M.P.H.	Research Center of Psychological Medicine Shashi Psychiatric Hospital Shashi, Hubei People's Republic of China
Korean	Kwang-Soo Kim, M.D. Tae-Yul Lew, M.D.	Department of Neuropsychiatry St. Mary's Hospital 62 Yeoido-Dong Young Deung Po-Keu Seoul, 150-010 Korea
Turkish	Dr. Mehmet Bulent Akman	Bakirköy Mental Hospital Psychiatry Clinic Bakirköy Akil Hastanesi H. 1 Servisi Bakirköy–Istanbul Turkey
Russian	Dr. L. Lukianova Dr. M. Drobizhev	USSR Academy of Medical Sciences National Mental Health Research Center Kashirskoye Shosse, 34 Moscow,113152 USSR

PROVISIONAL NORMS AND PERCENTILE RANKS FOR THE PANSS*

Conversion of Raw Scores to Percentile Ranks

Normative distribution	Raw Score on PANSS Scales								
	Positive	Negative	Com-posite	General Psycho-pathology	Anergia	Thought Distur-bance	Acti-vation	Paranoid Bellig-erence	Depres-sion
Mean	19.86	21.75	−1.89	39.68	10.05	12.33	6.50	7.38	9.23
Standard Deviation	6.27	6.21	7.74	9.48	3.30	4.62	2.60	2.95	3.49
Range: Min.	7	7	−49	16	4	4	3	3	4
Max.	49	49	49	112	28	28	21	21	28
Percentile Rank:									
99.9	39	41	22	69	20	26	14	16	20
99	34	36	16	62	18	23	13	14	17
98	33	35	13	59	17	22	12	13	16
95	30	32	11	55	15	20	11	12	15
90	28	30	8	52	14	18	10	11	14
85	26	28	6	50	—	17	9	—	13
80	25	27	5	48	13	16	—	10	12
75	24	26	3	46	—	—	—	—	—
70	23	25	2	45	12	15	8	9	11
65	22	24	1	43	—	14	—	—	—
60	21	23	0	42	11	—	—	8	10
55	—	—	−1	41	—	13	7	—	—
50	20	22	−2	40	10	12	—	—	9
45	19	21	−3	38	—	—	6	7	—
40	18	20	−4	37	—	11	—	—	—
35	—	19	−5	36	9	—	—	—	8
30	17	—	−6	35	—	10	5	6	—
25	16	18	−7	33	8	9	—	—	7
20	15	17	−8	32	—	8	—	5	6
15	13	15	−10	30	7	7	4	—	—
10	12	14	−12	28	6	6	3	4	5
5	10	12	−15	24	5	5	—	3	4
2	7	9	−18	20	—	—	—	—	—
1	—	7	−20	18	—	—	—	—	—
0.1	—	—	−26	—	—	—	—	—	—

*Based on a sample of 240 medicated schizophrenic inpatients (see text for details). From Kay, Opler, & Fiszbein (1990), reproduced with permission courtesy of Multi-Health Systems Inc.

Appendix D

POSITIVE AND NEGATIVE SYNDROME SCALE
(PANSS)—RATING FORM

INSTRUCTIONS: Circle the appropriate rating for each dimension following the specified clinical interview. Refer to the Rating Manual for item definitions, description of anchoring points, scoring procedure, and norms.

Patient's name _____ Age _____ Sex _____ ID# _____
Study _____ Observation period _____
Diagnosis _____ Years since first hosp._____
Ward/location _____ Date _____ Rater_____

		ABS	MIN	MILD	MOD	MOD SEV	SEV	EXT
Positive Scale								
P1. Delusions	P1.	1	2	3	4	5	6	7
P2. Conceptual disorganization	P2.	1	2	3	4	5	6	7
P3. Hallucinatory behavior	P3.	1	2	3	4	5	6	7
P4. Excitement	P4.	1	2	3	4	5	6	7
P5. Grandiosity	P5.	1	2	3	4	5	6	7
P6. Suspiciousness/persecution	P6.	1	2	3	4	5	6	7
P7. Hostility	P7.	1	2	3	4	5	6	7
Negative Scale								
N1. Blunted affect	N1.	1	2	3	4	5	6	7
N2. Emotional withdrawal	N2.	1	2	3	4	5	6	7
N3. Poor rapport	N3.	1	2	3	4	5	6	7
N4. Passive/apathetic social withdrawal	N4.	1	2	3	4	5	6	7
N5. Difficulty in abstract thinking	N5.	1	2	3	4	5	6	7
N6. Lack of spontaneity and flow of conversation	N6.	1	2	3	4	5	6	7
N7. Stereotyped thinking	N7.	1	2	3	4	5	6	7
General Psychopathology Scale								
G1. Somatic concern	G1.	1	2	3	4	5	6	7
G2. Anxiety	G2.	1	2	3	4	5	6	7
G3. Guilt feelings	G3.	1	2	3	4	5	6	7
G4. Tension	G4.	1	2	3	4	5	6	7
G5. Mannerisms and posturing	G5.	1	2	3	4	5	6	7
G6. Depression	G6.	1	2	3	4	5	6	7

G7. Motor retardation	G7.	1	2	3	4	5	6	7
G8. Uncooperativeness	G8.	1	2	3	4	5	6	7
G9. Unusual thought content	G9.	1	2	3	4	5	6	7
G10. Disorientation	G10.	1	2	3	4	5	6	7
G11. Poor attention	G11.	1	2	3	4	5	6	7
G12. Lack of judgment and insight	G12.	1	2	3	4	5	6	7
G13. Disturbance of volition	G13.	1	2	3	4	5	6	7
G14. Poor impulse control	G14.	1	2	3	4	5	6	7
G15. Preoccupation	G15.	1	2	3	4	5	6	7
G16. Active social avoidance	G16.	1	2	3	4	5	6	7

PROFILE SUMMARY

Scales*	Raw Total	Percentile	Range
Positive syndrome			
Negative syndrome			
Composite index			
General psychopathology			
Cluster scores**			
Anergia			
Thought disturbance			
Activation			
Paranoid/belligerence			
Depression			

*Positive syndrome	= Sum of P1 through P7
Negative syndrome	= Sum of N1 through N7
Composite index	= Positive syndrome minus negative syndrome
General psychopathology	= Sum of G1 through G16
**Anergia	= N1 + N2 + G7 + G10
Thought disturbance	= P2 + P3 + P5 + G9
Activation	= P4 + G4 + G5
Paranoid/belligerence	= P6 + P7 + G8
Depression	= G1 + G2 + G3 + G6

NOTES:

Appendix E

PANSS MANUAL OF DEFINITIONS

P1. *Delusions.* Beliefs that are unfounded, unrealistic, and idiosyncratic. *Basis for rating*: thought content expressed in the interview and its influence on social relations and behavior.

1. *Absent*—Definition does not apply.

2. *Minimal*—Questionable pathology; may be at the upper extreme of normal limits.

3. *Mild*—Presence of one or two delusions which are vague, uncrystallized, and not tenaciously held. Delusions do not interfere with thinking, social relations, or behavior.

4. *Moderate*—Presence of either a kaleidoscopic array of poorly formed, unstable delusions or of a few well-formed delusions that occasionally interfere with thinking, social relations, or behavior.

5. *Moderate severe*—Presence of numerous well-formed delusions that are tenaciously held and occasionally interfere with thinking, social relations, or behavior.

6. *Severe*—Presence of a stable set of delusions which are crystallized, possibly systematized, tenaciously held, and clearly interfere with thinking, social relations, and behavior.

7. *Extreme*—Presence of a stable set of delusions which are either highly systematized or very numerous, and which dominate major facets of the patient's life. This frequently results in inappropriate and irresponsible action, which may even jeopardize the safety of the patient or others.

P2. *Conceptual disorganization.* Disorganized process of thinking characterized by disruption of goal-directed sequencing, e.g., circumstantiality, tangentiality, loose associations, non sequiturs, gross illogicality, or thought block. *Basis for rating*: cognitive-verbal processes observed during the course of interview.

1. *Absent*—Definition does not apply.

2. *Minimal*—Questionable pathology; may be at the upper extreme of normal limits.

3. *Mild*—Thinking is circumstantial, tangential, or paralogical. There is some difficulty in directing thoughts toward a goal, and some loosening of associations may be evidenced under pressure.

4. *Moderate*—Able to focus thoughts when communications are brief and structured, but becomes loose or irrelevant when dealing with more complex communications or when under minimal pressure.

5. *Moderate severe*—Generally has difficulty in organizing thoughts, as evidenced by frequent irrelevancies, disconnectedness, or loosening of associations even when not under pressure.

6. *Severe*—Thinking is seriously derailed and internally inconsistent, resulting in gross irrelevancies and disruption of thought processes, which occur almost constantly.

7. *Extreme*—Thoughts are disrupted to the point where the patient is incoherent. There is marked loosening of associations, which results in total failure of communication, e.g., "word salad" or mutism.

P3. *Hallucinatory behavior.* Verbal report or behavior indicating perceptions which are not generated by external stimuli. These may occur in the auditory, visual, olfactory, or somatic realms. *Basis for rating*: Verbal report and physical manifestations during the course of interview as well as reports of behavior by primary care workers or family.

1. *Absent*—Definition does not apply.

2. *Minimal*—Questionable pathology; may be at the upper extreme of normal limits.

3. *Mild*—One or two clearly formed but infrequent hallucinations, or else a number of vague abnormal perceptions which do not result in distortions of thinking or behavior.

4. *Moderate*—Hallucinations occur frequently but not continuously, and the patient's thinking and behavior are affected only to a minor extent.

5. *Moderate severe*—Hallucinations are frequent, may involve more than one sensory modality, and tend to distort thinking and/or disrupt behavior. Patient may have a delusional interpretation of these experiences and respond to them emotionally and, on occasion, verbally as well.

6. *Severe*—Hallucinations are present almost continuously, causing major disruption of thinking and behavior. Patient treats these as real perceptions, and functioning is impeded by frequent emotional and verbal responses to them.

7. *Extreme*—Patient is almost totally preoccupied with hallucinations, which virtually dominate thinking and behavior. Hallucinations are provided a rigid delusional interpretation and provoke verbal and behavioral responses, including obedience to command hallucinations.

P4. *Excitement.* Hyperactivity as reflected in accelerated motor behavior, heightened responsivity to stimuli, hypervigilance, or excessive mood lability. *Basis for rating*: Behavioral manifestations during the course of interview as well as reports of behavior by primary care workers or family.

1. *Absent*—Definition does not apply.

2. *Minimal*—Questionable pathology; may be at the upper extreme of normal limits.

3. *Mild*—Tends to be slightly agitated, hypervigilant, or mildly overaroused throughout the interview, but without distinct episodes of excitement or marked mood lability. Speech may be slightly pressured.

4. *Moderate*—Agitation or overarousal is clearly evident throughout the interview, affecting speech and general mobility, or episodic outbursts occur sporadically.

5. *Moderate severe*—Significant hyperactivity or frequent outbursts or motor activity are observed, making it difficult for the patient to sit still for longer than several minutes at any given time.

6. *Severe*—Marked excitement dominates the interview, delimits attention, and to some extent affects personal functions such as eating and sleeping.

7. *Extreme*—Marked excitement seriously interferes in eating and sleeping and makes interpersonal interactions virtually impossible. Acceleration of speech and motor activity may result in incoherence and exhaustion.

P5. *Grandiosity*. Exaggerated self-opinion and unrealistic convictions of superiority, including delusions of extraordinary abilities, wealth, knowledge, fame, power, and moral righteousness. *Basis for rating*: thought content expressed in the interview and its influence on behavior.

1. *Absent*—Definition does not apply.

2. *Minimal*—Questionable pathology; may be at the upper extreme of normal limits.

3. *Mild*—Some expansiveness or boastfulness is evident, but without clear-cut grandiose delusions.

4. *Moderate*—Feels distinctly and unrealistically superior to others. Some poorly formed delusions about special status or abilities may be present but are not acted upon.

5. *Moderate severe*—Clear-cut delusions concerning remarkable abilities, status, or power are expressed and influence attitude but not behavior.

6. *Severe*—Clear-cut delusions of remarkable superiority involving more than one parameter (wealth, knowledge, fame, etc.) are expressed, notably influence interactions, and may be acted upon.

7. *Extreme*—Thinking, interactions, and behavior are dominated by multiple delusions of amazing ability, wealth, knowledge, fame, power, and/or moral stature, which may take on a bizarre quality.

P6. *Suspiciousness/persecution*. Unrealistic or exaggerated ideas of persecution, as reflected in guardedness, a distrustful attitude, suspicious hypervigilance, or frank delusions that others mean one harm. *Basis for rating*: thought content expressed in the interview and its influence on behavior.

1. *Absent*—Definition does not apply.

2. *Minimal*—Questionable pathology; may be at the upper extreme of normal limits.

3. *Mild*—Presents a guarded or even openly distrustful attitude, but thoughts, interactions, and behavior are minimally affected.

4. *Moderate*—Distrustfulness is clearly evident and intrudes on the interview and/ or behavior, but there is no evidence of persecutory delusions. Alternatively, there may be indication of loosely formed persecutory delusions, but these do not seem to affect the patient's attitude or interpersonal relations.

5. *Moderate severe*—Patient shows marked distrustfulness, leading to major disruption of interpersonal relations, or else there are clear-cut persecutory delusions that have limited impact on interpersonal relations and behavior.

6. *Severe*—Clear-cut pervasive delusions of persecution which may be systematized and significantly interfere in interpersonal relations.

7. *Extreme*—A network of systematized persecutory delusions dominates the patient's thinking, social relations, and behavior.

P7. *Hostility.* Verbal and nonverbal expressions of anger and resentment, including sarcasm, passive-aggressive behavior, verbal abuse, and assaultiveness. *Basis for rating*: interpersonal behavior observed during the interview and reports by primary care workers or family.

1. *Absent*—Definition does not apply.

2. *Minimal*—Questionable pathology; may be at the upper extreme of normal limits.

3. *Mild*—Indirect or restrained communication of anger, such as sarcasm, disrespect, hostile expressions, and occasional irritability.

4. *Moderate*—Presents an overtly hostile attitude, showing frequent irritability and direct expression of anger or resentment.

5. *Moderate severe*—Patient is highly irritable and occasionally verbally abusive or threatening.

6. *Severe*—Uncooperativeness and verbal abuse or threats notably influence the interview and seriously impact upon social relations. Patient may be violent and destructive but is not physically assaultive toward others.

7. *Extreme*—Marked anger results in extreme uncooperativeness, precluding other interactions, or in episodes(s) of physical assault toward others.

NEGATIVE SCALE (n)

N1. *Blunted affect.* Diminished emotional responsiveness as characterized by a reduction in facial expression, modulation of feelings, and communicative gestures. *Basis for rating*: observation of physical manifestations of affective tone and emotional responsiveness during the course of interview.

1. *Absent*—Definition does not apply.

2. *Minimal*—Questionable pathology; may be at the upper extreme of normal limits.

3. *Mild*—Changes in facial expression and communicative gestures seem to be stilted, forced, artificial, or lacking in modulation.

4. *Moderate*—Reduced range of facial expression and few expressive gestures result in a dull appearance.

5. *Moderate severe*—Affect is generally "flat," with only occasional changes in facial expression and a paucity of communicative gestures.

6. *Severe*—Marked flatness and deficiency of emotions exhibited most of the time. There may be unmodulated extreme affective discharges, such as excitement, rage, or inappropriate uncontrolled laughter.

7. *Extreme*—Changes in facial expression and evidence of communicative gestures are virtually absent. Patient seems constantly to show a barren or "wooden" expression.

N2. *Emotional withdrawal.* Lack of interest in, involvement with, and affective commitment to life's events. *Basis for rating*: reports of functioning from primary care workers or family and observation of interpersonal behavior during the course of interview.

1. *Absent*—Definition does not apply.

2. *Minimal*—Questionable pathology; may be at the upper extreme of normal limits.

3. *Mild*—Usually lacks initiative and occasionally may show deficient interest in surrounding events.

4. *Moderate*—Patient is generally distanced emotionally from the milieu and its challenges but, with encouragement, can be engaged.

5. *Moderate severe*—Patient is clearly detached emotionally from persons and events in the milieu, resisting all efforts at engagement. Patient appears distant, docile, and purposeless but can be involved in communication at least briefly and tends to personal needs, sometimes with assistance.

6. *Severe*—Marked deficiency of interest and emotional commitment results in limited conversation with others and frequent neglect of personal functions, for which the patient requires supervision.

7. *Extreme*—Patient is almost totally withdrawn, uncommunicative, and neglectful of personal needs as a result of profound lack of interest and emotional commitment.

N3. *Poor rapport.* Lack of interpersonal empathy, openness in conversation, and sense of closeness, interest, or involvement with the interviewer. This is evidenced by interpersonal distancing and reduced verbal and nonverbal communication. *Basis for rating*: interpersonal behavior during the course of interview.

1. *Absent*—Definition does not apply.

2. *Minimal*—Questionable pathology; may be at the upper extreme of normal limits.

3. *Mild*—Conversation is characterized by a stilted, strained, or artificial tone. It may lack emotional depth or tend to remain on an impersonal, intellectual plane.

4. *Moderate*—Patient typically is aloof, with interpersonal distance quite evident. Patient may answer questions mechanically, act bored, or express disinterest.

5. *Moderate severe*—Disinvolvement is obvious and clearly impedes the productivity of the interview. Patient may tend to avoid eye or face contact.

6. *Severe*—Patient is highly indifferent, with marked interpersonal distance. Answers are perfunctory, and there is little nonverbal evidence of involvement. Eye and face contact are frequently avoided.

7. *Extreme*—Patient is totally uninvolved with the interviewer. Patient appears to be completely indifferent and consistently avoids verbal and nonverbal interactions during the interview.

N4. *Passive/apathetic social withdrawal.* Diminished interest and initiative in social interactions due to passivity, apathy, anergy, or avolition. This leads to reduced interpersonal involvements and neglect of activities of daily living. *Basis for rating*: reports on social behavior from primary care workers or family.

1. *Absent*—Definition does not apply.

2. *Minimal*—Questionable pathology; may be at the upper extreme of normal limits.

3. *Mild*—Shows occasional interest in social activities but poor initiative. Usually engages with others only when approached first by them.

4. *Moderate*—Passively goes along with most social activities but in a disinterested or mechanical way. Tends to recede into the background.

5. *Moderate severe*—Passively participates in only a minority of activities and shows virtually no interest or initiative. Generally spends little time with others.

6. *Severe*—Tends to be apathetic and isolated, participating very rarely in social activities and occasionally neglecting personal needs. Has very few spontaneous social contacts.

7. *Extreme*—Profoundly apathetic, socially isolated, and personally neglectful.

N5. *Difficulty in abstract thinking.* Impairment in the use of the abstract-symbolic mode of thinking, as evidenced by difficulty in classification, forming generalizations, and proceeding beyond concrete or egocentric thinking in problem-solving tasks. *Basis for rating*: responses to questions on similarities and proverb interpretation, and use of concrete vs. abstract mode during the course of the interview.

1. *Absent*—Definition does not apply.

2. *Minimal*—Questionable pathology; may be at the upper extreme of normal limits.

3. *Mild*—Tends to give literal or personalized interpretations to the more difficult proverbs and may have some problems with concepts that are fairly abstract or remotely related.

4. *Moderate*—Often utilizes a concrete mode. Has difficulty with most proverbs and some categories. Tends to be distracted by functional aspects and salient features.

5. *Moderate severe*—Deals primarily in a concrete mode, exhibiting difficulty with most proverbs and many categories.

6. *Severe*—Unable to grasp the abstract meaning of any proverbs or figurative expressions and can formulate classifications for only the most simple of similarities. Thinking is either vacuous or locked into functional aspects, salient features, and idiosyncratic interpretation.

7. *Extreme*—Can use only concrete modes of thinking. Shows no comprehension of proverbs, common metaphors or similes, and simple categories. Even salient and functional attributes do not serve as a basis for classification. This rating may apply to those who cannot interact even minimally with the examiner due to marked cognitive impairment.

N6. *Lack of spontaneity and flow of conversation.* Reduction in the normal flow of communication associated with apathy, avolition, defensiveness, or cognitive deficit. This is manifested by diminished fluidity and productivity of the verbal-interactional process. *Basis for rating*: cognitive-verbal processes observed during the course of interview.

1. *Absent*—Definition does not apply.

2. *Minimal*—Questionable pathology; may be at the upper extreme of normal limits.

3. *Mild*—Conversation shows little initiative. Patient's answers tend to be brief and unembellished, requiring direct and leading questions by the interviewer.

4. *Moderate*—Conversation lacks free flow and appears uneven or halting. Leading questions are frequently needed to elicit adequate responses and proceed with conversation.

5. *Moderate severe*—Patient shows a marked lack of spontaneity and openness, replying to the interviewer's questions with only one or two brief sentences.

6. *Severe*—Patient's responses are limited mainly to a few words or short phrases intended to avoid or curtail communication. (e.g., *"I don't know," "I'm not at liberty to*

say.") Conversation is seriously impaired as a result, and the interview is highly unproductive.

7. *Extreme*—Verbal output is restricted to, at most, an occasional utterance, making conversation not possible.

N7. *Stereotyped thinking.* Decreased fluidity, spontaneity, and flexibility of thinking, as evidenced in rigid, repetitious, or barren thought content. *Basis for rating*: cognitive-verbal processes observed during the interview.

1. *Absent*—Definition does not apply.

2. *Minimal*—Questionable pathology; may be at the upper extreme of normal limits.

3. *Mild*—Some rigidity shown in attitudes or beliefs. Patient may refuse to consider alternative positions or have difficulty in shifting from one idea to another.

4. *Moderate*—Conversation revolves around a recurrent theme, resulting in difficulty in shifting to a new topic.

5. *Moderate severe*—Thinking is rigid and repetitious to the point that, despite the interviewer's efforts, conversation is limited to only two or three dominating topics.

6. *Severe*—Uncontrolled repetition of demands, statements, ideas, or questions which severely impairs conversation.

7. *Extreme*—Thinking, behavior, and conversation are dominated by constant repetition of fixed ideas or limited phrases, leading to gross rigidity, inappropriateness, and restrictiveness of patient's communication.

GENERAL PSYCHOPATHOLOGY SCALE (G)

G1. *Somatic concern.* Physical complaints or beliefs about bodily illness or malfunctions. This may range from a vague sense of ill being to clear-cut delusions of catastrophic physical disease. *Basis of rating*: thought content expressed in the interview.

1. *Absent*—Definition does not apply.

2. *Minimal*—Questionable pathology; may be at the upper extreme of normal limits.

3. *Mild*—Distinctly concerned about health or somatic issues, as evidenced by occasional questions and desire for reassurance.

4. *Moderate*—Complains about poor health or bodily malfunction, but there is no delusional conviction, and overconcern can be allayed by reassurance.

5. *Moderate severe*—Patient expresses numerous or frequent complaints about physical illness or bodily malfunction, or else patient reveals one or two clear-cut delusions involving these themes but is not preoccupied by them.

6. *Severe*—Patient is preoccupied by one or a few clear-cut delusions about physical disease or organic malfunction, but affect is not fully immersed in these themes, and thoughts can be diverted by the interviewer with some effort.

7. *Extreme*—Numerous and frequently reported somatic delusions, or only a few somatic delusions of a catastrophic nature, which totally dominate the patient's affect and thinking.

G.2. *Anxiety.* Subjective experience of nervousness, worry, apprehension, or restlessness, ranging from excessive concern about the present or future to feelings of panic. *Basis for rating*: verbal report during the course of interview and corresponding physical manifestations.

1. *Absent*—Definition does not apply.

2. *Minimal*—Questionable pathology; may be at the upper extreme of normal limits.

3. *Mild*—Expresses some worry, overconcern, or subjective restlessness, but no somatic and behavioral consequences are reported or evidenced.

4. *Moderate*—Patient reports distinct symptoms of nervousness, which are reflected in mild physical manifestations such as fine hand tremor and excessive perspiration.

5. *Moderate severe*—Patient reports serious problems of anxiety which have significant physical and behavioral consequences, such as marked tension, poor concentration, palpitation, or impaired sleep.

6. *Severe*—Subjective state of almost constant fear associated with phobias, marked restlessness, or numerous somatic manifestations.

7. *Extreme*—Patient's life is seriously disrupted by anxiety, which is present almost constantly and at times reaches panic proportion or is manifested in actual panic attacks.

G3.*Guilt feelings*. Sense of remorse or self-blame for real or imagined misdeeds in the past. *Basis for rating*: verbal report of guilt feelings during the course of interview and the influence on attitudes and thoughts.

1. *Absent*—Definition does not apply.

2. *Minimal*—Questionable pathology; may be at the upper extreme of normal limits.

3. *Mild*—Questioning elicits a vague sense of guilt or self-blame for a minor incident, but the patient clearly is not overly concerned.

4. *Moderate*—Patient expresses distinct concern over his responsibility for a real incident in his life but is not preoccupied with it, and attitude and behavior are essentially unaffected.

5. *Moderate severe*—Patient expresses a strong sense of guilt associated with self-deprecation or the belief that he deserves punishment. The guilt feelings may have a delusional basis, may be volunteered spontaneously, may be a source of preoccupation and/or depressed mood, and cannot be allayed readily by the interviewer.

6. *Severe*—Strong ideas of guilt take on a delusional quality and lead to an attitude of hopelessness or worthlessness. The patient believes he should receive harsh sanctions for the misdeeds and may even regard his current life situation as such punishment.

7. *Extreme*—Patient's life is dominated by unshakable delusions of guilt, for which he feels deserving of drastic punishment, such as life imprisonment, torture, or death. There may be associated suicidal thoughts or attribution or others' problems to one's own past misdeeds.

G4. *Tension*. Overt physical manifestations of fear, anxiety, and agitation, such as stiffness, tremor, profuse sweating, and restlessness. *Basis for rating*: verbal report attesting to anxiety and, thereupon, the severity of physical manifestations of tension observed during the interview.

1. *Absent*—Definition does not apply.

2. *Minimal*—Questionable pathology; may be at the upper extreme of normal limits.

3. *Mild*—Posture and movements indicate slight apprehensiveness, such as minor rigidity, occasional restlessness, shifting of position, or fine rapid hand tremor.

4. *Moderate*—A clearly nervous appearance emerges from various manifestations, such as fidgety behavior, obvious hand tremor, excessive perspiration, or nervous mannerisms.

5. *Moderate severe*—Pronounced tension is evidenced by numerous manifestations, such as nervous shaking, profuse sweating, and restlessness, but conduct in the interview is not significantly affected.

6. *Severe*—Pronounced tension to the point that interpersonal interactions are disrupted. The patient, for example, may be constantly fidgeting, unable to sit still for long, or show hyperventilation.

7. *Extreme*—Marked tension is manifested by signs of panic or gross motor acceleration, such as rapid restless pacing and inability to remain seated for longer than a minute, which makes sustained conversation not possible.

G5. *Mannerisms and posturing.* Unnatural movements or posture as characterized by an awkward, stilted, disorganized, or bizarre appearance. *Basis for rating*: observation of physical manifestations during the course of interview as well as reports from primary care workers or family.

1. *Absent*—Definition does not apply.

2. *Minimal*—Questionable pathology; may be at the upper extreme of normal limits.

3. *Mild*—Slight awkwardness in movements or minor rigidity of posture.

4. *Moderate*—Movements are notably awkward or disjointed, or an unnatural posture is maintained for brief periods.

5. *Moderate severe*—Occasional bizarre rituals or contorted posture are observed, or an abnormal position is sustained for extended periods.

6. *Severe*—Frequent repetition of bizarre rituals, mannerisms, or stereotyped movements, or a contorted posture is sustained for extended periods.

7. *Extreme*—Functioning is seriously impaired by virtually constant involvement in ritualistic, manneristic, or stereotyped movements or by an unnatural fixed posture which is sustained most of the time.

G6. *Depression.* Feelings of sadness, discouragement, helplessness, and pessimism. *Basis for rating*: verbal report of depressed mood during the course of interview and its observed influence on attitude and behavior.

1. *Absent*—Definition does not apply.

2. *Minimal*—Questionable pathology; may be at the upper extreme of normal limits.

3. *Mild*—Expresses some sadness or discouragement only on questioning, but there is no evidence of depression in general attitude or demeanor.

4. *Moderate*—Distinct feelings of sadness or hopelessness, which may be spontaneously divulged, but depressed mood has no major impact on behavior or social functioning, and the patient usually can be cheered up.

5. *Moderate severe*—Distinctly depressed mood is associated with obvious sadness, pessimism, loss of social interest, psychomotor retardation, and some interference in appetite and sleep. The patient cannot be easily cheered up.

6. *Severe*—Markedly depressed mood is associated with sustained feelings of misery,

occasional crying, hopelessness, and worthlessness. In addition, there is major interference in appetite and/or sleep as well as in normal motor and social functions, with possible signs of self-neglect.

7. *Extreme*—Depressive feelings seriously interfere in most major functions. The manifestations include frequent crying, pronounced somatic symptoms, impaired concentration, psychomotor retardation, social disinterest, self-neglect, possible depressive or nihilistic delusions, and/or possible suicidal thoughts or action.

G7. *Motor retardation.* Reduction in motor activity as reflected in slowing or lessening of movements and speech, diminished responsiveness to stimuli, and reduced body tone. *Basis for rating:* manifestations during the course of interview as well as reports by primary care workers or family.

1. *Absent*—Definition does not apply.

2. *Minimal*—Questionable pathology; may be at the upper extreme of normal limits.

3. *Mild*—Slight but noticeable diminution in rate of movements and speech. Patient may be somewhat underproductive in conversation and gestures.

4. *Moderate*—Patient is clearly slow in movements, and speech may be characterized by poor productivity, including long response latency, extended pauses, or slow pace.

5. *Moderate severe*—A marked reduction in motor activity renders communication highly unproductive or delimits functioning in social and occupational situations. Patient can usually be found sitting or lying down.

6. *Severe*—Movements are extremely slow, resulting in a minimum of activity and speech. Essentially the day is spent sitting idly or lying down.

7. *Extreme*—Patient is almost completely immobile and virtually unresponsive to external stimuli.

G8. *Uncooperativeness.* Active refusal to comply with the will of significant others, including the interviewer, hospital staff, or family, which may be associated with distrust, defensiveness, stubbornness, negativism, rejection of authority, hostility, or belligerence. *Basis for rating:* interpersonal behavior observed during the course of interview, as well as reports by primary care workers or family.

1. *Absent*—Definition does not apply.

2. *Minimal*—Questionable pathology; may be at the upper extreme of normal limits.

3. *Mild*—Complies with an attitude of resentment, impatience, or sarcasm. May inoffensively object to sensitive probing during the interview.

4. *Moderate*—Occasional outright refusal to comply with normal social demands, such as making own bed, attending scheduled programs, etc. The patient may project a hostile, defensive, or negative attitude but usually can be worked with.

5. *Moderate severe*—Patient frequently is incompliant with the demands of his milieu and may be characterized by others as an "outcast" or having "a serious attitude problem." Uncooperativeness is reflected in obvious defensiveness or irritability with the interviewer and possible unwillingness to address many questions.

6. *Severe*—Patient is highly uncooperative, negativistic, and possibly also belligerent. Refuses to comply with most social demands and may be unwilling to initiate or conclude the full interview.

7. *Extreme*—Active resistance seriously impacts on virtually all major areas of functioning. Patient may refuse to join in any social activities, tend to personal hygiene, converse with family or staff, and participate even briefly in an interview.

G9. *Unusual thought content.* Thinking characterized by strange, fantastic, or bizarre ideas, ranging from those which are remote or atypical to those which are distorted, illogical, and patently absurd. *Basis for rating*: thought content expressed during the course of interview.

1. *Absent*—Definition does not apply.

2. *Minimal*—Questionable pathology; may be at the upper extreme of normal limits.

3. *Mild*—Thought content is somewhat peculiar or idiosyncratic, or familiar ideas are framed in an odd context.

4. *Moderate*—Ideas are frequently distorted and occasionally seem quite bizarre.

5. *Moderate severe*—Patient expresses many strange and fantastic thoughts (e.g., being the adopted son of a king, being an escapee from death row) or some which are patently absurd (e.g., having hundreds of children, receiving radio messages from outer space through a tooth filling).

6. *Severe*—Patient expresses many illogical or absurd ideas or some which have a distinctly bizarre quality (e.g., having three heads, being a visitor from another planet).

7. *Extreme*—Thinking is replete with absurd, bizarre, and grotesque ideas.

G10. *Disorientation.* Lack of awareness of one's relationship to the milieu, including persons, place, and time, which may be due to confusion or withdrawal. *Basis for rating*: responses to interview questions on orientation.

1. *Absent*—Definition does not apply.

2. *Minimal*—Questionable pathology; may be at the upper extreme of normal limits.

3. *Mild*—General orientation is adequate but there is some difficulty with specifics. For example, patient knows his location but not the street address, knows hospital staff names but not their functions, knows the month but confuses the day of week with an adjacent day, or errs in the date by more than two days. There may be narrowing of interest evidenced by familiarity with the immediate but not extended milieu, such as ability to identify staff, but not the Mayor, Governor, or President.

4. *Moderate*—Only partial success in recognizing persons, places, and time. For example, patient knows he is in a hospital but not its name, knows the name of his city but not the borough or district, knows the name of his primary therapist but not many other direct care workers, knows the year and season but not sure of the month.

5. *Moderate severe*—Considerable failure in recognizing persons, place, and time. Patient has only a vague notion of where he is and seems unfamiliar with most people in his milieu. He may identify the year correctly or nearly so but not know the current month, day of week, or even the season.

6. *Severe*—Marked failure in recognizing persons, place, and time. For example, patient has no knowledge of his whereabouts, confuses the date by more than one year, can name only one or two individuals in his current life.

7. *Extreme*—Patient appears completely disoriented with regard to persons, place, and time. There is gross confusion or total ignorance about one's location, the cur-

rent year, and even the most familiar people, such as parents, spouse, friends, and primary therapist.

G11. *Poor attention*. Failure in focused alertness manifested by poor concentration, distractibility from internal and external stimuli, and difficulty in harnessing, sustaining, or shifting focus to new stimuli. *Basis for rating*: manifestations during the course of interview.

1. *Absent*—Definition does not apply.

2. *Minimal*—Questionable pathology; may be at the upper extreme of normal limits.

3. *Mild*—Limited concentration evidenced by occasional vulnerability to distraction or faltering attention toward the end of the interview.

4. *Moderate*—Conversation is affected by the tendency to be easily distracted, difficulty in long sustaining concentration on a given topic, or problems in shifting attention to new topics.

5. *Moderate severe*—Conversation is seriously hampered by poor concentration, distractibility, and difficulty in shifting focus appropriately.

6. *Severe*—Patient's attention can be harnessed for only brief moments or with great effort due to marked distraction by internal or external stimuli.

7. *Extreme*—Attention is so disrupted that even brief conversation is not possible.

G12. *Lack of judgment and insight*. Impaired awareness or understanding of one's own psychiatric condition and life situation. This is evidenced by failure to recognize past or present psychiatric illness or symptoms, denial of need for psychiatric hospitalization or treatment, decisions characterized by poor anticipation of consequences, and unrealistic short-term and long-range planning. *Basis of rating*: thought content expressed during the interview.

1. *Absent*—Definition does not apply.

2. *Minimal*—Questionable pathology; may be at the upper extreme of normal limits.

3. *Mild*—Recognizes having a psychiatric disorder but clearly underestimates its seriousness, the implications for treatment, or the importance of taking measures to avoid relapse. Future planning may be poorly conceived.

4. *Moderate*—Patient shows only a vague or shallow recognition of illness. There may be fluctuations in acknowledgement of being ill or little awareness of major symptoms which are present, such as delusions, disorganized thinking, suspiciousness, and social withdrawal. The patient may rationalize the need for treatment in terms of its relieving lesser symptoms, such as anxiety, tension, and sleep difficulty.

5. *Moderate severe*—Acknowledges past but not present psychiatric disorder. If challenged, the patient may concede the presence of some unrelated or insignificant symptoms, which tend to be explained away by gross misinterpretation or delusional thinking. The need for psychiatric treatment similarly goes unrecognized.

6. *Severe*—Patient denies ever having had a psychiatric disorder. He disavows the presence of any psychiatric symptoms in the past or present and, though compliant, denies the need for treatment and hospitalization.

7. *Extreme*—Emphatic denial of past and present psychiatric illness. Current hospitalization and treatment are given a delusional interpretation (e.g., as punishment for misdeeds, as persecution by tormentors, etc.), and the patient may thus refuse to cooperate with therapists, medication, or other aspects of treatment.

G13. *Disturbance of volition.* Disturbance in the willful initiation, sustenance, and control of one's thoughts, behavior, movements, and speech. *Basis for rating:* thought content and behavior manifested in the course of interview.

1. *Absent*—Definition does not apply.

2. *Minimal*—Questionable pathology; may be at the upper extreme of normal limits.

3. *Mild*—There is evidence of some indecisiveness in conversation and thinking, which may impede verbal and cognitive processes to a minor extent.

4. *Moderate*—Patient is often ambivalent and shows clear difficulty in reaching decisions. Conversation may be marred by alternation in thinking, and in consequence verbal and cognitive functioning are clearly impaired.

5. *Moderate severe*—Disturbance of volition interferes in thinking as well as behavior. Patient shows pronounced indecision that impedes the initiation and continuation of social and motor activities, and which also may be evidenced in halting speech.

6. *Severe*—Disturbance of volition interferes in the execution of simple, automatic motor functions, such as dressing and grooming, and markedly affects speech.

7. *Extreme*—Almost complete failure of volition is manifested by gross inhibition of movement and speech, resulting in immobility and/or mutism.

G14. *Poor impulse control.* Disordered regulation and control of action on inner urges, resulting in sudden, unmodulated, arbitrary, or misdirected discharge of tension and emotions without concern about consequences. *Basis for rating:* behavior during the course of interview and reported by primary care workers or family.

1. *Absent*—Definition does not apply.

2. *Minimal*—Questionable pathology; may be at the upper extreme of normal limits.

3. *Mild*—Patient tends to be easily angered and frustrated when facing stress or denied gratification but rarely acts on impulse.

4. *Moderate*—Patient gets angered and verbally abusive with minimal provocation. May be occasionally threatening, destructive, or have one or two episodes involving physical confrontation or a minor brawl.

5. *Moderate severe*—Patient exhibits repeated impulsive episodes involving verbal abuse, destruction of property, or physical threats. There may be one or two episodes involving serious assault, for which the patient requires isolation, physical restraint, or p.r.n. sedation.

6. *Severe*—Patient frequently is impulsively aggressive, threatening, demanding, and destructive, without any apparent consideration of consequences. Shows assaultive behavior and may also be sexually offensive and possibly respond behaviorally to hallucinatory commands.

7. *Extreme*—Patient exhibits homicidal attacks, sexual assaults, repeated brutality, or self-destructive behavior. Requires constant direct supervision or external constraints because of inability to control dangerous impulses.

G15. *Preoccupation.* Absorption with internally generated thoughts and feelings and with autistic experiences to the detriment of reality orientation and adaptive behavior. *Basis for rating:* interpersonal behavior observed during the course of interview.

1. *Absent*—Definition does not apply.

2. *Minimal*—Questionable pathology; may be at the upper extreme of normal limits.

3. *Mild*—Excessive involvement with personal needs or problems, such that conversation veers back to egocentric themes and there is diminished concern exhibited toward others.

4. *Moderate*—Patient occasionally appears self-absorbed, as if daydreaming or involved with internal experiences, which interferes with communication to a minor extent.

5. *Moderate severe*—Patient often appears to be engaged in autistic experiences, as evidenced by behaviors that significantly intrude on social and communicational functions, such as the presence of a vacant stare, muttering or talking to oneself, or involvement with stereotyped motor patterns.

6. *Severe*—Marked preoccupation with autistic experiences, which seriously delimits concentration, ability to converse, and orientation to the milieu. The patient frequently may be observed smiling, laughing, muttering, talking, or shouting to himself.

7. *Extreme*—Gross absorption with autistic experiences, which profoundly affects all major realms of behavior. The patient constantly may be responding verbally and behaviorally to hallucinations and show little awareness of other people or the external milieu.

G16. *Active social avoidance.* Diminished social involvement associated with unwarranted fear, hostility, or distrust. *Basis for rating*: reports of social functioning by primary care workers or family.

1. *Absent*—Definition does not apply.

2. *Minimal*—Questionable pathology; may be at the upper extreme of normal limits.

3. *Mild*—Patient seems ill at ease in the presence of others and prefers to spend time alone, although he participates in social functions when required.

4. *Moderate*—Patient begrudgingly attends all or most social activities but may need to be persuaded or may terminate prematurely on account of anxiety, suspiciousness, or hostility.

5. *Moderate severe*—Patient fearfully or angrily keeps away from many social interactions despite others' efforts to engage him. Tends to spend unstructured time alone.

6. *Severe*—Patient participates in very few social activities because of fear, hostility, or distrust. When approached, the patient shows a strong tendency to break off interactions, and generally he tends to isolate himself from others.

7. *Extreme*—Patient cannot be engaged in social activities because of pronounced fears, hostility, or persecutory delusions. To the extent possible, he avoids all interactions and remains isolated from others.

Bibliography

Abramsky, O., & Litvin, O. (1978). Autoimmune response to dopamine as a possible mechanism in the pathogenesis of Parkinson's disease and schizophrenia. *Perspectives in Biology and Medicine*, 24, 104–114.

Agid, Y., Javoy-Agid, F., Ruberg, M., Pillon, B., Dubois, B., Duyckaerts, C., Hauw, J. J., Baron, J. C., & Scatton, B. (1986). Progressive supranuclear palsy: Anatomoclinical and biochemical consideration. In M. D. Yahr & K. J. Bergmann (Eds.), *Advances in Neurology*, Vol. 45. New York: Raven Press, pp. 191–206.

Albrecht, P., Torrey, E. F., & Boone, E. (1980). Raised cytomegalovirus antibody level in cerebrospinal fluid of schizophrenic patients. *Lancet*, 2, 769–772.

Alizan, T. S., Terasaki, P. I., & Yahr, M. D. (1980). MLA-BI4 antigen and postencephalitic Parkinson's disease: Their association in an American Jewish ethnic group. *Archives of Neurology*, 37, 542–544.

Alpert, M., Diamond, F., Weisenfreund, J., Taleporos, E., & Friedhoff, A. J. (1978). The neuroleptic hypothesis: Study of the covariation of the extrapyramidal and therapeutic drug effects. *British Journal of Psychiatry*, 133, 169–175.

Alpert, M., & Rush, M. (1983). Comparison of affect in Parkinson's disease and schizophrenia. *Psychopharmacology Bulletin*, 196, 118–120.

American Psychiatric Association (1980). *DSM-III: Diagnostic and Statistical Manual of Mental Disorders* (3rd ed.) Washington, DC: American Psychiatric Association.

American Psychiatric Association. (1987). *DSM-III-R: Diagnostic and Statistical Manual of Mental Disorders* (3rd ed., Rev.) Washington, DC: American Psychiatric Association.

American Psychological Association. (1985). *Standards for Educational and Psychological Tests*. Washington, DC: American Psychological Association.

Ammons, R. B., & Ammons, C. H. (1962). The Quick Test (QT): Provisional manual. *Psychological Reports*, 11, 111–162.

Andreasen, N. C. (1982). Negative symptoms in schizophrenia: Definition and reliability. *Archives of General Psychiatry*, 39, 784–788.

Andreasen, N. C. (1985). Positive vs. negative schizophrenia: A critical evaluation. *Schizophrenia Bulletin*, 11, 380–389.

Andreasen, N. C., & Olsen, S. A. (1982). Negative vs. positive schizophrenia: Definition and validation. *Archives of General Psychiatry*, 39, 789–794.

Andreasen, N. C., Olsen, S. A., Dennert, J. W., & Smith, M. R. (1982). Ventricular enlargement in schizophrenia: Relationship to positive and negative symptoms. *American Journal of Psychiatry*, 139, 297–302.

Angrist, B., Rotrosen, J., & Gershon, S. (1980). Differential effects of amphetamine and neuroleptics on negative vs. positive symptoms in schizophrenia. *Psychopharmacology*, 72, 17–19.

Anthony, W. A., Cohen, M. R., & Vitalo, R. (1978). The measurement of rehabilitation outcome. *Schizophrenia Bulletin*, 4, 365–383.

Anthony, W. A., & Farkas, M. (1982). Client outcome model for assessing psychiatric rehabilitation interventions. *Schizophrenia Bulletin*, 8, 13–38.

Ashcroft, G. W., Crawford, T. B. B., Eccelson, D., Sharman, D. F., Macdougal, E. G., Stanton, J. B., & Binnis, J. K. (1966). 5-hydroxyindole compounds in the cerebrospinal fluid of patients with psychiatric or neurological diseases. *Lancet*, 2, 1049–1052.

Becker, H., Grau, H., & Schneider, E. (1976). CT examination series of Parkinson patients. In W. Laukisch & E. Kazner (Eds.), *Cranial Computerized Tomography*. New York: Springer Varlag, pp. 249–251.

Benedek, L. (1925). Zwangmassiges Schreinen in Anfallen als Postencephalitische Hyperkinesie. *Zeitschrift fir die Gesamte Neurologie und Psychiatrie*, 98, 17–26.

Berkanovic, E. (1980). The effect of adequate language translation on Hispanics' response to health surveys. *American Journal of Public Health*, 70, 1273–1276.

Berry, J. W. (1969). On cross-cultural compatibility. *International Journal of Psychology*, 4, 119–128.

Bes, A., Guell, A., & Fabre, N. (1983). Cerebral blood flow studied by xenon-133 inhalation technique in parkinsonism: Loss of hyperfrontal pattern. *Journal of Cerebral Blood Flow and Metabolism*, 3, 33–37.

Bilder, R. M., Mukherjee, S., Reider, R. O., & Pandurangi, A. K. (1985). Symptomatic and neuropsychological components of defect states. *Schizophrenia Bulletin*, 11, 409–419.

Birkmayer, W., Dannielzyk, W., Neumacher, E., & Riederer, P. (1974). Nucleus ruber and L-DOPA psychosis: Biochemical postmortem findings. *Journal of Neural Transmission*, 35, 93–116.

Birkmayer, W., Knoll, J., Riederer, P., Youdim, M. B. H., Hars, V., & Marton, J. (1985). Increased life expectancy resulting from addition of L-deprenyl to madopar treatment in Parkinson's disease: A longterm study. *Journal of Neural Transmission*, 64, 113–127.

Bjorklund, A., & Lindvall, O. (1979). Regeneration of normal terminal innervation patterns by central noradrenergic neurons after 5,7-dihydroxytryptamine-induced axotomy in the adult rat. *Brain Research*, 171, 271–294.

Blatt, S. J., & Wild, C. M. (1976). *Schizophrenia: A Developmental Analysis*. New York: Academic Press.

Bleuler, E. (1908). *Dementia Praecox or the Group of Schizophrenias*. Trans., J. Zinkin (1950). New York: International Universities Press.

Blumer, D., & Benson, D. F. (1975). Personality changes with frontal and temporal lobe lesions. In D. F. Benson & D. Blumer (Eds.), *Psychiatric Aspects of Neurological Disease*. New York: Grune & Stratton, pp. 151–170.

Bobon, J., Pinchard, A., Collard, J., & Bobon, D. P. (1972). Clinical classification of neuroleptics with special reference to their antimanic, antiautistic, and ataraxic properties. *Comprehensive Psychiatry*, 13, 123–131.

Bock, R. D. (1975). *Multivariate Statistical Methods in Behavioral Research*. New York: McGraw-Hill.

Bogerts, B., Meertz, E., & Schonfeldt-Bausch, R. (1985). Basal ganglia and limbic system pathology in schizophrenia: A morphometric study of brain volume and shrinkage. *Archives of General Psychiatry*, 42, 784–791.

Bowdler, H., Martin, R. S., Reinsch, C., & Wilkinson, J. H. (1968). The QR and QL algorithm for symmetric metrices. *Numerische Mathematik*, 11, 293–306.

Bowers, M. B. (1974). Central dopamine turnover in schizophrenic syndromes. *Archives of General Psychiatry*, 31, 50–54.

Bowers, M. B., Goodman, E., & Sim, V. M. (1964). Some behavioral changes in man following anticholinesterase administration. *Journal of Nervous and Mental Diseases*, 138, 383–389.

Bowman, M., & Lewis, M. S. (1980). Sites of subcortical damage in diseases which resemble schizophrenia. *Neuropsychologia*, 18, 597–601.

Boyd, A. E., Lebovits, H. E., & Feldman, J. M. (1971). Endocrine function and glucose metabolism in patients with Parkinson's disease and their alteration by L-dopa. *Journal of Clinical Endocrinology and Metabolism*, 33, 829–837.

Braff, D. L., & Saccuzzo, D. P. (1985). The time course of information processing deficits in schizophrenia. *American Journal of Psychiatry*, 142, 170–174.

Brambilla, F., Guastalla, A., & Guerrini, A. (1976). Glucose-insulin metabolism in chronic schizophrenia. *Diseases of the Nervous System*, 37, 98–103.

Breier, A., Wolkowitz, O. M., Doran, A. R., Roy, A., Hommer, D. W., & Pickar, D. (1987). Neuroleptic responsivity of negative and positive symptoms in schizophrenia. *American Journal of Psychiatry*, 144, 1549–1555.

Brown, G. W. (1960). Length of hospital stay and schizophrenia: A review of the statistical studies. *Acta Psychiatrica Neurologica Scandinavica*, 35, 414–430.

Bucci, L. (1987). The negative symptoms of schizophrenia and monoamine oxidase inhibitors. *Psychopharmacology*, 91, 104–108.

Buchanan, F. H., Parton, R. V., Warren, J. W., & Baker, E. P. (1975). Double-blind trial of L-dopa in chronic schizophrenia. *Australian and New Zealand Journal of Psychiatry*, 9, 269–271.

Buchsbaum, M. S., Ingvar, D. S., Kessler, R., Waters, R. N., Cappelleti, J., van Kamron, D. P., King, A. C., Johnson, J. L., Manning, R. G., Flynn, R. W., Mann, L. S., Bunney, W. E., & Sokoloff, L. (1982). Cerebral glucography with emission tomography: Use in normal subjects and in patients with schizophrenia. *Archives of General Psychiatry*, 39, 251–259.

Burdock, E. I., & Hardesty, S. (1973). *Structured Clinical Interview (SCI)*. Nutley, NJ: Hoffman LaRoche.

Buscaino, V. M. (1920). Le cause anatoma-pathologiche della manifetatione schizophrenica della demenza precoce. *Ric Pathologia Nervus Mental*, 25, 193–226.

Carpenter, W. T., Jr., Heinrichs, D. W., & Alphs, L. D. (1985). Treatment of negative symptoms. *Schizophrenia Bulletin*, 11, 440–452.

Carpenter, W. T., Jr., Heinrichs, D. W., & Wagman, A. M. I. (1988). Deficit and nondeficit forms of schizophrenia: The concept. *American Journal of Psychiatry*, 145, 578–583.

Cash, R., Dennis, T., L'Heureux, R., Raisman, R., Javoy-Agid, F., & Scatton, B. (1987). Parkinson's disease and dementia: Norepinephrine and dopamine in locus coeruleus. *Neurology*, 39, 42–46.

Chapman, L. J., Cameron, R., Cocke, J. G., & Pritchett, T. (1975). Effects of phenothiazine withdrawal on proverb interpretation of chronic schizophrenics. *Journal of Abnormal Psychology*, 84, 24–29.

Chase, T. N. (1974). Catecholamine metabolism and neurological disease. *Biochemical Pharmacology*, 23 (Suppl.), 941–946.

Chien, C., DiMascio, A., & Cole, J. O. (1974). Antiparkinson agents and depot phenothiazines. *American Journal of Psychiatry*, 131, 86–90.

Cornblatt, B. A., Lenzenweger, M. F., Dworkin, R. M., & Erlenmeyer-Kimling, L. (1985). Positive and negative schizophrenic symptoms, attention, and information processing. *Schizophrenia Bulletin*, 11, 397–408.

Cox, S. M., & Ludwig, A. M. (1979). Neurological soft signs and psychopathology: Findings in schizophrenia. *Journal of Nervous and Mental Disease*, 167, 161–165.

Crow, T. J. (1980a). Molecular pathology of schizophrenia: More than one disease process? *British Medical Journal*, 280, 66–68.

Crow, T. J. (1980b). Positive and negative schizophrenic symptoms and the role of dopamine: Discussion, 2. *British Journal of Psychiatry*, 137, 383–386.

Crow, T. J. (1983). Is schizophrenia an infectious disease? *Lancet*, 1, 173–175.

Crow, T. J. (1985). The two-syndrome concept: Origins and current status. *Schizophrenia Bulletin*, 11, 471–486.

Crow, T. J., Johnstone, E. C., & McClelland, H. A. (1976). The coincidence of schizophrenia and parkinsonism: Some neurochemical implications. *Psychological Medicine*, 6, 227–233.

Crunch Statistical Package: Reference Manual (1986). Oakland, CA.: Crunch Software Corp.

Csernansky, J. G., Brown, K., & Hollister, L. E. (1986). Is there drug treatment for negative schizophrenic symptoms? *Hospital Formulary*, 21, 790–792.

D'Antona, R., Baron, J. C., Samson, Y., Serdaru, M., Viader, F., Agid, Y., & Cambier, J. (1985). Subcortical dementia: Frontal cortex hypometabolism detected by positron tomography in patients with progressive supranuclear palsy. *Brain*, 108, 785–799.

Davis, K. L., Hollister, L. E., Overall, J., Johnson, A., & Train, K. (1976). Physostigmine: Effects on cognition and affect in normal subjects. *Psychopharmacology*, 51, 23–27.

Davis, T. M., & Rodriguez, V. L. (1979). Comparison of WAIS and EIWA scores in an institutionalized Latin American psychiatric population. *Journal of Consulting and Clinical Psychology*, 47, 181–182.

De Buck, R., Hoffman, G., & De Smet, S. (1989). A polysomnographic study of chronic schizophrenic patients treated with risperidone. In C. N. Stefanis, C. R. Soldatos, & A. D. Rabavilas (Eds.), *Psychiatry Today: Accomplishments and Promises*. Amsterdam: Excerpta Medica, p. 559.

De Cuyper, H. J. A. (1989). Risperidone in the treatment of chronic psychotic patients: An overview of the double-blind comparative studies. In F. J. Ayd, Jr. (Ed.), *Thirty Years of Janssen Research in Psychiatry*. Baltimore: Ayd Medical Communications, pp. 115–122.

De Jong, D. (1966). Parkinson's disease: Statistics. *Journal of Neurosurgery*, 24(suppl.), 149–155.

Den Hartog Jager, W. A., & Bethlem, J. (1960). The distribution of Lewy bodies in the central and autonomic nervous system in idiopathic paralysis agitans. *Journal of Neurology, Neurosurgery, and Psychiatry*, 23, 283–290.

Deniker, P. (1978). Impact of neuroleptic chemotherapies on schizophrenic psychosis. *American Journal of Psychiatry*, 135, 923–927.

Desai, N. G., Ganghadar, B. N., Pradham, N., & Chanabasavanna, S. M. (1984). Treatment of negative schizophrenia with d-amphetamine. *American Journal of Psychiatry*, 141, 723–724.

Dewan, M. J., Pandurangi, A. K., Lee, S. M., Ramacharan, T., Levy, B., Boucher, M., Yuzawitz, A., & Major, L. F. (1983). Central brain morphology in chronic schizophrenic patients: A controlled CT study. *Biological Psychiatry*, 18, 1133–1140.

Di Leo, J. H. (1973). *Children's Drawings as Diagnostic Aids*. New York: Brunner/Mazel.

Domino, E. F., & Olds, M. E. (1968). Cholinergic inhibition of self-stimulation behavior. *Journal of Pharmacology*, 164, 202–211.

Dworkin, R. H., & Lenzenweger, M. F. (1984). Symptoms and the genetics of schizophrenia: Implication for diagnosis. *American Journal of Psychiatry*, 141, 1541–1546.

Economo, C. (1931). *Encephalitis Lethargica: Its Sequelae and Treatment*. Trans., K. O. Newman. Oxford: Oxford University Press.

Elner, A. M., & Kandel, E. I. (1965). Study of carbohydrate metabolism in parkinsonism. *ZH Neurvpathology Psikhiatry IM SS Korsakova*, 65, 46–50.

Fabrega, H. (1974). Problems implicit in the cultural and social study of depression. *Psychosomatic Medicine*, 36, 377–398.

Fairweather, D. S. (1947). Psychiatric aspects of postencephalitic syndrome. *Journal of Mental Science*, 93, 201–254.

Falloon, I., Watt, D. C., & Shepherd, M. (1978). The social outcome of patients in a trial of long-term continuation therapy in schizophrenia: Pimozide vs. fluphenazine. *Psychological Medicine*, 8, 265–274.

Fanget, F., Claustrat, B., Delery, J., Brun, J., Terra, J. L., Marie-Cardine, M., & Guyotat, J. (1989). Nocturnal plasma melatonin levels in schizophrenic patients. *Biological Psychiatry*, 25, 499–501.

Fayen, M., Goldman, M. B., Moulthrop, M. A., & Luchins, D. J. (1988). Differential memory function with dopaminergic versus anticholinergic treatment of drug-induced extrapyramidal symptoms. *American Journal of Psychiatry*, 145, 483–486.

Feighner, J., Robins, E., Guze, S. B., Woodruff, R. A., Winokur, G., & Munoz, R. (1972). Diagnostic criteria for use in psychiatric research. *Archives of General Psychiatry*, 26, 57–63.

Feinberg, S. S., Kay, S. R., Elijovich, L. R., Fiszbein, A., & Opler, L. A. (1988). Pimozide treatment of the negative schizophrenic syndrome: An open trial. *Journal of Clinical Psychiatry*, 49, 235–238.

Ferrier, I. N., Arendt, J., Johnstone, E. C., & Crow, T. J. (1982). Reduced nocturnal melatonin secretion in chronic schizophrenia: Relationship to body weight. *Clinical Endocrinology*, 17, 181–187.

Ferrier, I. N., Roberts, G.W., Crow, T. J., Johnstone, E. C., Owens, D. G. C., Lee, Y. C., O'Shaughnessy, D., Adrian, T. E., Polak, J. M., & Bloom, S. R. (1983). Reduced cholecystokinin-like and somatostatin-like immunoreactivity is associated with negative symptoms in schizophrenia. *Life Sciences*, 33, 475–482.

Fields, J. H., Kay, S. R., Grosz, D., Levin, L., Pawl, G., & Alexander, G. (1990). *The Positive and Negative Syndrome Scale for Children (Kiddie-PANSS)*. New York: Albert Einstein College of Medicine.

Fishman, M. (1975). The brain stem in psychosis. *British Journal of Psychiatry*, 126, 414–422.

Flaherty, J. A., Gavaria, F. M., Pathak, D., Mitchell, T., Wintrob, R., Richman, J. A., & Birz, S. (1988). Developing instruments for cross-cultural psychiatric research. *Journal of Nervous and Mental Disease*, 176, 257–263.

Fleischhaker, W. W., Barnas, C., Stuppack, C., Unterweger, B., & Hinterhuber, H. (1987). Zotepine in the treatment of negative symptoms in chronic schizophrenia. *Pharmacopsychiatry*, 20, 58–60.

Flint, A. J., & Wastwood, R. (1988). Frontal lobe syndrome and depression in old age. *Journal of Geriatric Psychiatry and Neurology*, 1, 53–55.

Forno, L. S. (1986). The Lewy body in Parkinson's disease. In M. D. Yahr & K. J.

Bergmann (Eds.), *Advances in Neurology*, Vol. 45. New York: Raven Press, pp. 35–43.

Friedberg, J. (1961). Shock treatment, brain damage, and memory loss: A neurological perspective. *American Journal of Psychiatry*, 117, 1113–1118.

Friedhoff, A. J. (1983). A strategy for developing novel drugs for the treatment of schizophrenia. *Schizophrenia Bulletin*, 9, 555–562.

Friedman, J. H., & Lannon, M. C. (1989). Clozapine in the treatment of psychosis in Parkinson's disease. *Neurology*, 39, 1219–1221.

Friedman, J. M., Max, J., & Swift, R. (1987). Idiopathic Parkinson's disease in a chronic schizophrenic patient: Long-term treatment with clozapine and L-dopa. *Clinical Neuropharmacology*, 10, 470–475.

Garrett, H. E. (1964). *Statistics in Psychology and Education*. New York; David McKay, pp. 337–370.

Gath, J., Jorgensen, A., & Sjaastad, O. (1975). Pneumoencephalographic findings in parkinsonism. *Archives of Neurology*, 32, 769–773.

Gelders, Y. E., Heylen, S. L. E., Vanden Bussche, A. J. M., Reyntjens, A. J. M., & Janssen, P. A. J. (1989). Risperidone: A breakthrough in antipsychotic therapy. In F. J. Ayd, Jr. (Ed.), *Thirty Years of Janssen Research in Psychiatry*. Baltimore: Ayd Medical Communications, pp. 123–128.

Gellenberg, A. J., & Doller, J. C. (1979). Clozapine vs. chlorpromazine for the treatment of schizophrenia. Preliminary results from a double-blind study. *Journal of Clinical Psychiatry*, 40, 238–240.

George, L., & Neufeld, R. W. J. (1985). Cognition and symptomatology in schizophrenia. *Schizophrenia Bulletin*, 11, 264–285.

Gerlach, J., Behnke, K., Heltberg, J., Munk-Anderson, E., & Nielsen, H. (1985). Sulpiride and haloperidol in schizophrenia: A double-blind cross-over study of its therapeutic effect, side effects, and plasma concentrations. *British Journal of Psychiatry*, 147, 283–288.

Gerlach, J., & Luhdorf, K. (1985). The effect of L-dopa on young patients with simple schizophrenia treated with neuroleptic drugs: A double-blind cross-over trial with madopar and placebo. *Psychopharmacologia*, 44, 105–110.

Gibbs, W. R. G., & Lees, A. J. (1989). Prevalence of Lewy body in Alzheimer's disease. *Annals of Neurology*, 26, 691–692.

Goldberg, E. (1985). Akinesia, tardive dysmentia, and frontal lobe disorder in schizophrenia. *Schizophrenia Bulletin*, 11, 255–263.

Goldberg, T. E., Weinberger, D. R., Berman, K. F., Pliskin, N. H., & Podd, M. H. (1987). Further evidence for dementia of the prefontal type in schizophrenia? A controlled study of teaching the Wisconsin Card Sorting Test. *Archives of General Psychiatry*, 44, 1008–1014.

Golden, C. J., Graber, B., Coffman, J., Berg, R. A., Newlin, D. B., & Bloch, S. (1981). Structural brain deficits in schizophrenia: Identification by computed tomographic scan density measurement. *Archives of General Psychiatry*, 38, 1014–1017.

Gould, R. J., Murphy, K. M., Reynolds, I. J., & Snyder, S. H. (1983). Antischizophrenic drugs of the diphenylbutylpiperidine type acts as calcium channel antagonists. *Proceedings of the National Academy of Science, USA*, 80, 5122–5125.

Graham, F. K., & Kendall, B. S. (1960). Memory-for-Designs Test: Revised general manual. *Psychological Reports*, 11, 147–188.

Green, M., & Walker, E. (1984). Susceptibility to backward masking in schizophrenia patients with positive and negative symptoms. *American Journal of Psychiatry*, 141, 1273–1275.

Green, M., & Walker, E. (1986). Symptom correlates of vulnerability to backward masking in schizophrenia. *American Journal of Psychiatry*, 143, 181–186.

Green, R. F., & Martinez, J. N. (1968). *Escala de Inteligencia Wechsler para Adultos*. New York: Psychological Corporation.

Greenfield, J. G., & Bosanquet, F. D. (1953). The brainstem in parkinsonism. *Journal of Neurology, Neurosurgery, and Psychiatry*, 16, 213–226.

Gross, H., & Langner, E. (1970). The neuroleptic 100–129/HF 1854 (clozapine) in psychiatry. *International Pharmacopsychiatry*, 4, 220–230.

Growdon, J. M., & Corkin, S. (1986). Cognitive impairments in Parkinson's disease. In M. D. Yahr & K. J. Bergmann (Eds.), *Advances in Neurology*, Vol. 45. New York: Raven Press, pp. 383–392.

Gruzelier, J. H., & Hammond, N. V. (1978). The effect of chlorpromazine upon psychophysiological, endocrine, and information processing measures in schizophrenia. *Journal of Psychiatric Research*, 14, 167–182.

Guy, W. (1976). *ECDEU Assessment Manual for Psychopharmacology* (Rev. ed.) Washington, DC: U.S. Department of Health, Education, and Welfare.

Hall, A. (1945). The origin and purpose of blinking. *British Journal of Ophthalmology*, 29, 445–467.

Harnyrd, C., Bjerkenstedt, L., Bjork, K., Gullberg, B., Orenstierna, G., Sedvall, G., Wiesal, F. A., Wik, C., & Aberg-Wistedt, A. (1984). Clinical evaluation of sulpiride in schizophrenic patients: A double-blind comparison with chlorpromazine. *Acta Psychiatrica Scandinavica*, (Suppl.), 311, 7–30.

Harris, R. J. (1975). *A Primer of Multivariate Statistics*. New York: Academic Press.

Haubrich, D. R., & Pfleugler, A. B. (1982). The autoreceptor control of dopamine synthesis. *Molecular Pharmacology*, 21, 114–120.

Hedlund, J. L., & Viewig, B. W. (1980). The Brief Psychiatric Rating Scale (BPRS): A comprehensive review. *Journal of Operational Psychiatry*, 11, 48–65.

Heinrichs, D. W., Hanlon, T. E., & Carpenter, W. T., Jr. (1984). The Quality of Life Scale: An instrument for rating the schizophrenic deficit syndrome. *Schizophrenia Bulletin*, 10, 388–398.

Hoehn, M. M., Crowley, T. J., & Rutledge, C. O. (1976). Dopamine correlates of neurological and psychological status in untreated parkinsonism. *Journal of Neurology, Neurosurgery, and Psychiatry*, 39, 941–951.

Hoffman, W. F., Labs, S. M., & Casey, D. E. (1987). Neuroleptic-induced parkinsonism in older schizophrenics. *Biological Psychiatry*, 22, 427–439.

Hollister, L. E., & Glazener, F. S. (1961). Concurrent paralysis agitan and schizophrenia. *Disease of the Nervous System*, 22, 187–189.

Honigfeld, G., Patin, J., & Singer, J. (1984). Clozapine: Antipsychotic activity in treatment-resistant schizophrenics. *Advances in Therapy*, 1, 77–97.

Hopf, A. (1952). Uber histopathologische veranderungen im Pallidum und Striatum bei Schizophrenie. *Proceedings of the International Congress of Neuropathology*, 3, 629–635.

Hornykiewicz, O., & Kish, S. J. (1986). Biochemical pathology of Parkinson's disease. In M. D. Yahr & K. J. Bergmann (Eds.), *Advances in Neurology*, Vol. 45. New York: Raven Press, pp. 19–34.

Houston, J. P., Mass, J. W., Bowden, C. L., Contreras, S. A., McIntyre, K. L., & Javors, M. A. (1986). Cerebrospinal fluid HVA, central brain atrophy, and clinical state in schizophrenia. *Psychiatry Research*, 19, 207–214.

Howard, R. S., & Lees, A. J. (1987). Encephalitis lethargica: A report of four recent cases. *Brain*, 110, 19–33.

Hurst, J. H., Lewitt, P. A., Burns, R. S., Foster, N. L., & Lovenberg, W. (1985). CSF dopamine-beta-hydroxylase activity in Parkinson's disease. *Neurology*, 35, 565–568.

Iager, A.-C., Kirch, D. C., & Wyatt, R. J. (1985). A negative symptom rating scale. *Psychiatry Research*, 16, 27–36.

Inanaga, K., Nakazawa, Y., Inoue, E., Tachibana, H., & Oshima, M. (1975). Double-blind controlled study of L-dopa therapy in schizophrenia. *Folia Psychiatrica Neurologica Japan*, 29, 123–143.

Jackson, J. A., Free, G. B. M., and Pike, H. V. (1923). The psychic manifestation in paralysis agitans. *Archives of Neurology and Psychiatry*, 10, 680–684.

Jackson, J. Hughlings (1887). Remarks on evolution and dissolution of the nervous system. *Journal of Mental Science*, 23, 25–48.

Jansen, A. A. I., & Boom, A. J. (1989). Risperidone in the treatment of chronic psychosis. In C. N. Stefanis, C. R. Soldatos, & A. D. Rabavilas (Eds.), *Psychiatry Today: Accomplishments and Promises*. Amsterdam: Excerpta Medica, p. 551.

Janssen Research Foundation (1989). Risperidone in the Treatment of Chronic Schizophrenia: A Double-blind, Parallel Group Phase III Study (protocol # 64766/0204). Piscataway, NJ: Janssen Research Foundation.

Javoy-Agid, F., & Agid, F. (1980). Is the mesocortical dopaminergic system involved in Parkinson's disease? *Neurology*, 30, 1326–1330.

Javoy-Agid, F., Ruberg, M., Hirsch, E., Cash, R., Raisman, R., Taquet, H., Epelbaum, J., Scatton, B., Duychkaerts, C., & Agid, Y. (1986). Recent progress in the neurochemistry of Parkinson's disease. In S. Fahn, C. D. Marsden, P. Jenner, & P. Teychenne (Eds.), *Recent Developments in Parkinson's Disease*. New York: Raven Press, pp. 67–83.

Jelliffe, S. E. (1927). The mental pictures in schizophrenia and in epidemic encephalitis. *American Journal of Psychiatry*, 6, 413–465.

Jellinger, K. (1986a). Overview of morphological changes in Parkinson's disease. In M. D. Yahr & K. J. Bergmann (Eds.), *Advances in Neurology*, Vol. 45. New York; Raven Press, pp. 1–18.

Jellinger, K. (1986b). Pathology of parkinsonism. In S. Fahn, C. D. Marsden, P. Jenner, & P. Teychenne (Eds.), *Recent Developments in Parkinson's Disease*. New York: Raven Press, pp. 33–66.

Johnstone, E. C., Crow, T. J., Ferrier, I. N., Frith, C. D., Owens, D. G. C., Bourne, R. C., & Gamble, S. J. (1983). Adverse effects of anticholinergic medication on positive schizophrenic symptoms. *Psychological Medicine*, 13, 513–527.

Johnstone, E. C., Crow, T. J., Frith, C. D., Carney, M. P. W., & Price, J. S. (1978a). Mechanisms of the antipsychotic effect in the treatment of acute schizophrenia. *Lancet*, 1, 848–851.

Johnstone, E. C., Crow, T. J., Frith, C. D., Stevens, M., Kreel, L., & Husband, J. (1978b). The dementia of dementia praecox. *Acta Psychiatrica Scandinavica*, 57, 305–324.

Johnstone, E. C., Owens, D. G. C., Frith, C. D., & Crow, T. J. (1987). The relative stability of positive and negative features in chronic schizophrenia. *British Journal of Psychiatry*, 150, 60–64.

Kane, J. M., Honigfeld, G., Singer, J., & Meltzer, A. (1988). Clozapine in treatment resistant schizophrenia. *Archives of General Psychiatry*, 45, 789–795.

Kane, J. M., Rifkin, A., Woener, M., Reardon, G., Kreisman, D., Blumenthal, R., & Borenstein, M. (1985). High dose versus low dose strategies in treatment of schizophrenia. *Psychopharmacology Bulletin*, 22, 533–537.

Kanofsky, J. D., Kay, S. R., Lindenmayer, J. P., & Opler, L. A. (1987). Catatonic schizo-phrenia and negative syndrome. *Canadian Journal of Psychiatry, 32,* 162.

Karson, C. N. (1983). Spontaneous eye blink rates and dopaminergic systems. *Brain, 106,* 643–653.

Katz, M. M. (1968). The dimensional and typological approaches to assessment and prediction in psychopathology. In D. E. Ephron (Ed.), *Psychopharmacology: A Review of Progress, 1957–1967.* Washington, D.C.: Public Health Service Publication No. 1836.

Katz, M. M., & Itil, J. M. (1974). Video methodology for research in psychopathology and psychopharmacology. *Archives of General Psychiatry, 31,* 204–210.

Kawamura, T., Kinoshita, M., Iwasaki, Y., & Nemoto, H. (1987). Low-dose dexametha-sone suppression test in Japanese patients with Parkinson's disease. *Journal of Neurology, 234,* 264–265.

Kay, S. R. (1977). Developmental assessment of cognitive style in mentally retarded psychotics. *Journal of Clinical Psychology, 33,* 953–958.

Kay, S. R. (1978). Qualitative differences in human figure drawings according to schizo-phrenic subtype. *Perceptual and Motor Skills, 47,* 923–932.

Kay, S. R. (1980). Progressive figure drawings in the developmental assessment of men-tally retarded psychotics. *Perceptual and Motor Skills, 50,* 583–590.

Kay, S. R. (1981). Arousal and schizophrenia: Toward a dual-process model and frame-work for research. *JSAS Catalog of Selected Documents in Psychology, 11,* 35–36 (Whole No. 2256).

Kay, S. R. (1982). *The Cognitive Diagnostic Battery: Evaluation of Intellectual Disorders.* Odessa, FL: Psychological Assessment Resources.

Kay, S. R. (1986). Diagnosis of mental retardation in schizophrenia: Psychometric dis-tinction between intellectual subnormality and abnormality. *Journal of Psychoeducational Assessment, 4,* 13–25.

Kay, S. R. (1988). Differential diagnosis of mental subnormality and abnormality: The contribution of psychometrics. *Psychiatric Quarterly, 59,* 47–61.

Kay, S. R. (1989). Cognitive diagnostic assessment. In S. Wetzler & M. M. Katz (Eds.), *Contemporary Approaches to Psychological Assessment.* New York: Brunner/Mazel, pp. 177–200.

Kay, S. R. (1990). Pyramidical model of syndromes in schizophrenia. In *Treatment of Negative Symptoms in Schizophrenia.* Oxford: Oxford Clinical Communications, pp. 9–17.

Kay, S. R. (in press-a). The longitudinal course of negative symptoms in schizophrenia. In J. F. Greden & R. Tandon (Eds.), *Negative Schizophrenic Symptoms: Pathophysiology and Clinical Implications.* Washington, D. C.: American Psychiatric Press.

Kay, S. R. (in press-b). Methods of assessing negative symptoms. *Archives of Psychiatric Diagnostics and Clinical Evaluation.*

Kay, S. R. (in press-c). New perspectives on the positive-negative distinction in schizo-phrenia. In J. P. Lindenmayer & S. R. Kay (Eds.), *New Biological Vistas on Schizo-phrenia.* New York: Brunner/Mazel.

Kay, S. R. (in press-d). Significance of the positive-negative distinction in schizophrenia. *Schizophrenia Bulletin.*

Kay, S. R., Fiszbein, A., Gorelick, A., Opler, L. A., Spitzer, R. L., Williams, J. B. W., Gibbon, M., & First, M. B. (1990). Two-tier diagnostic system for psychotic disor-ders. 143rd Annual Meeting of the American Psychiatric Association, New York.

Kay, S. R., Fiszbein, A., Lindenmayer, J. P., & Opler, L. A. (1986). Positive and negative syndromes in schizophrenia as a function of chronicity. *Acta Psychiatrica Scandinavica*, 74, 507–518.

Kay, S. R., Fiszbein, A., & Opler, L. A. (1986). Negative symptom rating scale: Limitations in psychometric and research methodology. *Psychiatry Research*, 19, 169–170.

Kay, S. R., Fiszbein, A., & Opler, L. A. (1987). The Positive and Negative Syndrome Scale (PANSS) for schizophrenia. *Schizophrenia Bulletin*, 13, 261–276.

Kay, S. R., Fiszbein, A., Vital-Herne, M., & Fuentes, L. S. (in press). The Positive and Negative Syndrome Scale, Spanish adaptation (PANSS-S). *Journal of Nervous and Mental Disease*.

Kay, S. R., Kanofsky, J. D., Lindenmayer, J. P., & Opler, L. A. (1987). The changing presentation of catatonia. *American Journal of Psychiatry*, 144, 834–835.

Kay, S. R., & Lindenmayer, J. P. (1987). Outcome predictors in acute schizophrenia: Prospective significance of background and clinical dimension. *Journal of Nervous and Mental Disease*, 175, 152–160.

Kay, S. R., & Murrill, L. M. (1990). Predicting outcome of schizophrenia: Significance of symptom profiles and outcome dimension. *Comprehensive Psychiatry* 31, 91–102.

Kay, S. R., Murrill, L. M., & Opler, L. A. (1989). Characteristics of verbal encoding in positive and negative syndromes of schizophrenia. *Proceedings and Abstracts of the Annual Meeting of Eastern Psychological Association*, 60, 52.

Kay, S. R., & Opler, L. A. (1985). L-dopa in the treatment of negative schizophrenic symptoms. *International Journal of Psychiatry in Medicine*, 15, 293–298.

Kay, S. R., & Opler, L. A. (1987). The positive-negative dimension in schizophrenia: Its validity and significance. *Psychiatric Developments*, 5, 79–103.

Kay, S. R., & Opler, L. A. (1989). Deficit or negative syndrome? *American Journal of Psychiatry*, 149, 282–283.

Kay, S. R., & Opler, L. A. (1990). Structured Clinical Interview for the Positive and Negative Syndrome Scale (SCI-PANSS). Toronto: Multi-Health Systems Inc.

Kay, S. R., Opler, L. A., & Fiszbein, A. (1985). Genetics of schizophrenia and the positive-negative dimension. *American Journal of Psychiatry*, 142, 994–995.

Kay, S. R., Opler, L. A., & Fiszbein, A. (1986). Significance of positive and negative syndromes in chronic schizophrenia. *British Journal of Psychiatry*, 149, 439–448.

Kay, S. R., Opler, L. A., & Fiszbein, A. (1987). *Positive and Negative Syndrome Scale (PANSS) Rating Manual*. San Raphael, Calif.: Social and Behavioral Sciences Documents.

Kay, S. R., Opler, L. A., & Fiszbein, A. (1989a). *The Positive and Negative Syndrome Scale: Tape 1. Demonstration of Interview Technique*. Piscataway, NJ: Janssen Research Foundation.

Kay, S. R., Opler, L. A., & Fiszbein, A. (1989b). *The Positive and Negative Syndrome Scale: Tape 2. Self-assessment and Determination of Inter-rater Reliability*. Piscataway, NJ: Janssen Research Foundation.

Kay, S. R., Opler, L. A., & Fiszbein, A. (1990). *Positive and Negative Syndrome Scale (PANSS) Manual*. Toronto: Multi-Health Systems Inc.

Kay, S. R., Opler, L. A., & Lindenmayer, J. P. (1988). Reliability and validity of the Positive and Negative Syndrome Scale for schizophrenics. *Psychiatry Research*, 23, 99–110.

Kay, S. R., Opler, L. A., & Lindenmayer, J. P. (1989). The Positive and Negative Syndrome Scale (PANSS): Rationale and standardization. *British Journal of Psychiatry*, 155, (Suppl. 7), 59–65.

Kay, S. R., Opler, L. A., Spitzer, R. L., Williams, J. B. W., Gibbon, M., & First, M. B.

(1989). *Structured Clinical Interview for DSM-III-R: PANSS Version*. New York: New York State Psychiatric Institute, Biometrics Research.

Kay, S. R., & Sevy, S. (in press). Pyramidical model of schizophrenia. *Schizophrenia Bulletin*.

Kay, S. R., & Singh, M. M. (1974). A temporal measure of attention in schizophrenia and its clinical significance. *British Journal of Psychiatry*, 125, 146–151.

Kay, S. R., & Singh, M. M. (1975a). A developmental approach to delineate components of cognitive dysfunction in schizophrenia. *British Journal of Social and Clinical Psychology*, 14, 387–399.

Kay, S. R., & Singh, M. M. (1975b). Pulse rate and sleeplessness in relation to nosological distinctions in schizophrenia. *Perceptual and Motor Skills*, 40, 178.

Kay, S. R., & Singh, M. M. (1979). Cognitive abnormality in schizophrenia: A dual-process model. *Biological Psychiatry*, 14, 155–176.

Kay, S. R., & Singh, M. M. (1989). The positive-negative distinction in drug-free schizophrenic patients: Stability, response to neuroleptics, and prognostic significance. *Archives of General Psychiatry*, 46, 711–718.

Kay, S. R., Singh, M. M., & Smith, J. M. (1975). Color Form Representation Test: A developmental method for the study of cognition in schizophrenia. *British Journal of Social and Clinical Psychology*, 14, 401–411.

Kay, S. R., Wolkenfeld, F., & Murrill, L. M. (1988a). Profiles of aggression among psychiatric patients. I. Nature and prevalence. *Journal of Nervous and Mental Disease*, 176, 539–546.

Kay, S. R., Wolkenfeld, F., & Murrill, L. M. (1988b). Profiles of aggression among psychiatric patients: II. Covariates and predictors. *Journal of Nervous and Mental Disease*, 176, 547–557.

Knight, R. A., & Roff, J. D. (1985). Affectivity in schizophrenia. In M. Alpert (Ed.), *Controversies in Schizophrenia*. New York: Guilford Press.

Kolb, B., and Whishaw, I. (1983). Performance of schizophrenic patients on tests sensitive to left or right frontal, temporal, or parietal function in neurological patients. *Journal of Nervous and Mental Disease*, 171, 435–443.

Kraepelin, E. (1919). *Dementia Praecox and Paraphrenia*. Trans., R. M. Barclay (1971). Huntington, NY: Krieger.

Krawiecka, M., Goldberg, D., & Vaughan, H. (1977). A standardized psychiatric assessment scale for rating chronic psychiatric patients. *Acta Psychiatrica Scandinavica*, 55, 299–308.

Lader, M. (1983). *Introduction to Psychopharmacology*. Kalamazoo, MI.: Scope Publications.

Langston, J. W., & Forno, L. S. (1978). The hypothalamus in Parkinson's disease. *Annals of Neurology*, 3, 129–133.

Lecrubier, Y., Puech, A. J., & Aubin P. (1988). Improvement by amisulpride of the negative syndrome in nonpsychotic subjects: A preliminary study. *Psychiatry and Psychobiology*, 3, 329–333.

Lepine, J. P., Piron, J., & Chapotot, E. (1989). Factor analysis of the PANSS in schizophrenic patients. In C. N. Stefanis, C. R. Soldatos, and A. D. Rabavilas (Eds.), *Psychiatry Today: Accomplishments and Promises*. Amsterdam: Excerpta Medica, p. 828.

Lesch, A., & Bogerts, B. (1984). The diencephalon in schizophrenia: Evidence for reduced thickness of the periventricular grey matter. *European Archives of Psychiatry and Neurological Sciences*, 234, 212–219.

Lewine, R. R. J., Fogg, L., & Meltzer, H. Y. (1983). Assessment of negative and positive symptoms in schizophrenia. *Schizophrenia Bulletin*, 9, 368–378.

Lewy, F. H. (1923). Die Lehre vom Tonus und der Bewegung. Berlin: Springer.

Liddle, P. F. (1987). The symptoms of chronic schizophrenia: A re-examination of the positive-negative dichotomy. *British Journal of Psychiatry*, 151, 145-151.

Lidsky, T. I., Weinhold, D. M., & Levine, F. M. (1979). Implications of basal ganglionic dysfunction for schizophrenia. *Biological Psychiatry*, 14, 3-12.

Lindenmayer, J. P., & Kay, S. R. (1987). Affective impairment in young acute schizophrenics: Its structure, course, and prognostic significance. *Acta Psychiatrica Scandinavica*, 75, 287-296.

Lindenmayer, J. P., & Kay, S. R. (1989). Depression, affective impairment, and negative symptoms in schizophrenia. *British Journal of Psychiatry*, 155 (Suppl. 7), 108-114.

Lindenmayer, J. P., Kay, S. R., & Friedman, C. (1986). Negative and positive schizophrenic syndromes after the acute phase: A prospective follow-up. *Comprehensive Psychiatry*, 27, 276-286.

Lindenmayer, J. P., Kay, S. R., & Opler, L. A. (1984). Positive and negative subtypes in acute schizophrenia. *Comprehensive Psychiatry*, 25, 454-464.

Lindenmayer, J. P., Kay, S. R., & van Praag, H. M. (1989). Distinction of schizoaffective from schizophrenic profile: Independent validation. *Schizophrenia Research*, 2, 423-424.

Lindenmayer, J. P., Mabugat, L. B., Kay, S. R., Murrill, L. M., & Sevy, S. (1990). Clozapine effects on positive vs. negative symptoms of schizophrenia. 143rd Annual Meeting of the American Psychiatric Association, New York.

Lindstrom, L. H. (1985). Low HVA and normal 5-HIAA CSF level in drug-free schizophrenic patients compared to healthy volunteers: Correlations to symptomatology and family history. *Psychiatry Research*, 14, 265-273.

Lipman, I. J., Boykin, M. E., & Flora, R. E. (1974). Glucose intolerance in Parkinson's disease. *Journal of Chronic Diseases*, 27, 573-579.

Lorr, M. (1962). Measurement of major psychotic syndromes. *Annals of the New York Academy of Sciences*, 93, 851-866.

Luchins, D. J., Jackman, H., & Meltzer, H. Y. (1983). Lateral ventricular size and drug-induced parkinsonism. *Psychiatry Research*, 9, 9-16.

Luria, A. R. (1966). *Higher Cortical Functions in Man*. New York: Basic Books.

MacKay, A. V. P. (1980). Positive and negative schizophrenic symptoms and the role of dopamine: Discussion, 1. *British Journal of Psychiatry*, 137, 379-383.

Marangell, L. B., Kay, S. R., & Lindenmayer, J. P. (1989). Low dose bromocriptine in the treatment of schizophrenia and tardive dyskinesia. Fourth Annual Meeting of the Society for Research in Psychopathology, Coral Gables, Florida.

Marascuilo, L. A., & Levin, J. R. (1983). *Multivariate Statistics in the Social Sciences*. Monterey, CA: Brooks/Cole.

Markianos, M., & Tripodianakis, J. (1985). Low plasma dopamine beta-hydroxylase in demented schizophrenics. *Biological Psychiatry*, 20, 94-119.

Marttila, R. J., Eskola, J., Paivarina, M., & Rinne, U. K. (1984). Immune functions in Parkinson's disease, In R. G. Hassler & J. F. Christ (Eds.), *Advances in Neurology*, Vol. 40. New York: Raven Press, pp. 315-323.

Maser, J. D., & Keith, S. J. (1983). CT scan and schizophrenia: Report on a workshop. *Schizophrenia Bulletin*, 9, 265-273.

Mason, S. T. (1979). Noradrenaline and behavior. *Trends in Neuroscience*, 2, 82-84.

Maudsley, H. (1899). *The Pathology of the Mind* (3rd ed.). New York: Appleton.

Mayeux, R. (1982). Depression and dementia in Parkinson's disease. In C. D. Maraden & S. Fahn (Eds.), *Movement Disorders*. London: Butterworths International Medical Reviews, pp. 75-95.

McCowan, P. K., & Cook, L. C. (1928). The mental aspect of chronic epidemic encephalitis. *Lancet*, 1, 1316–1320.

McGlashan, T. (1984). The Chestnut Lodge follow-up study: Long-term outcome of schizophrenia and affective disorders. *Archives of General Psychiatry*, 41, 586–601.

Meltzer, H. Y. (1987). Biological studies in schizophrenia. *Schizophrenia Bulletin*, 13, 77–111.

Meltzer, H. Y., Sommers, A. A., & Luchins, D. J. (1986). The effect of neuroleptics and other psychotropic drugs on negative symptoms in schizophrenia. *Journal of Clinical Psychopharmacology*, 6, 329–338.

Merriam, A. E., Kay, S. R., Opler, L. A., Kushner, S. F., & van Praag, H. M. (in press). Neurological signs and the positive-negative dimension in schizophrenia. *Biological Psychiatry*.

Mettler, F. A. (1955). Perceptual capacity, functions of the corpus striatum, and schizophrenia. *Psychiatric Quarterly*, 29, 89–97.

Mettler, F. A., & Crandell, A. (1959). Relation between parkinsonism and psychiatric disorder. *Journal of Nervous and Mental Disease*, 129, 551–557.

Mindham, R. H. S. (1970). Psychiatric symptoms in parkinsonism. *Journal of Neurology, Neurosurgery, and Psychiatry*, 32, 188–191.

Misra, P. C., & Hay, G. G. (1971). Encephalitis presenting as acute schizophrenia. *British Medical Journal*, 1, 532–533.

Morel-Maroger, A. (1977). Effects of levodopa on frontal signs in parkinsonism. *British Medical Journal*, 2, 1543.

Morgan, L. O., & Gregory, H. S. (1935). Pathological changes in the tuber cinereum in a group of psychoses. *Journal of Nervous and Mental Disease*, 82, 286–298.

Morrison, D. F. (1973). *Multivariate Statistical Methods* (2nd ed.). New York: McGraw-Hill.

Narabayashi, M., Kondo, T., Nagatsu, T., Hayashi, A., & Suzuki, T. (1984). DL-thereo-3,4,-dihydroxyphenylserine for freezing symptom in parkinsonism. In R. G. Hassler & J. F. Christ (Eds.), *Advances in Neurology*, Vol. 40. New York: Raven Press, pp. 497–502.

Nasrallah, H. A., Kuperman, S., Jacoby, C. G., McCalley-Whitters, M., & Hamra, B. (1983). Clinical correlates of sulcal widening in chronic schizophrenia. *Psychiatry Research*, 10, 237–242.

National Institute of Mental Health (1974). *Abnormal Involuntary Movement Scale*. Washington, DC: U. S. Department of Health, Education, and Welfare.

Neppe, V. M. (1989). *Innovative Psychopharmacotherapy*. New York: Raven Press.

Niemegeers, C. J. E. (1989). Serotonin receptor antagonism. In F. J. Ayd, Jr. (Ed.), *Thirty Years of Janssen Research in Psychiatry*. Baltimore: Ayd Medical Communications, pp. 99–107.

Nieto, A., & Nieto, D. (1988). The red nucleus, the substantia nigra, and the pineal gland responsible for mental illness. *International Journal of Neuroscience*, 32, 277–278.

Nieto, D., & Escobar, A. (1972). Major psychoses. In J. Minckler (Ed.), *Pathology of the Nervous System*, Vol. 3. New York: McGraw-Hill, pp. 2654–2665.

Nimatoudis, J., Fotiadis, H., Kokantzis, N., Karavatos, A., & Fotiadou, M. (1989). Main causes for the readmission of schizophrenic patients. In C. N. Stefanis, C. R. Soldatos, & A. D. Rabavilas (Eds.), *Psychiatry Today: Accomplishments and Promises*. Amsterdam: Excerpta Medica, p. 288.

Nunnally, J. C. (1978). *Psychometric Theory* (2nd ed.). New York: McGraw-Hill.

Ogura, C., Kishimoto, A., & Nakao, T. (1976). Clinical effects of L-dopa on schizophrenia. *Current Therapeutic Research, 20,* 308–318.

Olmedo, E. L. (1981). Testing linguistic minorities. *American Psychologist, 36,* 1078–1985.

Opler, L. A., & Kay, S. R. (1985). Birth seasonality and schizophrenia. *Archives of General Psychiatry, 42,* 106–108.

Opler, L. A., Kay, S. R., & Fiszbein, A. (1987). Positive and negative syndromes in schizophrenia: Typological, dimensional, and pharmacological validation. In P. D. Harvey & E. Walker (Eds.), *Positive and Negative Symptoms in Psychosis: Description, Research, and Future Directions.* Hillside, NJ: Lawrence Erlbaum Associates, pp. 124–154.

Opler, L. A., Kay, S. R., Rosado, V., & Lindenmayer, J. P. (1984). Positive and negative syndromes in chronic schizophrenic inpatients. *Journal of Nervous and Mental Disease, 172,* 317–325.

Overall, J. E. (1976). The Brief Psychiatric Rating Scale in psychopharmacological research. In *Psychological Measurements in Psychopharmacology: Modern Problems in Psychopharmacology,* Vol. 7. Basel: Karger.

Overall, J. E., & Gorham, D. R. (1962). Brief Psychiatric Rating Scale. *Psychological Reports, 10,* 799–912.

Owens, D. G. C., & Johnstone, E. C. (1980). The disabilities of chronic schizophrenia: Their nature and the factors contributing to their development. *British Journal of Psychiatry, 136,* 384–395.

Paunović, V. R., Jasović, M., Bogdanović, M. R., & Totić, S. D. (1988). Clozapine in the treatment of negative symptoms in schizophrenia. In *Proceedings of the Collegium Internationale Neuropsychopharmacologium,* Munich.

Payne, R. W. (1973). Cognitive abnormalities. In H. J. Eysenck (Ed.), *Handbook of Abnormal Psychology.* London: Pitman Medical Press, pp. 420–483.

Pearce, J. M. S., Flowers, K., Pearce, I., & Pratt, A. E. (1981). Clinical, psychometric, and CAT scan correlations in Parkinson's disease. In F. Rose & R. Capiladeo (Eds.), *Research Progress in Parkinson's Disease.* Kent: Pitman Medical Press, pp. 43–52.

Pearce, J. M. S., Hassan, A., & Gallagher, D. (1968). Primitive reflex activity in primary and symptomatic parkinsonism. *Journal of Neurology, Neurosurgery, and Psychiatry, 31,* 501–504.

Peuskins, J., De Cuyper, H. J. A., Bollen, J., Eneman, M., & Wilms, G. (1989). Risperidone: A new approach in the treatment of schizophrenia. In *Treatment of Negative Symptoms in Schizophrenia.* Oxford: Oxford Clinical Communications.

Pfeiffer, R. F., Hsieh, H. H., Diercks, M. J., Glaeske, C., Jefferson, A., & Cheng, S. C. (1986). Dexamethasone suppression test in Parkinson's disease. In M. D. Yahr & K. J. Bergmann (Eds.), *Advances in Neurology,* Vol. 45. New York: Raven Press, pp. 439–442.

Phillips, L. (1953). Case history data and prognosis in schizophrenia. *Journal of Nervous and Mental Disease, 117,* 515–525.

Piaget, J. (1952). *The Origins of Intelligence in Children.* New York: International Universities Press.

Pinder, R. M., Brogden, R. N., Sawyer, P. R., Speight, T. M., Spenser, R., & Avery, G. S. (1976). Pimozide: A review of its pharmacological properties and therapeutic uses in psychiatry. *Drugs, 12,* 1–40.

Pirozzolo, F. J., Hansch, E. C., & Mortimer, J. A. (1982). Dementia in Parkinson's disease: A neuropsychological analysis. *Brain and Cognition, 1,* 71–83.

Pogue-Geile, M. F., & Harrow, M. (1985). Negative and positive symptoms in schizophrenia and depression: A followup. *Schizophrenia Bulletin*, 10, 371–387.

Pogue-Geile, M. F., & Harrow, M. (1984). Negative symptoms in schizophrenia: Their longitudinal course and prognostic significance. *Schizophrenia Bulletin*, 11, 427–439.

Pogue-Geile, M. F., & Zubin, J. (1988). Negative symptomatology in schizophrenia: A conceptual and empirical review. *International Journal of Mental Health*, 16, 3–45.

Portin, R., Raininko, R., & Rinne, U. K. (1984). Neuropsychological disturbances in cerebral atrophy determined by computerized tomography in parkinsonian patients with long-term levodopa treatment. In R. G. Hassler & J. F. Christ (Eds.), *Advances in Neurology*, Vol. 40. New York: Raven Press, pp. 219–227.

Post, R. M., Jimerson, D. C., Bunney, W. E., Jr., & Goodwin, F. K. (1980). Dopamine and mania: Behavioral and biochemical effects of the dopamine receptor blocker, pimozide. *Psychopharmacology*, 67, 295–307.

Potkin, S. G., Weinberger, D. R., Linnoila, M., & Wyatt, R. J. (1983). Low CSF 5-hydroxyindoleacetic acid in schizophrenic patients with enlarged cerebral ventricles. *American Journal of Psychiatry*, 140, 21–25.

Pouplard, A., & Emile, J. (1984). Autoimmunity in Parkinson's disease. In R. G. Hassler & J. F. Christ (Eds.). *Advances in Neurology*, Vol. 40. New York: Raven Press, pp. 307–313.

Prasad, A. J., & Kumar, N. (1988). Suicidal behavior in hospitalized schizophrenics. *Suicide and Life-Threatening Behavior*, 18, 265–269.

Prosser, E. S., Csernansky, J. G., Kaplan, J., Thiemann, S., Becker, T. J., & Hollister, L. E. (1987). Depression, parkinsonian symptoms, and negative symptoms treated with neuroleptics. *Journal of Nervous and Mental Disease*, 175, 100–105.

Rafal, R. D., Posner, M., Walker, J. A., & Friedrich, F. J. (1984). Cognition and basal ganglia: Separating mental and motor components of performance in Parkinson's disease. *Brain*, 107, 1083–1094.

Ramirez, P. M. (1989). *Phenomenological and Neuropsychological Correlates of Positive and Negative Dimensionality in Schizophrenia*. Ann Arbor, MI: Dissertation Abstracts International.

Redmond, D. E., Maas, J. W., Kling, A., & Dekirmenjian, H. (1971). Changes in primate social behavior after treatment with alpha-methyl-para-tyrosine. *Psychosomatic Medicine*, 33, 97–113.

Reilly, T. M. (1989). Pimozide: A selective clinical review. In F. J. Ayd, Jr. (Ed.), *Thirty Years of Janssen Research in Psychiatry*. Baltimore: Ayd Medical Communications, pp. 72–84.

Reilly, T. M., Livingston, M. G., Hammond, G. L., & Batchelor, D. H. (1989). Preliminary U. K. experience with risperidone (R 64 766) in acute schizophrenia. In C. N. Stefanis, C. R. Soldatos, & A. D. Rabavilas (Eds.), *Psychiatry Today: Accomplishments and Promises*. Amsterdam: Excerpta Medica, p. 130.

Rifkin, A. (1981). The risks of long-term neuroleptic treatment of schizophrenia, especially depression and akinesia. *Acta Psychiatrica Scandinavica*, Suppl. 63, 129–134.

Rifkin, A., Quitkin, F., & Klein, D. F. (1975). Akinesia: A poorly recognized drug-induced extrapyramidal behavioral disorder. *Archives of General Psychiatry*, 32, 672–674.

Rogers, D., Lees, A. J., Trimble, M., & Stern, G. M. (1986). Concept of bradyphernia: A neuropsychiatric approach. In M. D. Yahr & K. J. Bergmann (Eds.), *Advances in Neurology*, Vol. 45. New York: Raven Press, pp. 447–455.

Rose, R. M., & Sachar, E. (1981). Endocrine disturbance in psychiatric disorders. In R. H. Williams (Ed.), *Textbook of Endocrinology*. Philadelphia: W. B. Saunders.

Rosen, J., Silk, K. R., Rice, H. E., & Smith, C. B. (1985). Platelet alpha-2 adrenergic dysfunction in negative symptom schizophrenia: A preliminary study. *Biological Psychiatry*, 20, 539–545.

Saffer, D., Metcalfe, M., & Coopen, A. (1985). Abnormal dexamethasone suppression test in Type II schizophrenia? *British Journal of Psychiatry*, 147, 721–723.

Sandyk, R. (in press). Pineal melatonin functions: Possible relevance to Parkinson's disease. *International Journal of Neuroscience*.

Sandyk, R., & Fisher, H. (1988). Serotonin in involuntary movement disorders. *International Journal of Neuroscience*, 42, 185–205.

Sandyk, R., & Iacono, R. P. (in press). Early vs. late onset Parkinson's disease: The role of locus coeruleus. *International Journal of Neuroscience*.

Sandyk, R., & Kay, S. R. (in press-a). Bradykinesia is associated with ventricular enlargement in chronic schizophrenia. *International Journal of Neuroscience*.

Sandyk, R., & Kay, S. R. (in press-b). Diabetes mellitus as a clinical marker of idiopathic Parkinson's disease in schizophrenic patients with neuroleptic-induced parkinsonism. *International Journal of Neuroscience*.

Sandyk, R., & Kay, S. R. (in press-c). The effects of anticholinergic therapy on negative schizophrenia. *International Journal of Neuroscience*.

Sandyk, R., & Kay, S. R. (in press-d). Habituation of the glabellar tap reflex as a marker of negative schizophrenia. *International Journal of Neuroscience*.

Sandyk, R., & Kay, S. R. (in press-e). Negative schizophrenia and abnormal melanocyte-stimulating hormone functions. *International Journal of Neuroscience*.

Sandyk, R., & Kay, S. R. (in press-f). Pineal calcification is related to drug-induced parkinsonism. *International Journal of Neuroscience*.

Sandyk, R., & Kay, S. R. (in press-g). The role of pineal melatonin functions in the pathophysiology of schizophrenia: A review and hypothesis. *Schizophrenia Bulletin*.

Sandyk, R., Kay, S. R., & Iacono, R. P. (in press). Diabetes mellitus as a risk factor for drug-induced parkinsonism in schizophrenia. *International Journal of Neuroscience*.

Schneider, K. (1959). *Clinical Psychopathology*. Trans., M. W. Hamilton (1959). New York: Grune and Stratton.

Schwartz, L. & Munoz, R. (1968). Blood sugar levels in patients treated with chlorpromazine. *American Journal of Psychiatry*, 125, 253–255.

Seidman, L. J. (1983). Schizophrenia and brain dysfunctions: An integration of recent neurodiagnostic findings. *Psychological Bulletin*, 94, 195–238.

Selby, G. (1968). Cerebral atrophy and parkinsonism. *Journal of the Neurological Sciences*, 6, 517–559.

Simoes, M. (1989). Cannabis use in the schizophrenic shift. In C. N. Stefanis, C. R. Soldatos, & A. D. Rabavilas (Eds.), *Psychiatry Today: Accomplishments and Promises*. Amsterdam: Excerpta Medica, p. 122.

Singh, M. M., & Kay, S. R. (1975a). A comparative study of haloperidol and chlorpromazine in terms of clinical effects and therapeutic reversal with benztropine in schizophrenia: Theoretical implications for potency differences among neuroleptics. *Psychopharmacologia*, 43, 103–113.

Singh, M. M., & Kay, S. R. (1975b). A longitudinal therapeutic comparison between two prototypic neuroleptics (haloperidol and chlorpromazine) in matched groups of schizophrenics: Nontherapeutic interactions with trihexyphenidyl; theoretical implications for potency difference. *Psychopharmacologia*, 43, 115–123.

Singh, M. M., & Kay, S. R. (1976). Wheat gluten as a pathogenic factor in schizophrenia. *Science*, 191, 401–402.

Singh, M. M., & Kay, S. R. (1978). Therapeutic antagonism between anticholinergics and neuroleptics: Possible involvement of cholinergic mechanisms in schizophrenia. *Schizophrenia Bulletin*, 4, 3–6.

Singh, M. M., & Kay, S. R. (1979a). Dysphoric response to neuroleptic treatment in schizophrenia: Its relationship to autonomic arousal and prognosis. *Biological Psychiatry*, 14, 277–294.

Singh, M. M., & Kay, S. R. (1979b). Therapeutic antagonism between anticholinergic anti-parkinsonism agents and neuroleptics in schizophrenia: Implications for a neuropharmacological model. *Neuropsychobiology*, 5, 74–86.

Singh, M. M., & Kay, S. R. (1984). Exogenous peptides and schizophrenia. In N. S. Shah & A. G. Donald (Eds.), *Psychoneuroendocrine Dysfunction*. New York: Plenum Medical Book Co., pp. 517–548.

Singh, M. M., & Kay, S. R. (1985). Pharmacology of central cholinergic mechanisms and schizophrenic disorders. In M. M. Singh, D. M. Warburton, & H. Lal (Eds.), *Central Cholinergic Mechanisms and Adaptive Dysfunctions*. New York: Plenum Press, pp. 247–308.

Singh, M. M., & Kay, S. R. (1987). Is the positive-negative distinction in schizophrenia valid? *British Journal of Psychiatry*, 150, 879–880.

Singh, M. M., Kay, S. R., & Opler, L. A. (1987). Anticholinergic-neuroleptic antagonism in terms of positive and negative symptoms of schizophrenia: Implications for psychobiological subtyping. *Psychological Medicine*, 17, 38–48.

Singh, M. M., Kay, S. R., & Pitman, R. K. (1981a). Aggression control and restructuring of social relations among recently admitted schizophrenics. *Psychiatry Research*, 5, 157–169.

Singh, M. M., Kay, S. R., & Pitman, R. K. (1981b). Territorial behavior of schizophrenics: A phylogenetic approach. *Journal of Nervous and Mental Disease*, 169, 503–512.

Singh, M. M., & Smith, J. M. (1973). Sleeplessness in acute and chronic schizophrenia: Response to haloperidol and anti-parkinsonism agents. *Psychopharmacology*, 29, 21–32.

Sommers, A. A. (1985). "Negative symptoms": Conceptual and methodological problems. *Schizophrenia Bulletin*, 11, 364–379.

Spitzer, R. L., Endicott, J. E., & Robins, E. (1978). *Research Diagnostic Criteria (RDC) for a Selected Group of Functional Disorders* (3rd ed.). New York: New York State Psychiatric Institute, Biometrics Research.

Spitzer, R. L., Williams, J. B. W., Gibbon, M., & First, M. B. (1988). *Structured Clinical Interview for DSM-III-R-Patient Version (SCID-P, 4/1/88)*. New York: New York State Psychiatric Institute, Biometrics Research.

Sroka, H., Elizan, T. S., Yahr, M. D., Burger, A., & Mendoza, M. R. (1981). Organic mental syndrome and confusional states in Parkinson's disease: Relationship to computerized tomographic signs of cerebral atrophy. *Archives of Neurology*, 38, 339–342.

Stein, L., & Wise, C. D. (1971). Possible etiology of schizophrenia: Progressive damage to the noradrenergic reward system by 6-hydroxydopamine. *Science*, 171, 1032–1036.

Steiner, I., Gomori, J. M., & Melamed, E. (1985). Features of brain atrophy in Parkinson's disease: A CT scan study. *Neuroradiology*, 27, 158–160.

Stevens, J. R. (1982). Neuropathology of schizophrenia. *Archives of General Psychiatry,* 39, 1131–1139.

Strauss, J. S., & Carpenter, W. T. Jr. (1972). The prediction of outcome in schizophrenia. *Archives of General Psychiatry,* 27, 739–745.

Strauss, J. S., Carpenter, W. T. Jr., & Bartko, J. J. (1974). The diagnosis and understanding of schizophrenia: II. Speculations on the processes that underlie schizophrenic symptoms and signs. *Schizophrenia Bulletin,* 11, 61–76.

Studler, J. M., Javoy-Agid, F., Cesselin, F., Legrand, J. C., & Agid, Y. (1982). CCK-8 immunoreactivity distribution in human brain: Selective decrease in the substantia nigra from parkinsonian patients. *Brain Research,* 243, 176–179.

Tamminga, C. A., & Schaeffer, M. H. (1979). Treatment of schizophrenia with ergot alkaloids. *Psychopharmacology,* 66, 229–242.

Tandon, R., Goodson, J., Silk, K. R., Kronfol, Z., Hariharan, M., & Greden, J. F. (1989). Positive and negative symptoms in schizophrenia and the dexamethasone suppression test. *Biological Psychiatry,* 25, 788–791.

Tandon, R., & Greden, J. F. (1987). Trihexyphenidyl treatment of negative schizophrenic symptoms. *Acta Psychiatrica Scandinavica,* 76, 732.

Tandon, R., & Greden, J. F. (1989). Cholinergic hyperactivity and negative schizophrenic symptoms: A model of cholinergic-dopaminergic interactions in schizophrenia. *Archives of General Psychiatry,* 46, 745–753.

Tandon, R., Greden, J. F., & Silk, K. R. (1988). Treatment of negative schizophrenic symptoms with trihexyphenidyl. *Journal of Clinical Psychopharmacology,* 8, 212–215.

Taylor, A. E., Saint-Cyr, J. A., & Lang, A. E. (1986). Frontal dysfunction in Parkinson's disease: The cortical focus of neostriatal outflow. *Brain,* 109, 845–883.

Tetrud, J. W., & Langston, J. W. (1989). The effects of deprenyl (selegiline) on the natural history of Parkinson's disease. *Science,* 245, 519–522.

Teuber, H. L. (1964). The riddle of frontal lobe function in man. In J. M. Warren & K. Akert (Eds.), *The Frontal Granular Cortex and Behavior.* New York: McGraw-Hill, pp. 410–444.

Thiemann, S., Csernansky, J. G., & Berger, P. A. (1987). Rating scales in research: The case of negative symptoms. *Psychiatry Research,* 20, 47–55.

Tinbergen, N. (1972). Functional ethology and the human sciences. *Proceedings of the Royal Society of Medicine,* 182, 385–410.

Todd, N. (1989). Scottish first episode schizophrenia study: Two year follow-up. In C. N. Stefanis, C. R. Soldatos, & A. D. Rabavilas (Eds.), *Psychiatry Today: Accomplishments and Promises.* Amsterdam: Excerpta Medica, p. 287.

Tonnard-Neuman, E. (1968). Phenothiazines and diabetes in hospitalized women. *American Journal of Psychiatry,* 124, 978–982.

Torrey, E. F. (1983). *Surviving Schizophrenia: A Family Manual.* New York: Harper and Row.

Turner, S. W., Lowe, M. R., & Hammond, G. L. (1989). Risperidone in acute episodes of schizophrenia: An open dose-escalating study. In C. N. Stefanis, C. R. Soldatos, & A. D. Rabivalas (Eds.), *Psychiatry Today: Accomplishments and Promises.* Amsterdam: Excerpta Medica, p. 130.

Tyrrell, D. A. J., Parry, R. P., Crow, T. J., Johnstone, E., & Ferrier, I. M. (1979). Possible virus in schizophrenia and some neurological disorders. *Lancet,* 2, 839–841.

U'Prichard, D. C., Bechtel, W. D., Rouot, B. M., & Snyder, S. H. (1971). Multiple apparent alpha-noradrenergic receptor binding sites in rat brain: Effect of 6 hydroxydopamine. *Molecular Pharmacology,* 16, 47–60.

Vaillant, G. E. (1964). Prospective prediction of schizophrenic remission. *Archives of General Psychiatry*, 11, 509–518.

Van Dongen, P. A. M. (1981). The human locus coeruleus in neurology and psychiatry. *Progress in Neurobiology*, 17, 97–139.

van Kammen, D. P., van Kammen, W. B., Mann, L. S., Seppala, T., & Linnoila, M. (1986). Dopamine metabolism in cerebrospinal fluid of drug-free schizophrenic patients with and without cortical atrophy. *Archives of General Psychiatry*, 43, 978–983.

van Praag, H. M., Kahn, R. S., Asnis, G. M., Wetzler, S., Brown, S. L., Bleich, A., & Korn, M. L. (1987). Denosologization of biological psychiatry or the specificity of 5-HT disturbances in psychiatric disorders. *Journal of Affective Disorders*, 13, 1–8.

van Praag, H. M., & Korf, J. (1971). Retarded depression and the dopamine metabolism. *Psychopharmacologia*, 19, 199–203.

van Praag, H. M., & Leijnse, B. (1965). Neubewertung des syndroms: Skizze einer funktionellen pathologie. *Psychiatry, Neurology, and Neurosurgery*, 68, 50–56.

Van Putten, T., & May, P. R. A. (1978). "Akinetic depression" in schizophrenia. *Archives of General Psychiatry*, 35, 1101–1107.

Van Putten, T., May, P. R. A., & Wilkins, J. N. (1980). Importance of akinesia: Plasma chlorpromazine and prolactin levels. *American Journal of Psychiatry*, 137, 1446–1448.

Vardy, M. M., & Kay, S. R. (1983). LSD psychosis or LSD-induced schizophrenia? A multimethod inquiry. *Archives of General Psychiatry*, 40, 877–883.

Venables, P. H. (1966). The psychophysiological aspects of schizophrenia. *British Journal of Medical Psychology*, 29, 289–297.

Watson, C. G., Kucala, T., Tilleskjor, C., & Jacobs, L. (1984). Schizophrenic birth seasonality in relation to the incidence of infectious diseases and temperature extremes. *Archives of General Psychiatry*, 41, 85–90.

Weinberger, D. R., Bigelow, L. B., Kleinman, J. E., Klein, S. T., Rosenblatt, J. E., & Wyatt, R. J. (1980). Cerebral ventricular enlargement in chronic schizophrenia: An association with poor response to treatment. *Archives of General Psychiatry*, 37, 11–13.

Weinberger, D. R., Cannon-Spoor, E., Potkin, S. G., & Wyatt, R. J. (1980). Poor premorbid adjustment and CT scan abnormalities in chronic schizophrenia. *American Journal of Psychiatry*, 137, 1410–1413.

Weinberger, D. R., Torrey, E. F., & Neophytides, A. N. (1979). Lateral cerebral ventricular enlargement in chronic schizophrenia. *Archives of General Psychiatry*, 36, 735–739.

Weinberger, D. R., & Wyatt, R. J. (1980). Structural brain abnormalities in chronic schizophrenia: Computed tomography findings. In C. Baxter & T. Melnuchek (Eds.), *Perspectives in Schizophrenia Research*. New York: Raven Press.

Weiner, R. U., Opler, L. A., Kay, S. R., Merriam, A. E., & Papouchis, N. (in press). Visual information processing in positive, mixed, and negative schizophrenic syndromes. *Journal of Nervous and Mental Disease*.

Widen, L., Bergstrom, M., Blomquist, C., Brismark, A., Elander, S., Eriksson, K., Grietz, T., Malmborg, P., & Nilsson, L. (1981). Glucose metabolism in patients with schizophrenia: Emission computed tomography measurements with 11-C-glucose. International Congress of Biological Psychiatry, Stockholm.

Wilkinson, D. G. (1981). Psychiatric aspects of diabetes mellitus. *British Journal of Psychiatry*, 138, 1–9.

Wise, C. D., & Stein, L. (1973). Dopamine beta-hydroxylase deficit in the brain of schizophrenic patients. *Science*, 181, 344–347.

Wise, R. A. (1982). Neuroleptics and operant behavior: The anhedonia hypothesis. *Behavioral and Brain Sciences*, 5, 39–87.

Woodard, J. C. (1962). Concentric hyaline inclusion body formation in mental disease: Analysis of 27 cases. *Journal of Neuropathology and Experimental Neurology*, 21, 442–449.

Zigmond, M. J., Acheson, A. L., Stachowiak, M. D., & Strickerm, E. M. (1984). Neurochemical compensation after nigro-striatal bundle injury in an animal model of preclinical parkinsonism. *Archives of Neurology*, 41, 856–861.

Zubin, J. (1985). Negative symptoms: Are they indigenous to schizophrenia? *Schizophrenia Bulletin*, 11, 461–470.

Name Index

Abramsky, O., 210
Agid, F., 200
Agid, Y., 200, 210
Albrecht, P., 209
Alizan, T.S., 210
Alpert, M., 133, 136, 144, 196, 201,
  205, 206
Alphs, L.D., 15, 19, 27, 28, 73,
  183, 191, 201, 202
American Psychiatric Association, 9,
  14, 73, 85, 104, 105, 107, 132,
  138, 181, 183, 189, 191
American Psychological Association,
  26, 28, 214
  *Standards for Educational and
  Psychological Tests* of, 83
Ammons, C.H., 133, 140
Ammons, R.B., 133, 140
Andreasen, N.C., 14, 15, 16, 17,
  18, 21, 31, 70, 132, 134, 137,
  154, 160, 182, 189, 191, 192,
  195, 196, 199, 201, 207, 210
Angrist, B., 16, 32, 164, 166, 201,
  205
Anthony, W.A., 7
Ashcroft, G.W., 203

Bartko,. J.J., 13, 15, 183
Becker, H., 207
Benedek, L., 199
Benson, D.F., 200

Berger, P.A., 31
Berkanovic, E., 84
Berry, J.W., 90
Bes, A., 200
Bethlem, J., 204
Bilder, R.M., 17, 18, 31, 152, 185
Birkmayer, W., 211, 213
Bjorklund, A., 211
Blatt, S.J., 10
Bleuler, E., xi, 8, 12, 14, 195, 212
Blumer, D., 200
Bobon, J., 178
Bock, R.D., 184
Bogerts, B., 208
Boom, A.J., 78
Boone, E., 209
Bosanquet, F.D., 208
Bowdler, H., 184
Bowers, M.B., 201, 202
Bowman, M., 199
Boyd, A.E., 204
Braff, D.L., 75, 144
Brambilla, F., 203
Breier, A., 77, 161, 196
Bronx Psychiatric Center, 41
Brown, G.W., 7, 152
Brown, K., 161
Bucci, L., 32
Buchanan, F.H., 20, 166
Burdock, E.I., 92
Buscaino, V.M., 208

267

Subject Index

About the Author

Stanley R. Kay, Ph.D., is Chief of the Schizophrenia Research Program and Associate Clinical Professor in the Department of Psychiatry (Psychology), Albert Einstein College of Medicine/Montefiore Medical Center. He also holds the appointment of Director of Psychological Research at Bronx Psychiatric Center, where he has engaged in clinical research since 1970.

A native of New York City, Dr. Kay completed his undergraduate studies in psychology at New York University and his Ph.D. in experimental psychology at the State University of New York at Stony Brook. His research directions have reflected his combined interests in methodology, psychometrics, cognition, and psychopathology. Although his work has revolved around schizophrenia, he has written on a wide range of topics, such as substance abuse disorders, mental retardation, aggression, nutritional factors in psychiatry, and differential diagnosis. Dr. Kay is the author of over 200 publications, including journal articles, chapters, and psychological tests and scales that are now widely used. Among his contributions, he is co-editor of *New Biological Vistas on Schizophrenia* (an upcoming volume in the Einstein Monograph Series), author of *The Cognitive Diagnostic Battery: Evaluation of Intellectual Disorders*, and originator of the *Positive and Negative Syndrome Scale* and the *Aggression Risk Profile*.